A Fan's Guide to Circle Track Racing

Facts, Tracks and Stats on NASCAR, Busch, Craftsman Truck, ARCA, ASA, World of Outlaws and Other Regional Racing Series

Tony Sakkis

HPBOOKS

HPBooks
are published by
The Berkley Publishing Group
A division of Penguin Putnam Inc.
375 Hudson Street
New York, New York 10014

First edition: February 2001
ISBN: 1-55788-351-3
© 2001 Tony Sakkis
10 9 8 7 6 5 4 3 2 1

Library of Congress Cataloging-in-Publication Data

Sakkis, Tony, 1960–
    A fan's guide to circle track racing : facts, tracks, and stats on NASCAR, Busch, Craftsman Truck, ARCA, ASA, World of Outlaws, and other regional racing series / Tony Sakkis.—1st ed.
       p. cm.
    ISBN 1-55788-351-3
    1. Automobile racing—United States.   2. Racetracks (Automobile racing)—United States.   I. Title.

GV1033 .S25   2001
796.72'0973—dc21
                                           00-066460

Book design & production by Michael Lutfy
Cover design by Bird Studios
All race track photos, including aerial views and maps, are courtesy of the respective race track.
All other interior photos by author unless otherwise noted.

All rights reserved. No part of this publication may be reproduced, stored in a retrieval system, or transmitted in any form, by any means electronic, mechanical, photocopying, recording or otherwise, without the prior written permission of the publisher.

NOTICE: The information in this book is true and complete to the best of our knowledge. All recommendations on parts and procedures are made without any guarantees on the part of the author or the publisher. Tampering with, altering, modifying or removing any emissions-control device is a violation of federal law. Author and publisher disclaim all liability incurred in connection with the use of this information.

CONTENTS

I wish to thank every promoter, PR person and official who lent and hand and a voice to this book. Hopefully, I have translated your thoughts into the right words.

I also wish to extend special thanks to Bob Latford, who has not only helped me with this guide, but on stories and background information for many years while at the *San Francisco Chronicle* and *Examiner*. He's a great asset to the sport. And a great guy.

As a longtime motorsports journalist, I cover a wide variety of racing series and have for many years. It is my job to know the ins and outs of racing, what goes on behind the scenes, the rules changes and how they affect strategy, car development, pit stops and ultimately championships. But the fan is often not privy to the same information. There is a lot that goes on that can't be seen from the stands or from the living room, and that is the purpose of this book.

What I've tried to do with this book is write a guide for fans of all types, from ardent gearheads and driver fan club members to novices that are just getting into it. It is a practical handbook for racing, so to speak. It will give you the whys, hows and wheres of the top circle track racing series in the country. Whether you're an armchair crew chief or a traveling fan with a motorhome painted in your favorite team's colors (you'd be surprised at how many fans do this), you'll find this to be an invaluable guide. It's a reference of rules, stats and strategy, as well as a virtual travel guide to get you to the track. Where to stay, how to get there and where to watch from are just some of the inside tips you won't get from the TV commentator.

At the same time, it is not meant to be a history book. For that, try HPBooks' *Stock Cars!* (ISBN: 1-55788-308-4), which traces the roots of all forms of stock car racing, from Winston Cup to ARCA. In fact, this book is an excellent companion guide, beginning where that one ends.

At the end of each section, I list the race tracks that host the events for each individual series. As you can imagine, there is quite a bit of overlap as many tracks host a variety of circle track events throughout the season. So rather than be redundant, I list the tracks that host Winston Cup events, for example, but in the Busch section, I will list only the tracks that were not mentioned in the Winston Cup section, and so on. So if you're looking for a particular track to attend a Busch event that also hosts Winston Cup events, you will find it in the Winston Cup section rather than with the Busch information.

If you are having trouble locating the track you want to go to, there is a track index on page 185 that lists each track by alphabetical order, not by series, so you can go directly to that track.

Another caveat: Although every effort was made to verify the information up to the last minute, it is a well known fact in our Internet/cell phone/pager age that phone numbers and area codes change frequently. What doesn't change as much is the physical location of the track—it's pretty hard to move a 2.5 mile speedway. So if you are getting a disconnect or wrong number, try information for the town listed with the track, and you should find the correct number. We plan on updating numbers as we reprint, but it's hard to keep up with daily changes.

Circle track racing, from a fan's point of view, offers some of the most exciting racing in the world. There is nothing quite like it. If you haven't been to one, then what are you waiting for? This is your guide to getting there.

NASCAR WINSTON CUP

NASCAR
P.O. Box 2875
1801 W. Int'l Speedway Blvd
Daytona Beach, FL 32114
PH: (904) 253-0611

Although there are quite a few forms of circle track racing, NASCAR is the King. In 1947, Bill France Sr., a stock car racer, decided that the very disorganized sport of circle track/stock racing needed a little organization and direction. In December of that year, he gathered several of his buddies and other car owners in Daytona Beach, Florida, and founded the National Association for Stock Car Auto Racing (NASCAR), and motorsports in the U.S. has never been the same. As a race-sanctioning body with a powerful racing lobby and body of support, there are few other series in the world with NASCAR's power and popularity. As one of the fastest growing sports of any kind in the

Winston Cup has become one of the world's fastest growing and most popular spectator sports. All races are sold out by Sunday, with some tracks seating more than 150,000 fans. What's the secret? Intense, tight compation, right up until the very last laps in most cases. NASCAR is quick to change the rules to keep cars equal so no one car or team dominates, which keeps the fans coming back for more.

United States, it has grown into many different branches and regional racing series. It is one of the few racing organizations with a "minor league," so to speak. Drivers with low budgets and pipe dreams can actually run a NASCAR event at a local track and work their way up through the system to the Winston Cup series, the biggest and most prestigious, although it is more difficult to do today than ever before. But it is still possible. NASCAR has series that go from the very bottom to the top so we'll start at the top and trickle down from there to the grassroots series.

THE WINSTON CUP SERIES

The Winston Cup was originally called Grand National, until R.J. Reynolds tobacco company signed on as a series sponsor in 1972 and changed the name, which is still the same today. Grand National was retained for the "B" Series, Busch Grand National, which is covered in the next section.

Winston Cup is pretty much a year-long affair, having grown to 36 races as of this writing. There are two championships up for grabs: the Driver's Championship and the Manufacturer's Championship. In addition to the 36 races on the schedule, there are two other non-points races, The Winston and the Busch Clash, which makes a total of 38. The team with the most points at the end of the season wins—it's that simple, but also rather complicated. As of 2000, there had been 52 national championships, and of them, 27 different Winston Cup champions

Point Scoring

One reason that NASCAR has remained so popular is because they have always gone out of their way to make sure no one car, driver, or team completely dominates, or at least they try to keep it close. The championships are often contested right down to the last couple of races, which keeps fans interested and tuned in. This is not necessarily true of other series, where many times the

WINSTON CUP POINT SYSTEM

1st: 175	2nd: 170	3rd: 165
4th: 160	5th: 155	6th: 150
7th: 146	8th: 142	9th: 138
10th: 134	11th: 130	12th: 127
13th: 124	14th: 121	15th: 118
16th: 115	17th: 112	18th: 109
19th: 106	20th: 103	21st: 100
22nd: 97	23rd: 94	24th: 91
25th: 88	26th: 85	27th: 82
28th:: 79	29th: 76	30th: 73
31st: 70	32nd: 67	33rd: 64
34th: 61	35th: 58	36th: 55
37th : 52	38th: 49	39th: 46
40th: 43	41st: 40	42nd: 37
43rd: 34	44th: 31	45th: 28

championship is decided two-thirds of the way through the season.

NASCAR's point system is one of the methods they use to keep the racing and competition close. Because points are awarded all the way through the field, teams are motivated to finish every race, even if they have an accident early on. If they can still go out an hour later after taping the car together in the garage and run around on the "apron" (the innermost portion of the track), they will do it for those precious few points.

NASCAR recognized the value of keeping the competition tight a long time ago, and they do it better than anyone else. One way they keep fan interest all year long is with a rather complicated point system that makes it very difficult for any one driver to completely dominate. In some other series, the championship is decided midway through the season, and that's no fun. NASCAR awards points just for completing one lap, finishing dead last, so there's a lot of incentive to keep running as much as you can.

Points are awarded all the way to last place, unlike many other series, which gives teams the incentive to keep running even if they don't have any chance of winning. Bonus points are also giving for winning the pole and for leading laps.

See the chart on the previous page for a look at how the points are scored.

So the difference between winning the race and finishing second is only five points; the difference between finishing second and tenth is only 36 points. But the difference between finishing tenth and failing to finish—or being involved in a first-lap crash—is a huge margin. So the points system motivates teams to keep the cars running on the track and in the top few for not just one race but the whole season. It keeps competition at any particular race exciting and usually keeps the season title up in the air until the last few races of the season.

Bonus Points—Of course, if points are awarded all the way down the grid (even if you don't finish after running just one lap, which would be 45th and 28 points), what's to keep a driver from doing his darndest to move up a spot or two? Are the 5 points between 1st and 2nd really worth it? Well, NASCAR has this figured out too. Running around in a circle and waiting for other cars to break down is not racing. So NASCAR offers bonus points.

There are two types: the first is based simply on leading a lap, any lap, the first one, the last one or any one in between. In fact, the driver doesn't have to lead the whole lap; all he has to do is lead the pack across the start/finish line at any point during the race. This can happen under caution or during pit stops. In other words, a driver could be second starting the lap, second all the way through four corners, take the lead just prior to the start/finish line and then lose the lead fifty feet across the line, and still be credited with leading a lap. At any rate, the bonus is 5 points, which is a significant number when you look at the above system. Sometimes you'll hear the announcer say "they're racing back to the line" after an accident or similar caution. That means the race will be temporarily halted next time past the start/finish line and whoever gets there first will be credited with a lap led, and actually extra laps run as the leader under caution—if the leader stays out and does not pit.

That brings up the second bonus: five points for leading the most laps. Since having the best car doesn't always mean a team will win a race, NASCAR gives a bonus of sorts for being the driver who has the best car—or more accurately, the driver who dominates the race. Five points are awarded to the driver who leads the most laps. If he should lead most laps, then crash, the bonus compensates him in a way for his troubles. Obviously, not enough, but it is something.

Jeff Gordon certainly has won his share of awards, and then some. This is the Fast Pace Award sponsored by MCI.

By the way, if two drivers happen to tie for lap leader with the same amount of laps led, each driver is awarded five points.

If you've done the math, you'll realize that there is a minor imperfection in this three decades-old standard. Since there are ten extra points available to each driver, there essentially can be two winners at any one race. The driver who wins the race obviously will have led a lap. You can't cross the finish line first without taking five bonus points for the win. That gives the winner 180 points—175 for the win and five for the last lap as leader—no matter how he won the race.

But if he didn't lead the most laps, the other five bonus points go to another driver. If that driver happens to finish second he will get the same 180 points—170 for second spot, five for leading a lap, and five for leading the most laps. That's the way the system works.

Often criticized for being too generous to the runners-up and too stingy with the winner of the race, even critics have to admit the current points system keeps the points battle tight all season long—which keeps fans interested. That's what NASCAR has been trying to accomplish for over 50 years now, and has arguably done better than anyone else.

And the points race, where drivers fight tooth and nail over just a few measly points, is one reason for the success of Winston Cup. But then there's the money.

PRIZE MONEY, SPECIAL EVENTS AND SPECIAL AWARDS

The prize money makes Winston Cup one of the richest sporting series in the world. For example, the 1998 season was worth five million dollars from series sponsor Winston. The 1998 Winston Cup Champion made two million dollars—just from the championship. That's not including the prize money from each race, or the bonuses paid by sponsors or suppliers. That's just the basic end-of-the-year prize money paid out as a bonus by NASCAR.

No Bull 5

Probably the most lucrative special event or bonus prize money award is the "No Bull 5," a five-race chance to win $1 million at each race. How it works is this: eligible drivers have a chance to win a million dollars by capturing a Winston No Bull event. The events that qualify a driver to win a million dollars are the Daytona 500, the Las Vegas 400, the Coca-Cola 600, the Richmond 400, and the Winston 500 at Talladega. To qualify for the money a driver must have finished

Kenny Irwin accepts his first Bud Pole Award. The $5000 prize isn't all that much, but the winner of the most poles by the end of the season can win an additional bonus of nearly $500,000.

in the top five at the previous No Bull event. So to be eligible for the No Bull award at the Coca Cola 600, which runs in May over Memorial Day Weekend, the driver would've had to finish in the top five at the Daytona 500 in February, and so on. If an eligible driver wins the race, he wins the million-dollar bonus available for that race. Provided he qualified for the first race, the winner of five No Bull races can win an additional five million dollars—that's in addition to the prize money for the race itself and in addition to the Winston Cup points fund. To date, no driver has won all five, but it could happen.

The Winston

Each season there is a single non-points event that is really as prestigious as any event on the 34-race calendar. "The Winston" is an All-Star race that pays extremely well, and is rather prestigious too.

Up to 20 racers maximum are selected from a pool of drivers who have either won a Winston Cup race in the past season, are past or current Winston Cup champions, and/or are past winners of The Winston itself. There is also a lone spot for the winner of the Winston Open, a sprint qualifying race that allows the winner to race in The Winston.

The Winston has evolved in recent years, but the most current version consists of three segments: two 30-lap races and one 10-lap event. Caution laps do not count in the total. Between segments one and two, the grids are inverted (they used to be completely inverted, so the driver in 20th would start first and so on, but now there is a complex formula where only about a dozen cars change position). The teams may elect to come in between segments two and three, but they may also stay on the track between segments to improve their track position. The segment winners are paid out of a $2 million dollar purse, making The Winston a lucrative way to spend a non-championship race weekend.

Bud Pole Award

There are also many awards given to drivers and teams for what seems like an endless variety of reasons. The Bud Pole Award is a $5,000 bonus awarded to the fastest qualifier, or pole sitter, of each race. At the end of the season, Anheuser-Busch awards the driver with the most poles an additional bonus (in 1998 it was $490,000). That's a lot of money by any standard.

Rookie of the Year

Rookie drivers (those in their first full season of Winston Cup), battle all year for the Rookie of the Year award. The "RoY," as it's commonly called, is like watching a championship within a championship. Just a few past RoYs include Dale Earnhardt, Ricky Rudd, Rusty Wallace, Alan Kulwicki,

NASCAR and the sponsors don't overlook the pit crew. Each race, a crew chief is honored with a special bonus. Frank Stoddard accepts his check from famed engine builder and owner Robert Yates.

Davey Allison, and Jeff Gordon. To qualify for the RoY, a driver must have not competed in more than a handful of Winston Cup races prior to his first full season. Winning the RoY gives the driver a nice spot in history—plus a substantial cash bonus.

Miscellaneous Awards

Now on to the endless variety of awards that change each season. At the time of this writing, some of the awards a driver or team could capture include:

• The Gatorade's Frontrunner Award, which recognizes the most competitive driver in the middle of the race. The drivers in the top three positions are awarded Frontrunner points at the halfway mark in each of the 36

Winston Cup races. The leader at the halfway mark in the race picks up a cash bonus, as well as Frontrunner points. At the 16th race a cash award is given to the driver with the most Frontrunner points. At the end of the season, the points leader for the year also receives another cash award, making it important not only for the Winston Cup title, but for helpful cash bonuses to be competitive all through each individual race.

• The True Value Man of the Year Award gives the winner of each race a bonus that is to be split between the driver and his favorite charity. The season is also split into four quarters and each driver is eligible for a bonus based on his off-track performances, for his participation in community charity and so forth. A panel of judges chooses four recipients per season, and one Man of the Year for his off-track contributions during the season.

• The Union 76 Challenge is an award for winning any race from the pole position. But the more complicated description of the 76 Challenge is that if a team runs 76 products, and wins the championship, they win at least an extra $100,000.

• Drivers and teams are also rewarded for just giving it their best shot, regardless of where they finish. The Exide All Charged Up Award gives the driver who has charged up through the pack, passing the most people, a cash bonus. In other words, the driver who finished highest from where he started, say for example from 28th to 3rd. At the end of the season, Exide pays the winner of the most awards a $50,000 bonus.

• MCI pays the driver who posts the fastest lap of the race, for each race, a bonus and a reward at the end of the season.

• The Goody's Headache Powder awards the driver with the worst luck during the race a

Most drivers are quick to credit the crew for the win, and NASCAR recognizes them too with awards and a competition for a cash prize. Mike Slade photo.

cash award—presumably to ease his pain. There is also a year-end award for the worst luck—but most teams try not to get that one.

Then there are the awards for using a specific product and doing something noteworthy. The DuPont fund awards the top ten drivers a season-ending $75,000 purse for using DuPont products, Goodyear Tire gives the top 10 teams using Goodyear tires cash awards, the Raybestos Top Stopper Award is for drivers using Raybestos brakes up to $50,000 for a championship season, and so on. There are many others, and the names change all the time.

Pit Crew Awards

But drivers are not the only people who participate in the awards. The Pit Crew Competition awards the guys who never seem to get enough publicity: the crew members. Usually held at the end of the year, the competition—which is not held during a race—has the crew competing against one another via the stopwatch. Each team must change all four tires and refuel. The fastest team wins, splitting approximately $50,000.

Plasti-Kote Winning and Quality Finish Awards gives a cash award to the winning Crew Chief of each race. At the end of the season, Plasti-Kote also awards the Crew Chief with an additional cash bonus for putting his driver in the highest overall finishing position during the season. The winner of this is frequently not the same Crew Chief whose team wins the Pit Crew Competition.

Crews are rewarded in other competitions as well. The AE Clevite Engine Parts rewards the best engine builders of the Winston Cup series. The award of nearly $100,000 rates engine builders and allots points toward a year-end bonus for the top three engine builders.

Sponsorship

Although NASCAR and their associate sponsors pay prize money that is far better than almost any other form of auto racing—

Do you think fans of Terry Labonte will buy Kellogg's Corn Flakes over another just because it's on his car? Kellogg's sure thinks so, and research proves this to be true. But such prime real estate costs quite a bit. To be primary sponsor of a top team can run as high as $10 million dollars a year or more. That's a lot of Corn Flakes. Mike Slade photo.

the real money to run the team comes from the sponsors, not the prize packages.

Sponsorship is the main reason NASCAR has continued to grow and prosper. The way NASCAR treats its sponsors and the way the fans respond to the products that sponsor their favorite drivers are what make NASCAR unique. Fans have been known to switch or support the brands of the products that sponsor their favorite driver, for example, Tide laundry detergent.

For a single-car team to run the entire Winston Cup series—all 38 races—they will need at least $3 million dollars. Primary sponsorships on cars range from $3 million to $10 million.

A sponsorship contract generally includes the sponsor's name on the car, the rights to use the car and the driver in sponsorship promotions, some clause in the contract that guarantees a certain number of personal appearances by the driver, the team owner, and maybe some of the other team personnel, and a general goodwill clause saying the team will promote the product whenever possible.

The team itself is generally funded and profitable before the season even begins. That is, all equipment, all salaries, all wear and tear and anything pertaining to running a Winston Cup championship campaign is generally paid for before the season begins. The winnings then are just icing on the cake. Obviously, if a team collects a big sponsorship check and squanders it by not being competitive, the team will lose the sponsorship deal and find it very difficult to get another one similar to it.

Drivers these days are generally paid a salary, or a retainer, and then are paid a bonus based on performance. The bonus can be paid as a percentage of winnings, a points-based bonus or any variation. There is really no set way to create a driver's contract and no way to keep track of every contingency in each contract. But just as the driver is paid to race based on his results, so too does the sponsor pay based on results. If the team doesn't get results it is penalized in the pocketbook.

A championship winning team is far more valuable to a sponsor than a team that typically runs in the back of the pack. The more times the car appears in the winner's circle

newspaper photos and news highlights the more exposure the sponsor gets. Exposure is the name of the game. A sure way to get it is to win.

WINSTON CUP CARS

In the first days of NASCAR, Bill France and his advisors thought the key to keeping fans interested in the racing was to ensure that they could identify with the cars on the track. Do you drive an Indy car to work? Probably not. But how about a Ford Taurus (millions do), or a Chevy Monte Carlo? France and NASCAR decided early on that the race cars must be identifiable with their street cousins. They have gone out of their way to ensure that this continues. Certain body panels of the car must be the same as the original, although the similarity basically ends there. In fact, today's Winston Cup cars haven't progressed much in terms of engine technology since the '60s. They are essentially still a pushrod, carbureted V8 running on pump gas. But although the cars seem like they are fairly simple from a technological standpoint, they are far from it. See the chart nearby for the technical specs as of the year 2000.

Tech Specs for Winston Cup

Height: 51 inches
Minimum Weight (w/driver): 3,400 lb
Wheelbase: 110 in.
Engine: 358 cubic inch V8
Induction: Holley 750 to 830 cfm 4-barrel carburetor
Horsepower: 720 @ 8500 rpm, Chevrolet; 700@ 8000 rpm, Ford; 715@ 6000 rpm, Pontiac
Torque: 525 ft-lb @ 6000 rpm, Chevrolet; 490 ft-lb @ 8000 rpm, Ford; 530 ft-lb @ 6000 rpm, Pontiac.
Transmission: 4 spd. Manual
Wheels: 9.5 x 15 inches
Tires: Goodyear Radials, 27.5 x 12.5"
Fuel: 104 octane gasoline
Fuel Cell: 22 gallon capacity
Brakes: Four-wheel discs
Chassis: Rectangular steel tubing with integral roll cage
Front Suspension: Independent coil springs with twin A-arms
Rear Suspension: Trailing arms, coil springs, Panhard rod, floating axle

Winston Cup cars have the same hood, roof and rear trunklid as those used on the street models. But that's about all they share in common. Actually, today's street car is far more advanced than today's Winston Cup car. Mike Slade photo.

Lift the hood of a Winston Cup car and you'll find that the engine closely resembles the same one used in the '60s: a carbureted pushrod V8. But old technology aside, it still pumps out an impressive 700-plus horsepow-

The numbers above are the basic specifications, subject to an endless interpretation by individual teams. This "interpretation" is what separates winners from losers and makes racing what it is. Without getting into too much detail, we can look at Winston Cup regulations as they apply to engines and suspensions so that you have a basic working knowledge of why one car might be faster than another.

Engines

As mentioned above, every NASCAR Winston Cup Series race car uses a pushrod V8. The engine is normally aspirated—meaning it has no components such as superchargers or turbochargers—and it doesn't even have fuel injection!

To get the fuel to the engine, a carburetor is used. The mandated carb is a Holley 750, a four-barrel flowing 830 cfm of air. As might be expected, no major alterations are permitted to the carb.

Restrictor Plates—You will hear track announcers and TV commentators frequently talk about "restrictor plates" when NASCAR runs at Daytona and Talledega. In order to keep speeds down and competition close, NASCAR requires that teams run these metal plates, mounted between the carb and the intake manifold, to restrict the flow of fuel and air. Without the plate, the opening is 1 9/16" in diameter, but the plate reduces it to 29/32".

Before each race, NASCAR officials hand out the plates to each team (which they do with great fanfare, with a NASCAR official to hold it up with a flourish before installing it beneath the carb). The team must run the plate it is given. Although the impact on speed is undeniable, there is some doubt as too how effective they are at promoting safety. Drivers complain that the plates equalize the cars to the point where they must all run nose to tail because no one car is able to break the draft and run up front. When an accident occurs, half the field can be wiped out.

Another aspect is that because the cars are now equal, the only way to get an advantage is to "hook up" with a drafting partner. As will be explained in a moment, two cars are

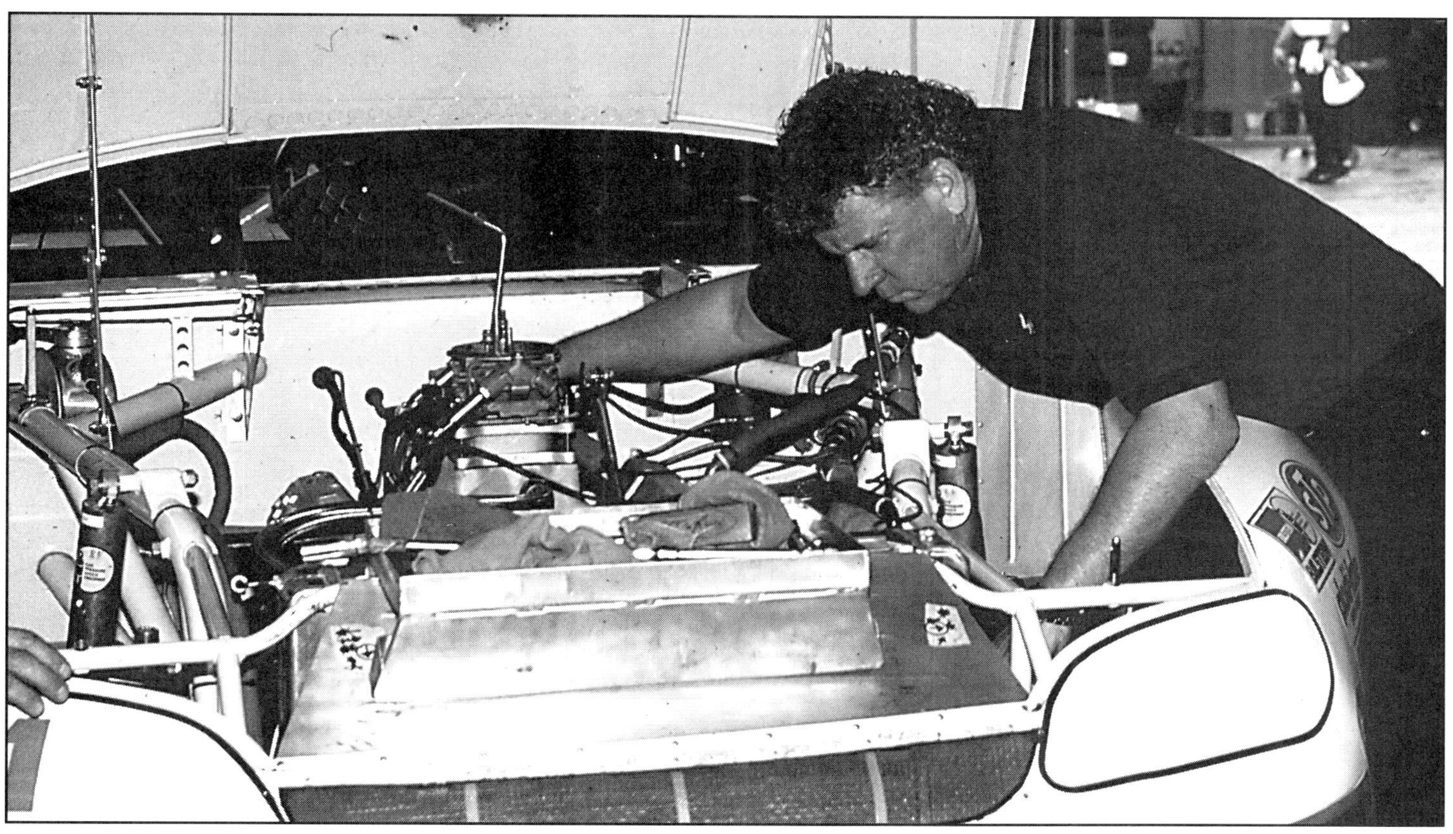

The carburetor needs to be tuned constantly to work in varying conditions, which is part of the art and science of the engine builder.

better than one, three better than two, etc. in a draft. If you don't have a partner, you basically don't have a chance The lead driver, no matter how dominant, can't fight a few cars working together in a draft. This will be discussed more when we get to the actual race and race strategy.

Each engine must match that of the original car manufacturer: a Taurus must run a Ford engine, a Monte Carlo a Chevy engine, etc. But that's where the similarities end. The manufacturers may supply the parts, but each team rebuilds, modifies and tunes their engines, or has them done privately. Everything inside the engine is different from what you see on a street car. The V8 you see on the track may be the same size and same basic design as what you run in your car, but it's completely different and heavily modified.

But not too modified. NASCAR's engine rules are designed to keep costs down, much less than say Indy cars or drag racing. They don't allow fuel injection, turbos, special heads, or the latest state-of-the-art technology because costs soon get out of hand, and then only those with the most money have the advantage. NASCAR's whole philosophy is to keep everyone on the same level as much as possible. That's what keeps the competition so tight, and the fans so interested.

One of the biggest engine controversies at the time this was written had to do with compression ratios. In an attempt to bring speeds down (or at least keep them from going up) NASCAR has looked at reducing the compression ratio. The higher the compression ratio, the more power the engine makes as a general rule, so by dropping the ratio NASCAR drops the horsepower and thereby the speeds.

At this point, Winston Cup rules limit compression ratios to 12:1. Busch Grand National is at 9.5:1. But 9.5:1 may soon become the engine rule for Winston Cup.

Many factors affect a car's handling. Weight distribution, springs, shocks, sway bars, spoilers and tires must all be dialed in to each track for optimum handling.

NASCAR is moving toward unleaded fuel. If you still think that's high compression, consider the fact that Winston Cup cars once had engines that were as high as 17:1, and were 14.5:1 as late as 1995.

Why do that if the engines all have the same components and same cubic-inch regulations? High compression is a way for engine builders to wring that extra bit of power out of an engine. But that power comes at a penalty. The penalty is increased engine failure.

Lowering the compression ratio creates less stress on components. Less stress means more reliability and more reliability, again, gets back to closer competition on the track.

Chassis and Suspension

At the speeds that Winston Cup cars run, just about every change has an effect on handling. The majority of the activity—and most of the problems—manifest themselves at the front end of the car. There are basically three conditions a driver experiences, and three things you will hear from time to time that explain how the car is handling: neutral, oversteer and understeer.

Neutral handling responds to every driver input. It is well balanced in cornering, with both the rear and front ends responding to cornering forces equally. A neutral car has also been set up to provide the best compromise between cornering ability and straightway speed. More downforce increases cornering speed at the expense of straightway speed, and vice versa. It allows a steady throttle through the corners without upsetting the car. In some forms of racing, the car is always set up to be neutral.

Oversteer is also called "loose" by racers. It means the car's tail end is steering through the corner faster than the front end, swinging out toward the outside of the turn. Too much oversteer and the car will spin. But in a slower speed turn, like at Martinsville or Bristol, the inertia of the rear end coming around can actually help push the car through the turn faster. Driving with oversteer requires more effort from the driver, who must modulate the throttle and steering wheel to keep the car on the edge of a spin. But loose is not always the way to go. At the speeds a Winston Cup car travels on superspeedways, you generally don't want a loose car in fast turns.

Understeer is often referred to as "push." This is where the front end of the car wants to head toward the outside of the turn, requiring the driver to turn the steering wheel further to get it to turn in. Sometimes, a push can be so bad that the front end will not turn in even with the wheels cocked all the way over. Quite often, if a car goes through a turn and into the wall face first, it is because of a push. Tail first would be oversteer. Push is almost never a good thing. It wears tires and is very difficult to use to an advantage. To compensate for push, a driver has to begin turning far from the apex, prolonging the turn and making him work hard just to get through it. Either that, or slow down, which isn't a good alternative for a race car driver either.

How a car handles is determined by many factors. Weight distribution, springs, shocks, tire components and pressure, sway bars and front and rear spoilers must all be tuned and adjusted to match each track and racing condition. Frequently, drivers and crews adjust their cars throughout the whole race. The track may heat up and become stickier, or get oiled and get slippery. A car will handle differently with a full load of fuel than with an empty tank.

Lately, NASCAR established a rule regarding shocks. At Daytona and Talladega, NASCAR issues shocks to the teams—four shocks (fronts and rear) at Daytona; and just the two rears at Talladega. The reason behind that new rule comes from the teams' use of qualifying shocks. In order to put up a fast qualifying lap, most teams were using shocks that allowed the back end to droop. So NASCAR decided to step in and force teams to run appropriate shocks. The only tracks that require them as of this writing are Talladega and Daytona—just like the restrictor plates.

Aerodynamics

NASCAR rules stipulate that the hood, the

Wind tunnel testing also is used to develop the front air dam, which should direct airflow around the car and help create downforce. Duct tape is often used across the grille opening, as seen on this Ford, to reduce airflow under the car. But it's a fine line between restricting airflow and overheating the car, so this tape has red tabs at either end so it can be stripped off in a hurry during a pit stop.

roof and the trunk lid must be completely stock, the same as you'd find on that same model car at your local dealer. Everything else is custom built from sheet metal by the teams for competition. If a manufacturer becomes interested in competing in the series, the appropriate representative would meet with NASCAR to discuss alterations if needed.

NASCAR rules stipulate that the car must be based on a two-door, rear-wheel drive street model. But how to explain the Ford Taurus, a four-door, front-wheel drive car? This is an example of the exceptions NASCAR will make to keep competition tight by stretching the rules for parity. For years the GM cars had had an advantage with their Monte Carlo.

These days, wind tunnel testing is critical. In a full-scale wind tunnel, the car is placed inside and a giant fan blows air over it. Smoke streams or strips of tape, along with sensors, indicate where the air is flowing. Trouble spots that might impede flow or create turbulence that would upset handling are noted and solutions within the rules are

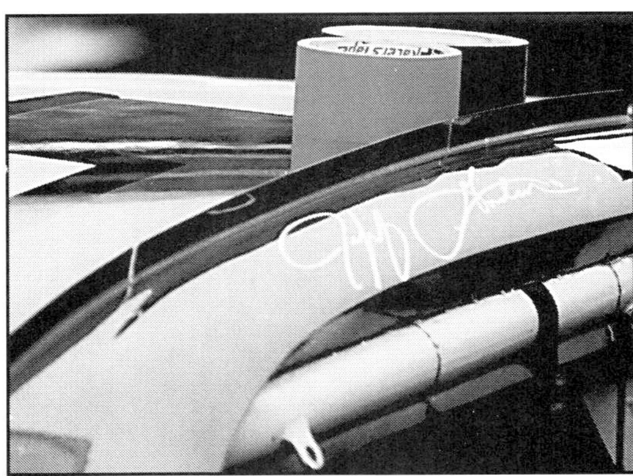

On superspeedways, it's all about how you manage airflow, especially on restrictor plate tracks. Hours spent in wind tunnel testing have pinpointed areas in the car where flow can be enhanced with the addition of a strip of metal here or there. That's how this stip of metal came to be on Jeff Gordon's roof.

The height and length of the rear wing had better meet NASCAR's measurements or the team will be disqualified. They can, however, adjust the wing angle to tune the car for cornering. That's the purpose of these Heim joints located at the rear.

looked for. Sometimes, moving a spoiler or front air dam a 1/4" can have a huge effect on speed or handling, something they would necessarily know from running on the track. But realistically, wind tunnel testing is very expensive and beyond the reach of many teams. Some teams can build a small scale model and run that in a mini–wind tunnel, which is obviously much less expensive.

Quite often, you'll see a Winston Cup car running colored duct tape on the front grille. Sometimes this tape is used to limit airflow to the radiator to increase water temperatures, but with the ambient temperature at most NASCAR tracks so high, it is more likely there to seal off the grille to limit airflow under the car or through the engine compartment.

Any small change—from something as small as a quarter inch angle change of the rear wing to a piece of tape on the grille—can have a significant effect on top speed, drafting and handling.

Tires

Tires in all forms of racing are exceptionally critical to handling. The tire size (width) relative to the weight of the car is one of many factors that determine cornering ability, and with a Winston Cup car, perhaps the heaviest of all race cars, you have a rather unbalanced ratio in this regard. This again is an attempt to keep speeds down. This is especially obvious when the Winston Cup series races at a road course like Sears Point or Watkins Glen. Road courses with tight right and left turns place a lot of demands on the tires, especially with a 3,400-lb racecar.

As comparison, oval track tires differ from road course tires in that they undergo a different duty cycle than the right side tires. Obviously, right side tires carry the majority of the load and cornering forces on an oval track. In road races they have to turn both directions. So for an oval track car, the tire sizes are different, the construction is different (the left side tires are softer and have more flex; the right side tires are stiffer). The right side tires will be "staggered," which means they will be slightly larger in diameter, which aids in turning ability.

Compared to sports car or Indy Car tires, there are some pretty dramatic differences.

In Indycar racing, CART allows a different tire to be used on each position of race car, which is the same with sports cars. They could have four individual compounds, sizes and construction of tires if they chose. In Winston Cup, teams are allowed one type of tire on each side, or two choices per car maximum.

Winston Cup tires are different from other racing tires because they employ an inner liner, which helps the driver keep control in the event of a catastrophic tire failure. The inner liner won't go flat even if the outside of the tire does. It keeps the carcass of the tire in one piece so the driver can slow down and regain control. At least that's the theory. It doesn't always work.

At the track, crew members refer to tires as "scuffs" and "stickers." A "sticker" tire is a brand-new tire that has never turned a wheel on the track. It often still has the sticker from the manufacturer on it, hence the term. A scuffed tire has been brought to temperature on the track and the compound is "cured." The tire is at its maximum grip. This is why a driver usually scuffs in his tires by weaving back and forth on the track during warm-up laps or during a caution period. Tires scuff in quickly, usually less than a lap.

Since Winston Cup teams must race on the same set of tires on which they qualify, they may do their qualifying laps on new stickers, or on slightly scuffed tires from practice, depending on the track and the conditions on that weekend. Being fast is important in qualifying, but there's also the race to think about. If the driver is unlucky enough to cut a tire after qualifying they're allowed to replace it; if they cut two they must start at the back of the pack.

There are not a lot of things that can be done to a tire to change its characteristics, but what can be done is very significant to the handling to the car. Mostly that relates to tire pressure. Tire pressure is a tactic frequently used during pit stops. When tire

A team will go through dozens of tires in a typical race weekend. These tires are laid out in order of when they'll go on for a pit stop. A tire man, who's only function is to tend to the tires, checks pressures and inspects tires so they're ready to go.

pressure changes, it changes the way the tire reacts to the cornering forces. In hard cornering a soft tire can pucker and lose some adhesion. Conversely an overfilled tire will expose too little contact patch to the road

Once a tire comes off after practice or during the race, it is checked for wear. How a tire is wearing can tell the crewmen how the car is handling, and how to adjust it for optimum handling.

A Hendrick's Motorsports tire man prepares a lug nut with adhesive so it can be installed on the car during a pit stop quickly. The adhesive keeps the lug nuts attached to the wheel, not only to help align the wheel, but to keep the lug nuts from bouncing all over pit lane.

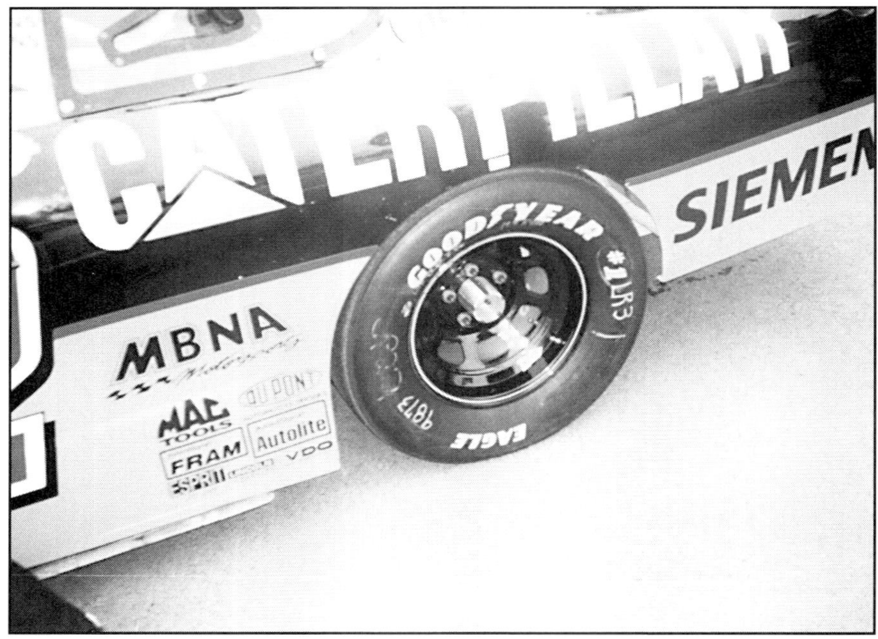

NASCAR rules state that you must begin the race on the same tires you qualified on. The only exception is if you cut a tire.

and will stiffen the ride and alter handling in a negative way.

Tire pressures also change during the race as the tires heat up, and it can have a dramatic effect on handling. Crews must often compensate for this change in tire pressure, and may adjust it throughout the race. They often have to consider and adjust for changing track temperatures, number of laps under yellow and so on.

Speaking of quick, you may see the wheel man taking a wheel, slapping it on, and tightening the lug nuts, one by one. It looks great and seems simple enough—until you think about how the lug nuts are attached. They have to be put on one by one. Yet the tire man just zooms all five lugnuts off and on in a snap.

The reason he can do that is because the lugnuts are held on by glue, or in some cases, very gooey grease. They are set in place on the rim and the rim is stored behind the pit wall, awaiting the pit stop. The wheel studs, on the other hand, are very long, more than three-quarters of an inch longer than they would normally be on a street car. The first inch or so are tapered and unthreaded, allowing the ends to be used like an alignment tool, getting the wheel lined up straight for the quick change. When the wheel goes on, the lug nuts hang on the ends of the studs, where the wheel man tightens up the lugs in a blink of an eye.

Safety

Many of you have witnessed a horrific accident, where the car disintegrates, yet the driver walks away unscathed. This is no "accident," if you will. Over the years, NASCAR has continually refined the safety equipment required on a Winston Cup car. From any view, race fans can see the equipment: roll cages to protect the driver, fireproof suits to keep the driver safe in case of fire, aerodynamic roof flaps to keep the car from becoming airborne if it starts sliding backward. But there are many more things about a Winston Cup car that you may not see from the stands.

Roll cages are designed to take some serious abuse, and can withstand impacts that would kill all occupants in a street car.

Accidents are common, but injuries are not. That's because NASCAR rules stipulate a bunch of safety equipment, from roll cages to fuel cells. The driver is basically enclosed in a steel cage that is capable of withstanding 200 mph impacts with the wall and with other cars. Mike Slade photos.

Fuel tanks are called fuel cells because they are essentially indestructible tanks. The 1964 Indianapolis 500 and Charlotte's World 600 changed the way the racing world looked at fire and how gas is stored aboard a race car. Always a source of fear for crews and drivers, it wasn't until Fireball Roberts, Eddie Sachs and Dave MacDonald all died in May of 1964 in fire-related crashes at the two speedways.

The cells had been on the scene for several years, but became mandatory shortly afterward. They are now so reliable that fire is almost non-existent in racing accidents. The cells are created to do two jobs: first, they are flexible and will deform as opposed to rupturing or bursting on impact. Second, an anti-static, anti-explosive synthetic foam

These fuel cells can withstand the impact of another car that has been going 200 mph, and they won't rupture. They are designed to give and deform rather than burst open.

This is a good shot of the roof flap that deploys if the car should find itself going backward down the track. The flap flips up and provides downforce to keep the rear end planted on the track. It's a simple idea that has no doubt saved lives.

filler prevents fuel from sloshing inside the tank, thereby preventing it from aerating with oxygen, which of course makes it more flammable. It can withstand some 1000 psi without tearing or rupturing.

NASCAR tech inspectors check to make sure there is an adequate amount of foam filler in the cell. Believe it or not, teams have been caught trimming foam from the blocks of material in hopes of gaining a little extra fuel capacity.

You may have noticed fuel spilling from the back of race cars as they pull away from the pits after refueling. That's normal and expected. It comes from an overflow vent at the left rear corner of the car. What you see is the small amount of fuel that has found its way into the vent overflow.

In the final analysis, Winston Cup drivers tend to know more about their cars than most other race car drivers. Bill Elliott does his own suspension work, and drivers like Mark Martin or Rusty Wallace are critical to their teams' success because they understand how a race car works and can actually do the changes themselves if they had to. Knowing something about the cars as a fan will help you know what's going on out there on the track as well.

A TYPICAL RACE WEEKEND

For those of you who have not attended a Winston Cup event in person, the following section will let you know what to expect. If you've been going to races for a while, you'll know some of this, but you may also be missing out on some of the action, which can only make your race more enjoyable.

Most Winston Cup racing takes place on weekends, typically on Sunday, although not always, and usually in the afternoon, with races starting generally at 12:30 to 1:00 P.M. Oval track racing has always been a fair-weather sport. So if it rains, there is no racing.

The Winston Cup season begins mid-February and runs through the middle of November. Where the series used to race mostly in Southern states—Alabama, The Carolinas, Florida and Georgia—it now races throughout the country, from New Hampshire to California. NASCAR racing is closer to your hometown now than it ever has been. At the end of this section, you'll find information on the NASCAR Winston Cup tracks, with specific directions to the tracks, phone numbers to call for ticket information and so on.

Although most races are on Sunday, there are several exceptions. Of the 38 established races, 30 of them are held on Sunday afternoon. Some, like the Daytona 500, start mid-morning; some in the mid-afternoon, like the Coca-Cola 600 at Charlotte. But most get the green flag right at or just before noon Sunday.

Those that vary are as follows: Bristol holds one of its two races on Saturday night, Richmond's two races fall on Saturday, the Daytona July race (the Pepsi 400) runs Saturday night, and the Brickyard 400 is also run on Saturday.

With the exception of the Daytona 500, all Winston Cup races have a qualifying session the same weekend as the race. And as long-time fans know, qualifying and how the team sets up the car is a major part of the race weekend.

Look at a race weekend this way: it is a start-to-finish event based upon the team's ability to use the few minutes of track time, plus previous experience at the track, to dial in, adjust and tune a car to go as fast as possible under current track conditions.

During the initial practice sessions, the driver gives the team feedback about what the car is doing. If it needs more stagger, less rear wing, stiffer springs, different air pressure, whatever, the driver is the only true link to the car. The team can only make changes to the car based on what the driver tells them. Unlike higher tech Indy and F1 cars, there is no telemetry on a Winston Cup car to record data on what the car is doing. Onboard computers of any kind are not allowed.

So most die-hard fans don't see a race as a single 2 to 3 hour event. They see it as a story that begins at the last race and ends when the checkered flag falls that particular Sunday. In other words, practice, qualifying, and "happy hour" are all-important parts of the weekend.

Pre-Race Tech Inspection

Before filling out the entry form, the entire team must be licensed by NASCAR. Everybody from the team must have NASCAR's blessing before setting foot into

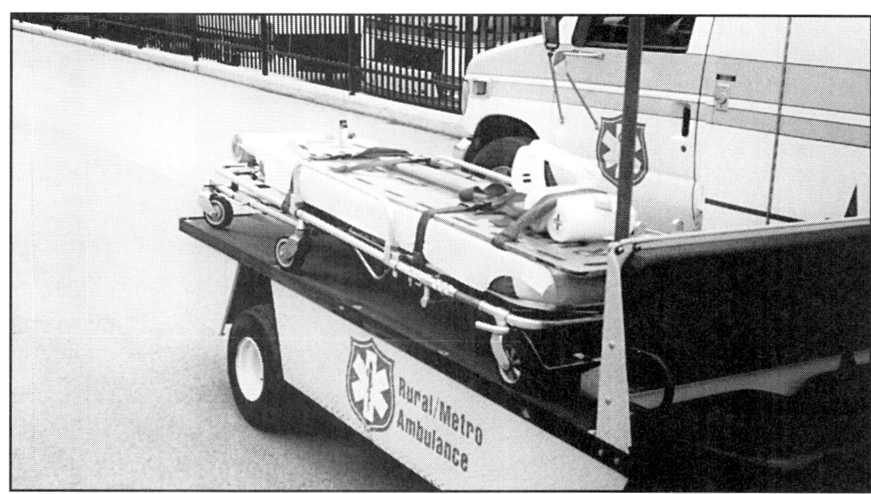

If a driver should be injured, he'll receive the very best care possible. Each race is staffed with appropriate medical personnel to treat drivers at the scene.

the garages.

Prior to running on the track, each car must pass NASCAR's rigorous pre-race tech inspection, which includes a template test. NASCAR has a set of aluminum forms, sort of like dressmakers' patterns, that fit on each individual car in the series. For Taurus they would use one template, for a Monte Carlo another template, and so on. The car must fit exactly within these dimensions—height, width and length. And it must have all the safety devices or components mandated by the rules. The car will be inspected and

One of the first things any car must do prior to turning a wheel on the track is pass NASCAR's rigorous pre-race tech inspection. Every area of the car is measured.

The car can weigh no less than 3400 lbs., including the driver and a full load of fuel. Any infraction usually means losing points at the very least.

Every car must pass a "template test." NASCAR manufactures these aluminum templates to very exact specifications. The car must fit the template exactly. This test is all part of NASCAR's overall strategy to keep the cars as equal as possible to ensure close competition.

This handy little block is actually built to a very precise measurement, and then placed under the car to check for the minimum ground clearance. If it doesn't fit, then the crew had better make some adjustments.

checked with the templates several times during a race weekend to ensure the teams don't change the dimensions at any time. Finally, the car will be weighed. It is weighed "wet," meaning it is weighed with fuel and oil. It must weigh no less than 3400 lbs.

Practice

The teams are only allowed to use three sets of tires prior to the start of the race. They will use the first set to practice, the second set to make sure the setup is correct and the final set to qualify. They must start the race on the same set of tires they qualify on. Once race day comes, they can use as many sets as they wish.

The first practice will be run Friday morning, depending on what the schedule at each particular track is. Teams will usually get three hours of practice prior to the first round of qualifying. During this time, they will come into the pits many times to play with suspension settings. Springs, shocks, weight distribution, carb jetting and many other adjustments are made during this three-hour period to dial in the car to the track and weather conditions.

Qualifying

Typically, the first day of qualifying will occur at 3 P.M. or so. The crews will try and establish a consistent set of times. Morning times are unofficial, but it gives you an idea of where the teams stand early. If one particular driver is ahead of the pack, he will probably be there in the afternoon for qualifying as well. Second round starts typically

Winston Cup cars qualify one car at a time. The order is determined by draw, and the teams have one warm-up lap, one flying lap, and one cool-down lap. They must also start the race on the same set of tires that they qualify on.

around 11 A.M. the next day.

NASCAR uses a single-car format for qualifying, just like the Indy 500. CART, Formula One and most other road racing series do not have such a format. Each car is timed separately, but all are run on the track at the same time.

In single-car qualifying only one car is allowed on the track at a time. A car will leave the pits and circle the track, accelerating up to speed by the time it reaches the start/finish stripe, then do a fast single lap, letting up after crossing the start/finish line before coming into the pits. The driver only crosses the start/finish line twice and only completes one full lap.

Teams get one shot at qualifying. Qualifying order is chosen by a drawing, using a machine with numbered balls, similar to a bingo caller. The car owner with the most points accumulated in the championship draws a qualifying spot. The ball he draws may be first it may be last, but that's the order of the one-lap qualifying attempts. They then line up and wait their turns. They can't wave off like at Indy and they can't change their qualifying position. They get one shot at it and have to make the most of that single lap.

Although teams may use a qualifying engine—an engine that might have just a little more power than a race engine, with perhaps less reliability (but still legal according to NASCAR specs)—they may not use qualifying tires. In fact, to keep teams from running tires that are good just for one lap, NASCAR mandates that the car must start the race on the exact same tires it qualifies on. The individual tires are marked by officials to make sure nobody switches the tires prior to the start. And, at the end of each practice day, the pits are cleared so no team can work on the car without supervision from NASCAR.

The times are recorded and the fastest driver wins the Bud Pole Award, taking the inside spot on the front row (there are two cars per row, and usually 21 to 22 rows, depending on the track size and the race). The other cars are gridded based on their times. Should there be a tie, the driver with the most wins, or most points accumulated so far during the season, will get the top spot.

Only the 25 fastest cars are able to make the grid the first day. The remainder of the pack—those who didn't make it into the top 25—have to try again the following day.

Should they fail to make the cut, there are still ways to start the race. Entrants can get

On race day, cars are gridded in the pit lane while opening ceremonies take place. At some tracks, drivers put on a parade for the fans prior to the start.

Once all the festivities are complete, the pit lane is cleared of all non-essential people—fans, media, etc.—and the teams get down to business.

into the race with such exceptions as promoter's option, past champion's option, and so on. Essentially, what it means is that no matter how poorly a driver performs on a particular day, he can still make the show if he was previously successful. Darrell Waltrip dreaded the day of the past champion's option, which he had to exercise several times in the twilight of his career. Most drivers would rather make it into the field on their own merit, but it makes sense for fans to see past champions race—regardless of how they got there or where they finish on race day. The rest of the field that didn't qualify goes home.

In case of rain or other delays, the qualifying will take place whenever possible.

Sometimes it's impossible to qualify the first 25 on Saturday because of rain. So they do it Sunday. If it rains Sunday and it becomes impossible to qualify, NASCAR will grid the cars based on current point standings.

Those who have to come back and try to qualify Sunday have added pressure. Now, instead of just having to concentrate on the race, they still have to qualify for it.

Happy Hour

After the last qualifying session, there will usually be a support race. It may be a Busch Grand National, ARCA or some other minor event. Then it is time for "Happy Hour," NASCAR style.

Happy Hour is the final practice before the race itself. A lot of fans leave after qualifying to beat the traffic, but if they do, they are missing out. Happy Hour is the last time the teams get to check out the car prior to a Sunday race, and it has become popular enough that sometimes it is televised.

The times set during Happy Hour can actually give an indication of who is going to be the fastest during the race. Oftentimes a team may not qualify well because they didn't get the car setup right. Then they go back, make some adjustments, and can be faster than the polesitter during Happy Hour.

Mark Martin is a model of intensity and concentration as he awaits word to start his engine.

The cars slowly make their way out onto the track in formation, to begin several warm-up laps. Once on track, they'll be weaving back and forth to scrub in the tires, and accelerating and braking to warm up the engine.

This creates a great deal of anticipation for those who are paying attention to the times. The cars will be running in full race trim, with heavy tanks, and the drivers will be checking to see if they have figured out the track. If they didn't, Happy Hour is their last opportunity to dial in the car.

Race Day

Race day will take on a carnival-like atmosphere, especially at the big events like the Daytona 500. The stands will be overflowing, there will be anticipation in the air. Although everyone involved seems to be relaxed, underneath they are just waiting, wishing for the race to get started. Time to get down to business. Everything's either ready or not.

The drivers will be introduced and they will sometimes take a parade lap in street cars for the crowd. Then they will get to their cars, ready for the signal for everyone to start their engines and be ready to race.

You'll see the cars on the track, accelerating, braking, acclerating, braking, then weaving back and forth on the track. The accelerating keeps the engine warm and up to operating temps, and the weaving brings up tire temperatures. Moving the car back and forth also scuffs the surface for grip. The tires need to be up to operating temperature before they can work properly.

The Start

Although the starts are really performed at the flagstand, by the flagman, the word for the start comes from the NASCAR scoring tower. The flagmen (there are now two who work all races, alternating between weekends) hear the command in their headphones and throw the appropriate flag.

Once NASCAR determines that all cars are in line, that no one driver has a jump on the others, they give the go-ahead for the green flag. If NASCAR feels the start should be aborted for some reason (perhaps one driver has jumped the start, or the cars are strung out too far, or any other situation that would be hazardous) the starter will throw the yellow flag. That calls the start off and they circulate at least one more lap before trying again.

Flags

We have discussed green flags (start or restart) and yellow flags (caution, accident), but there are several others. And, some of these flags mean something different in NASCAR than they do in, say, Formula 1.

Red Flag—A red flag means an extremely dangerous condition exists. The race has been stopped and there is no racing back to the yellow. Or in the case of a caution that is more extensive than first thought, the pace car will simply direct traffic to stop—not

Accidents happen—frequently in most races. With 45 cars running at 200 mph nose to tail for 500 miles, something is bound to happen.

usually in the pits since the crew could do work on the car and gain an unfair advantage.

Red Flag with Yellow—Pits closed and no one can enter.

White Flag—Means there is one more lap. More precisely, it indicates the start of the final lap of the race.

Blue and Yellow Flag—This is given to cars that are about to be passed by a faster car, and in theory, they are supposed to yield. Yeah, right.

Checkered Flag—Is there anyone reading this book who doesn't know what this one means? I didn't think so.

Accidents and Cautions

False starts are rare in Winston Cup, but first lap incidents are not. Racing around with forty other drivers nose to tail on a track like Bristol (a half-mile banked oval) is not an easy task.

At the beginning of any race, driver adrenaline will be high as the first laps at speed are completed. Conditions are crowded; everyone is jockeying for position, so the racing is pretty tight.

Frequently you'll see a driver in the middle of the pack make a mistake and a good percentage of the field will become involved in a major crash. Some of those involved may be out for the day—finished even before the race has really begun. Others may have damage so extensive they have to go back to the garage, fix the car and then will come back to racing many laps back. As mentioned earlier, they will still continue if they can to try and pick up points. Some drivers may just spin and need to get pointed in the right direction before they can get under way. Those are the lucky ones.

If a driver does have to go back to the garages before he can go back out onto the

Depending on the extent of the damage, crews will make every attempt to fix the car behind the wall or in the garage and get it back on the track to get as many points as possible.

A yellow flag is thrown and safety crews take to the track to clear up tire-cutting debris.

track to circulate for some points, a NASCAR official will always be on hand to make sure all the work is completed according to the rules. With the exception of the engine block, which can't be changed, almost everything on the car can be replaced. The team can replace a rear end, a transmission, or whatever, as long as they do it with approved replacement parts and under NASCAR supervision.

Longtime NASCAR fans remember the days when a car would go behind the wall and get a fresh engine. The best story of pit work happened in 1978 at Pocono, when Cale Yarborough, then in the series points lead, brought his car into the garages and the team changed an entire engine. He got the car back on the road in just over 15 minutes. He finished sufficiently high enough that he maintained the points lead. But that kind of

Once the yellow flag is thrown, the pace car comes out on the track. The NASCAR official at right is there to tell drivers whether or not pit lane is open during the yellow. There are also lights. If it's closed, he throws the red flag with a yellow cross in it (the flag on the ground). If pit lane is open, he flies the green like he is now.

Mark Martin heads for his pit, making a beeline for this Bosch marker.

thing doesn't happen anymore.

At any rate, being up front reduces the chance of getting knocked out if somebody at the back loses it. That's another reason qualifying up front is so important. It keeps a driver out of trouble during the first few laps of heavy traffic. Unfortunately, there are very few races where there are not at least two to three accidents. Fortunately, injuries are relatively rare.

Yellow Flags—Should there be an accident, NASCAR officials will throw a yellow flag. At the same time, yellow lights will appear around the track.

Depending on how big the track is, caution lights are placed as drivers head into all four turns, as well as the middle of backstretch, and of course at the start/finish line. The "Official Caution" is located at the flagstand. The driver leading that last lap, passing under the flagstand as the yellow first appears, will be credited with the race lap, and as mentioned earlier, pick up that extra point for leading a lap.

The other reason a driver will race to the flagstand is that he may be able to unlap himself. But say on the first lap an accident occurred. One of the drivers spun and had to get off the grass and then get back onto the track. Let's say he had to come into the pits to make sure everything was all right on the car. In the meantime, the pack has raced ahead. If he was never passed by the leader, but sits just in front of the leader when the race was given the green again, he is last.

Okay, at this moment in our scenario, he's on the same lap, albeit at the very end of the lap. Now let's say another accident happens and the yellow flag comes out again. If he manages to stay in front of the leader past the flagstand he can make up for all of the time he had lost. He hasn't been lapped yet, so he hasn't lost a lap. When the pace car enters the track to pick up the leader, the dri-

ver who was just about to get lapped can drive quickly around the track and join the other cars at the back of the pack. He (or anybody else for that matter) cannot pass another car while under yellow. But at least he has made up almost three-quarters of a lap.

Frankly, although NASCAR will deny it, they can throw a yellow flag to bunch up the field in order to keep the race tight. NASCAR will have full-course caution periods unlike road racing. Road racing has cautions that are frequently just at one corner, for minor wrecks or for a small piece of debris on the apron of the track away from any on-track action. Usually there is enough carnage at a race they don't need an excuse. But if the race is one-sided, they can find a reason to throw a yellow.

Yellow Flag Pit Stops

But they don't always have to pit while the race is going on. As mentioned, they can also do it under yellow. But there are some rules as to how it can be done.

First off, NASCAR knows that pitting under yellow is an ideal situation for teams.

A typical pit stop.

The crew is responsible for clearing their own gear, including the air hose. Failure to do so will mean a penalty, which could cost them the race.

They can get in and out while the rest of the field is held up behind the pace car, rejoining at the back of the grid. If everybody's pitting they can race back onto the track to improve position. By "race" that means speed in and out of the pits. But there is actually no real racing going on anywhere on the track during a caution. The race during the caution periods is in the pits. The driver who gets into and out of the pits first and crosses the line exiting the pits has the spot. He then speeds around the track to catch the field. But once past the yellow line, there is no more racing. Not during a caution.

So pitting under the yellow is advantageous. But the pits aren't always open under yellow flag conditions. That's because NASCAR wants to make sure there are no unfair advantages in pit stops.

A few years ago, pit lane was open at all times. So what was happening was some teams were able to dive into the pits before the pace car came out, depending on where they were when the caution came out. They would make the appropriate changes to the

car, then race back out. While the rest of the field was held up behind the pace car and didn't get an opportunity to pit, these cars would finally pit and drive around to find themselves behind the pace car and the drivers who dove into the pits first. It was an unfair situation based on coincidental track positioning and good radio contact.

Now, the pit lane is closed until the field is fully assembled and bunched up, then the pits are opened and a huge train of cars will travel down pit road for stops all at once. It gives everyone the same opportunity to pit under yellow and again, keeps the racing close.

Once the lapped and recently unlapped drivers sort themselves out, the field will most likely make pit stops. But based on the amount of fuel allowed in the tanks, which is 22 gallons, the cars will have to stop sometime during the race anyway. The fact is that near-two-ton cars eat up tires and need fresh ones to be competitive, teams need to come in to add gas and tires, and perhaps make changes to aerodynamics or

Many times, races are won or lost in the pits. A stubborn lug nut or just 1 second delay can cost the race.

chassis (see pages related to chassis, tires or aerodynamics). They can make these changes during green flag race laps, but they lose valuable time. A field slowed by caution may run 85 mph at Daytona behind the pace car. At speed, they're running 200+ even with restrictor plates. That's almost three times the distance lost between pitting on green and pitting on yellow. Everybody knows that and everybody tries to pit during a yellow caution if possible.

NASCAR knows that too, and they want to keep the stops orderly. That's why they keep pit lane closed for the initial lap. You'll see an official holding a red flag with a yellow "X" on it. That marks the "Pits Closed" condition. When the green flag appears in that same official's hand, it signals it's okay to enter.

Green Flag Pit Stops

A Winston Cup car is tricky enough to drive when the handling is perfect. But when the tires are worn, or when the car is not handling the way the driver wants it to, it's a handful just to keep on the track. And, you can't drive 500 miles flat-out on a single tank of gas.

Pit stops are a necessary evil, but they are also a key to winning. Many races are won or lost in the pits. Although teams need pit stops to change tires and add fuel, as well as give the driver a break, there are more things that can go wrong in the pits than just about anywhere else. Just coming into or leaving the pits can cost the race.

The best time to have a pit stop is when the yellow flag is out, during a caution period. Under caution the pace car comes out and bunches up the field. The entire field runs much slower; usually about one third of top speed, or somewhere around 70 to 80 mph.

Under green flag conditions—racing conditions—it takes a driver much more than the 22 seconds the television stopwatch says, because of the entrance and exit times going into and moving out of the pit. In other words, it isn't just the time spent at a dead stop that counts in the race, but the total time spent travelling down pit road to the stop, the stop itself, and accelerating back up to speed to join the other drivers. At a place like Dover or Martinsville, there's no way to not lose a lap during green flag racing. At Talladega, a driver will likely not lose a lap, but he'll be all the way in the back.

Pit stops themselves are choreographed more perfectly than a dance. Each person in

NASCAR also controls when drivers can can exit the pits, and to monitor that they don't cross the blend line too soon.

the pits has a job to do and must do it perfectly and in a space of about 20 seconds. A good stop is under 18 seconds; a bad one is 22. And when the entire field qualifies within a second of each other, pit stops can win or lose races.

Only seven people are allowed over the pit wall. The pit lane is separated from the pit area and pit box by a low wall. That's where you hear the expression "seven men over the wall." And that's why you'll see those long poles handing drivers drinks. They don't do it to be convenient. They can't be over the wall. Those are NASCAR rules and they are there to eliminate unfair advantages and reduce crowding in the pits to avoid accidents.

Generally teams will have four tire men, a jackman, a fuel man and the gas catch man, the guy who vents the tank and catches the excess fuel that comes back out of the car.

Obviously, the tire men change the tires. They do so with lightening quick moves and air wrenches that are finely tuned to whiz off a lug nut as quick as you can say, "take off that lug nut." As mentioned earlier, the lug nuts are held on to the replacement wheel studs by heavy grease or glue.

Sometimes you'll see a two-tire change as opposed to a four-tire change. The difference, frankly, is fuel. What that means is that you never see a two-tire stop if the team is refueling the car. Refueling takes all the time—sometimes nearly a half-minute. So a two-tire change is usually done right at the end of the race, with just a few laps to go, under caution. By the same token, sometimes they don't need a full tank of fuel. This is what's called a "splash and go," and it allows the driver to get just enough fuel to go to the end of the race without sacrificing extra time for unneeded fuel.

If the entire field pits for tires it makes no sense to stay out on old tires. But sometimes the driver doesn't need all new tires. Sometimes he wants the ones he has on the inside or outside to be changed, but the others left alone (the team will want to change outside, or right side). Like the splash and go, it shortens the stop.

Now if this stop is in the last ten laps, the driver has to hope it's the correct choice not to have put all four tires on. Maybe he got out just a few moments sooner than the dri-

NASCAR officials seem to be everywhere, watching every move, looking for any infractions. These guys keep things running smoothly.

ver who had all four changed. Maybe he went from fifth to first because he didn't take on new tires. About that time he's certainly wondering if he made the right choice.

Pit Location—The team's pits are assigned by qualifying order. They used to be set by point standings. The first pit selection was taken by the previous, or reigning, Winston Cup Champion, regardless of how badly his current season was going and regardless of where he qualifies in the race. The second spot was given to the current points leader, then the second place man in points, and so on.

That isn't the way it works anymore. Since all champions always took the last pit box on pit lane, it became obvious that the reigning champ's selection was becoming more than a perk, but a downright unfair advantage. Pit box positions are now decided by qualifying order. Whoever is on pole gets the first box he wants, second man gets whatever's left, and so on.

Pit Speed Limit—When cars come into the pits, they appear to be crawling, and they are relatively speaking. In the past, cars sped through the pits as if it were another part of the racetrack. Of course, a lot of injuries, and even some deaths, have occurred. Pit speed limits have reduced the likelihood of serious accidents, and they are taken very seriously.

The cars creep into the pits at a pre-deter-

mined pit speed. At most tracks it is 45 mph. The slowest is Martinsville at 35 mph.

To help drivers determine how fast their car is going, they need some sort of gauge. They don't have speedometers, so they must rely on the tach. During the parade laps, the pace car will turn off its lights, signalling that it is slowing down to the pit speed limit. The drivers can then slow down and note on their tach what engine rpm in a certain gear will give that speed.

NASCAR monitors the speed limit of the drivers as they come in. The cars are clocked via a set of lines painted on the pavement surface in pit lane. The tower watches to see how long it takes each driver to move from one line on pit lane to the next. If the driver travels the individual segment faster than he should, he's penalized. The lines are typically 100 to 150 yards apart.

Offending drivers who exceed the speed limit will be called in for a "stop and go," meaning that during green flag race conditions, the driver will have to come down pit road to his pit at the proper speed, stop his car, wait for NASCAR official to allow him to proceed again, then get back up to speed after exiting the pits. As you can imagine, that takes him from the front to the back real quick.

Other Pit Penalties—A driver will also be penalized for things he does driving in or out of the pits, or for mistakes his teams makes. For example, if the driver should run over

The jackman must carry the jack from side to side, rather than drag or whip it around. Too many people were getting struck in the legs with these things. Photo courtesy NASCAR.

the air hose for the pneumatic wrench, or the wrench itself because a crew member didn't clear it, he'll be brought in for a stop and go. Or if a car running a lap down on the leaders pits with the leaders, he will be brought in.

The way the crew does their job is also watched closely by officials. For example, the jackman must carry the hydraulic jack from one side of the car to the other; he can't just sling it around. Years ago, jackmen used to whip the jack around, and ankles were getting broken. So now they must carry it. Some teams decided to make things easy, and built their own lightweight aluminum jacks, but NASCAR outlawed those too (although for reasons that are less clear).

The pit lane is three lanes wide; one lane is for stopped cars and two lanes are for cars entering and exiting their pits. The rule on pit stops is that whomever is across the line marking the exit of the pits is in first position on the track. NASCAR has an official down at the end of pit lane to ensure exits are orderly.

So although there is a speed limit, there is still a race in the pits. And getting across the "Pit Exit Line" first is a top priority. Some drivers tend to get extremely single-minded getting to that line, often forsaking safety to beat their opponents out of the pits. You'll see a lot of mistakes made while trying to get out first. The most obvious is bumping another car in pit lane, shooting out of the pit too fast when trying to make it in front of another car that was also pitting.

Regardless, whoever is at that line first gets the position. They are generally good at relinquishing the position once it's clear they lost it—even if they only lost it by a few feet past the line.

Typically the pit road exit extends out of the actual pit lane some distance down the racetrack, marked with a yellow line called "the blend line." When the yellow line becomes white, the drivers can then move up onto the track. They must stay below the yellow line, or face a penalty. This is to ensure that they get up to a safe speed before jumping into traffic. It's the same concept as the on-ramp on your local highway

At places like Richmond or Martinsville, by the time the cars make it to the blend line they are travelling the same speed as the pack; at places like Daytona or Talladega, where it can take literally as much as two laps to work up to speed, they obviously won't be travelling the same rate of speed as the leaders, but the blend line will help.

Racing Lines

You'll often hear announcers talking of "lines" or "grooves." On a racetrack there are certain spots where the traffic runs smoother. It may start as a place where the asphalt has extra grip, but it becomes a place where the rubber from the entire field begins to accumulate and then becomes stickier. Some tracks have a couple of grooves; others only have one.

Many drivers consider Darlington to be a one-groove track. If you try to pass you'd better do it before a corner, because once you're in it, you're going to have a lot of trouble if you're not in that groove.

The groove, or racing line, is defined by the amount of rubber that has been laid down by the cars. There's more grip there, naturally. And, because tires compounds are so soft, they shed tiny bits of rubber, called "marbles," outside this groove. Needless to say, if you get "out of the groove and onto the marbles," the effect can be just as if you stepped on a bunch of marbles on a sidewalk. You're going to lose traction. Sometimes, the track surface outside the racing line is also sandy and dirty and contains debris.

Traction can also be questionable on the inside of the track, below the racing line. If a car blows an engine, the driver usually darts toward the apron as soon as possible to avoid spewing oil onto the racing line. The trouble is, he spews it onto the apron or below the racing line.

Some cars, however, just handle better

lower than the others do, and some handle better higher up. It depends on how the car was set up that day. Driving styles also dictate the racing line through a corner. The three photos above illustrate how three different drivers approach the same corner.

Three different drivers, three different lines through the turn. These are all taken at the same track, during the same practice session. Mike Slade photos.

Two of the best racing strategists in the business are Jack Roush (left) and Richard Childress. Roush owns (as of this writing) 5 different NASCAR teams, while Childress has partnered with Dale Earnhardt for 7 Winston Cup Championships. These guys call the shots during the race.

Restarts

If the driver should slide out and clip or smack the wall a caution will be thrown. If the accident is very severe or a lot of traffic is blocked, the race will be stopped, although that doesn't happen very often. Once the track is clear, the race is restarted.

Usually you'll see the cars restarted in a single row if they are all on the lead lap. If the race has just been given the green and there's an accident, you'll see the restart done with one long single-file line.

If the restart occurs in the middle to the end of the race, there will be two lines of cars, side by side, just as they do at the beginning of the race. This isn't because they're restarting the race in order, but because they essentially start the race in two groups, an outside row and an inside row. The outside row is for the slower cars. They determine that from the positions on the track at the time the caution occurred. More to the point, if you are a lap or more down, you'll be starting on the outside row. Additionally, the "25-lap rules" says that if you are not one of the frontrunners in the last 25 racing laps, you don't get to restart in the preferred groove, or racing line.

The pace car directs the drivers to take inside or outside, taking its cue via radio from NASCAR's timing and scoring officials. The scoring people can make a mistake and put a car on the wrong lap, but if that happens, the driver still needs to have the situation discussed by the team; he still needs to start where he's been told and hope an appeal gets him out for the next time.

Restarts early in the race, where there are no lapped cars, are done in single file after the pace car pulls in. The leader controls the pace of the restart and has an advantage because he can keep the pace slow until he decides to jump on the accelerator. It takes the people behind him a half-beat to get on full throttle and by then he's already moving out by the time the starter throws the green flag restarting the race.

RACING STRATEGY

Today's racing is much more than getting the car to go as fast as possible around the track ahead of everyone else. Crew chiefs and car owners have become crafty strategists that must adapt to the changing race conditions as they unfold during a race. It is likened to a battle, a war if you will, that is won or lost based on the spur of the moment decisions made in the pits. Drivers make them as well.

Drafting

When the track is a mile long and there are 43 cars on the track, it's obvious that cars will be running together. There's no way not to run together.

But there is a more important reason cars will run together, and that is wind resistance. Two cars punch through the air more easily than one car; three cars are faster than two and so on. At some point the length of this "train" will slow progress, but for the most part, cars running together are quicker than ones running alone.

The car in front pushes through the air mass first, creating a vacuum behind it. This vacuum has little wind resistance, so the car in the air pocket can actually go faster than the one in front of it. The second car also helps to push the front car by eliminating the turbulent mass of "dirty air" that is usually behind a car that can create drag. The air is swirling around the end of the second car now, but the effects on the two-cars is less than it would have been on just one. If another car joins the train, it will make the three of them faster still.

The Slingshot Pass—At the right moment in the draft, one of the cars behind can actually swing out and pass the car in front. It has more speed to pass. This passing technique is called the "slingshot." The car in the draft is faster than the car in front, so it can use the momentum through the corner to save power, then accelerate past the car in front, using the residual power saved while running just behind the leader to shoot past and take the lead. If he gets enough momentum, he can go far enough in front to break the draft. Many drivers do not want to lead the last lap of a long draft. It's tough to stay in front.

Drafting is important at all tracks, but it is

Drafting is a fact of life in NASCAR. If you don't draft well, or get hooked up with a partner, you will have trouble staying in front. Mike Slade photo.

absolutely critical at the longer tracks—especially the restrictor plate races like Daytona and Talladega.

You'll hear announcers talking about a certain driver getting a partner. What he means is that the lead driver needs to find someone who can work with him to draft to the front of the pack and keep it there, running nose to tail. Sure, they both want to win, but they can worry about that on the last lap. At that moment it's more important to get out front.

Here's a slingshot pass in progress. Just a moment ago, these three cars were single file. The Skoal car picked up enough speed in the draft to slingshot past, and he gets a push from the Hardees car. The Hardees car also gets a pull from the draft, so the two of them are hooked up and leave the Bud car behind. That's a classic NASCAR technique. Mike Slade photo.

Believe it or not, Jeff Gordon in the Dupont Monte Carlo is not in an ideal position. He's running all alone, and will likely get passed in the final laps unless he gets a push.

So they draft, two cars moving out and running together to get away from the confusion of the pack.

The air on the side of the cars makes a difference as well, an effect not unlike that of the wake from a boat. As two cars punch through the air, there is turbulence on the side, which can affect another car running alongside if it is too close by creating drag. This is called "side drafting," and is a defense strategy employed by drivers as they are being passed. A car being passed will often move as close to the passing car as possible to slow him down with this side air drag.

Daytona and Talladega frequently have 15- and 20-car drafts, and if you get caught out of one, you are in big trouble. In 1998, Jeff Gordon had probably the best car in the field at Talladega and was set to win the race. He was in second or third behind the leader. Behind him was Bobby Labonte. Behind him, the rest of the pack.

Gordon began gesturing to Labonte to move out, to work together. After a few minutes of hand signals (which Labonte wasn't responding to), Gordon moved out and tried to pass the leader. Labonte didn't go with him. Gordon went around, a six-car train passed him by. Gordon finished eighth. Labonte won the race.

So drafting can backfire too. If a driver doesn't have a partner it can be a disastrous situation. He will lose a race because of it, but if two cars run end to end and work together, they can run faster than a single car can. That's all through breaking through the mass of air and drafting.

Final Laps

The last 10 laps in a Winston Cup race are usually the best. NASCAR fans live for these last few laps. They watch qualifying and practice, follow the race's progress through cautions and pit stops for this moment, for these last ten laps of racing. And Winston Cup almost always delivers in these final minutes of competition.

Rarely can you pick a winner of a Winston Cup race before the race starts. There are so many different variables. But on the last ten laps, if you've been paying attention to lap times and watching who's been consistently fast and running clean, then you may have an idea of who should win. That's not to say that they actually will win.

Part of being successful in racing is based on creating opportunities. A race team that gives itself the ability to lead at the end has a great chance of winning. In other words, if a team is near the front in the final moments, anything can happen and it might get lucky and beat the best car on the day to win the race. It happens more often that you'd think.

Especially at restrictor plate races, the person who is leading at the end of the race has a good chance of losing in the final turn. The restrictor plate generally makes all cars equal by limiting power. Drafting is the only way to really gain a speed advantage. If you're leading without a partner, chances are the competitors behind are setting you up for a last-lap slingshot. Two or three other drivers will team up and drive right by, using the draft.

Regardless, the final few laps are the best, but you have to have been watching the whole race to get the same thrill out of the last laps. Hardened fans know its not the same thing watching the start, then coming back for the last few laps. You miss the intensity that way.

POST RACE INSPECTION

Once the race is over, the winning driver will head to the winner's circle, or victory lane (whatever it's called at each individual track) and step out to do the winner's interview. He'll do the hat dance (wearing maybe a dozen different sponsor's hats while a photographer takes his picture with each one on) and then goes into the media center for interviews.

Meanwhile his car is being torn apart.

To ensure fair play, NASCAR takes apart the winner's car. They check it with the templates once again, weigh it, check ride height and just inspect the car with the same attention to detail as pre-race tech inspection. Usually the teardown is limited to just the engine, but if they feel there are other irregularities the officials will scrutinize those as well. But typically, the officials remove the manifolds, the heads, and so forth. The teams will actually do the teardowns as NASCAR officials supervise, and then check the components themselves for infractions.

Should they find parts that are not legal— like heads that have different port configurations than they should have, or whatever, some sort of sanction will be placed upon the team, including losing the race should the infraction be serious enough.

As in any other form of racing, there are protests. NASCAR drivers tend to be more discreet. They make subtle statements through the press. There is still politics, it just isn't as blatant as in most other forms of motorsport. Which, frankly, is one of the appeals of NASCAR. Drivers and teams seem to sort out problems by themselves— or at least without a lot of official whining.

Finally, after three days of racing, the teams will pack up and move off.

Within an hour after the checkered flag, most transporters are already on the move, except those who must go thorugh the post race inspection. On to the next race, where they start all over again.

Miraculously, the cars will be loaded and moved within minutes of the checkered flag falling. It is by far the most efficient migration in all of racing. Where in most other series transporters will remain in the paddock well into the night, cleaning up and packing gear, Winston Cup teams are rarely in the garages more than an hour or two after the race. They will have stowed the unneeded gear during the race, put the pit equipment back first thing after the race, and pushed the car into the transporter within a half-hour after it comes back into the garages.

Forty or more transporters will move out of the garages at about the same time the fans do. Frequently, you'll be stuck in traffic with the same people you came to see race. NASCAR blending back into the real world.

The caravan will move on to the next stop and the teams will do it all over again. If you follow the sport, you'll know exactly where they're going and how they will get there. The only thing different will be what they accomplish at racing speeds.

WINSTON CUP TRACKS

2

Winston Cup tracks vary from short tracks to superspeedways and road courses. The following is a list of the tracks as of the year 2001. We've made every effort to update this list with the latest possible information, but you might want to check before you go to the race. These tracks are constantly being upgraded, and changes are inevitable. They are listed in alphabetical order.

Atlanta International Raceway

P.O. Box 500
Highways 19 & 41
Hampton, GA 30228
PH: (770) 946-4211
FAX: (770) 707-7853
Degree of banking in the corners: 24 degrees.
Degree of banking on the straight: 5 degrees.
Length of frontstretch: 1,415 feet.
Length of backstretch: 1,320 feet.
Track record: qualifying—Geoff Bodine (Ford), November 15, 1997, 197.478 mph; race Dale Earnhardt (Chevrolet), November 12, 1995, 163.633.
Location: In Hampton, 30 miles south of Atlanta, on 1500 Highway 19 and 41 South.
Circuit: 1.54 mile paved oval.
Major races: NASCAR Winston Cup (two races); NASCAR Busch Series Grand National Division.

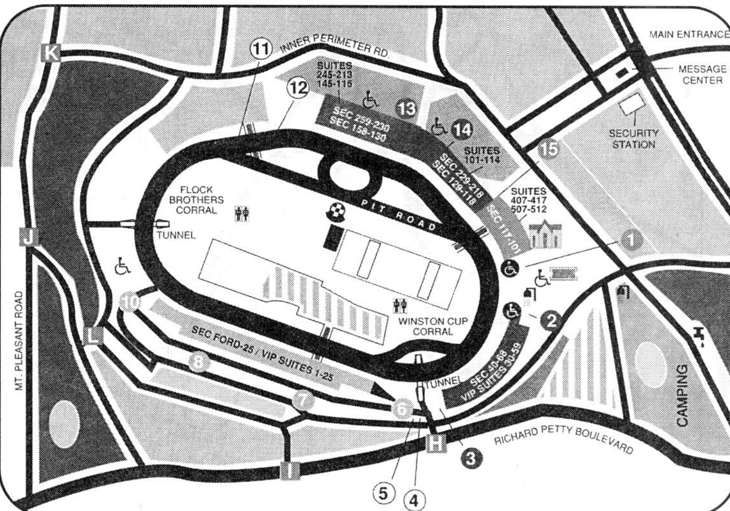

Atlanta Raceway's claim to fame is the annual staging of the final Winston Cup race of the Championship, the NAPA 500. Probably the most popular race in a season of spectacular events, Atlanta Raceway, built in 1960, is forever remembered for being a championship-deciding event.

It's fitting that the final race should be held here, since it is one of the most accessible tracks on the Winston Cup calendar, as well as being one of the best spectator facilities. There are very few seats at Atlanta Raceway where fans cannot see the entire track. In addition, the infield offers probably the best view in NASCAR racing. The speedway made a change recently. The start/finish line was switched to the opposite side of the track. Meanwhile, the seating on that side—the new start/finish—has been upgraded completely. Three new grandstands have appeared, more than doubling the capacity. A nine-story building with condos and suites has also been erected.

Both races sell out far in advance. But beware: the March race can be cold, although the rural countryside is usually known for its hot, humid weather.

But if you want tickets for the grandstands—especially with a view of the pits—you'll have to book tickets early in the season. You can buy tickets by phone with a credit card, or the track will reserve tickets for 10 days until they receive your check. Tickets sell out earlier each year, so act quickly.

There are general admission areas on the north hill backstretch. People bring lawn chairs, and there are small bleachers there as well. The infield offers a good view, and you can camp there Saturday of race weekend. There are several hotels in the immediate area, but the best place to stay is in Atlanta itself. There should be no problem getting rooms—even if you come into Atlanta at the last minute. Call the Georgia Department of Industry, Trade and Tourism at (404) 656-3590 in Atlanta for more information about lodging.

Bristol International Raceway

Highway 11 East & Volunteer Parkway
P.O. Box 3966
Bristol, TN 37625
PH: (423) 764-1161
FAX: (423) 764-1646
Degree of banking in the corners: 36 degrees.
Degree of banking on the straight: 16 degrees.
Length of frontstretch: 650 feet.
Length of backstretch: 650 feet.
Track record: qualifying—Rusty Wallace (Ford), April 9, 1999, 125.142 mph; race—Charlie Glotzbach (Chevrolet), July 11, 1971, 101.074 mph.
Location: Northern Tennessee, five miles from the Virginia border, off Interstate I -81 at Highway 11, in Bristol.
Circuit: .533 mile paved oval.
Major races: NASCAR Winston Cup (two races); NASCAR Busch Grand National (two races).

Touted as "The World's Fastest Half Mile," Bristol is the home of NASCAR's first major-league night race. Bristol is also remarkable in that it truly is an ultra fast half-mile circuit—mostly credited to its 36-degree banking.

It was sold in 1996 to Bruton Smith, who also owns Atlanta, Las Vegas, Texas, Charlotte and Sears Point Speedways. Smith's people expanded the facility dramatically, easing parking constraints, traffic flow and seating. In just one season the seating went from 71,000 to 130,000. That's 100,000 more seats then the track had when it opened in 1961.

The entire circuit is visible from anywhere in the stands, so any ticket will do the job. The problem is getting the seat in the first place. Tickets sell quickly, especially for August's night race. Longtime fans reserve seats a year in advance, and are on the waiting list for the following year, making life for one-timers difficult.

Staying in Bristol is not easy either. The hilly, forested area of northern Tennessee is a popular vacation spot, making the event even more difficult to see because tourists who often have only a passing interest in racing will come to Bristol while vacationing in nearby Cumberland National Park areas.

There are several hotels in Bristol, but they are quickly snatched up by teams. Try the Hampton Inn at (423) 764-3600, or the Ramada Inn at (540) 669-7171, or the Regency Inn at (423) 968-9474, or the Scottish Inn at (540) 669-4148, or the Red Carpet Inn at (540) 669-1151. Knoxville will have rooms, but is almost two hours away; or try Roanoke. Camping is probably the best way to do it. Camping exists outside the track, but there's nothing in the infield. In fact, you can't get into the infield at all.

Call the Tennessee Department of Tourist Development at (615) 741-2158. Or, for camping and cabin rental call the Tennessee Department of Conservation Division of Parks at (800) 421-6683.

California Speedway

9330 Cherry Ave.
Fontana, CA 92325
PH: (800) 944-7223
(909) 429-5200
Degree of banking in the corners: 14 degrees.
Degree of banking in the Tri-oval: 11 degrees.
Degree of banking on the back straight: three degrees.
Length of front stretch: 2,500 feet.
Length of back stretch: 3,100 feet.
Track record: qualifying – Greg Sacks (Chevrolet), June 21, 1997, 183.753 mph; race – Jeff Gordon (Chevrolet), June 22, 1997, 155.012 mph.
Circuit: Two-mile D-shaped oval.
Location/Directions: Located at the intersection of Interstates I-10, I-15 and I-60, approximately 45 miles east of Los Angeles, a few miles from Ontario International Airport. From I-10, exit at Cherry Ave, then go north approximately two miles to the track.
Major races: NASCAR Winston Cup; Busch Series, Craftsman Truck

Since the demise of Ontario Speedway and Riverside Raceway, Southern California fans have been without a permanent racetrack of stature. California Speedway's 1997 opening changed all that.

Roger Penske, of Indy and stock car team owner fame, built a modern showplace of a racetrack, with room for nearly 120,000 fans and wide flat-out racing surfaces almost identical in design to Michigan International Speedway, which he also owns.

The difference between the two—both D-shaped subtle tri-ovals—is the degree of banking. Michigan's corners are banked at 18 degrees while California Speedway's are banked at 14 degrees. Like at MIS, racing is fast and tight. The cars easily go three-wide in the turns for Winston Cup, and four-wide down the backstretch.

The facility definitely has a Californian feel to it, with palm trees lining the back straight, and brick, tile and stucco evident in the spectator areas.

From the beginning, the speedway has sold out for all its major races, be they CART or NASCAR. But NASCAR has a particular draw for the local race fans since it had been nearly 15 years since NASCAR has contested a race in southern California.

The first race was held in June 1997 with Jeff Gordon taking the win. The track sits five miles east of the old Ontario Speedway site (although all that's left of the old track is the Ontario Mills Mall) on the exact location of the historic 530-acre Kaiser Steel Mill. Remnants of that mill, a concrete water tower, still remain in the infield.

You can stay near Ontario Airport, where there's a Marriott, a Residence Inn, and a Doubletree, among others. Most of the teams stay in Ontario. Or check Riverside, where there's a Mariott (on University Ave.; call (909) 276-1200), a Hilton in Cucamunga (call (909) 980-0400), and the historic Mission Inn (call (909) 784-0300), among others.

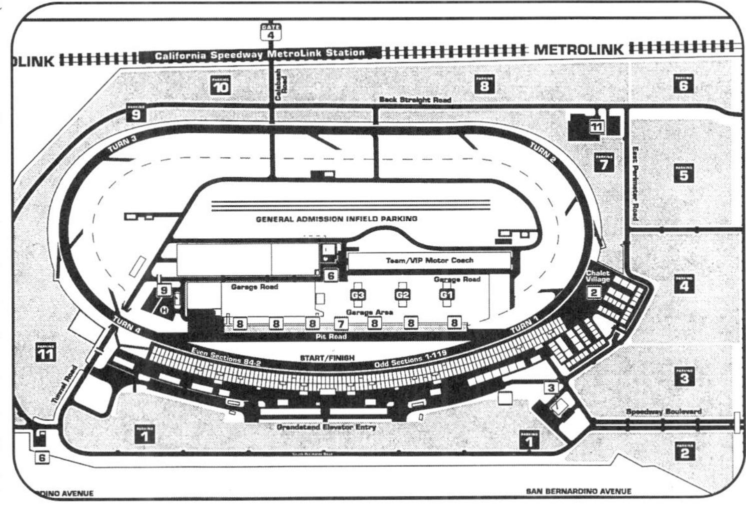

Chicagoland Speedway

3200 South Chicago St.,
Joliet, IL 60434
Mailing: P.P. Box 3339
Joliet, IL 60434
(815) 722-5500
Circuit: 1.5 mile paved tri-oval
Location/Directions: 30 miles southwest of downtown Chicago, in Joliet, IL on Old Historic Route 66 (three miles south of I-80 on Route 53). From the east, take I-80 West to the Route 53 South/Chicago St. exit (exit 132). Follow route 53 South. The Raceway will be 3 miles on the left. From the North, take I-55 South to I-80 east on the Route 53 South/Chicago St. exit (exit 132). Follow Route 53 South. The raceway will be 3 miles on the left.
Degree of banking in the corners: 18 degrees.
Degree of banking on the straight: 11 degrees frontstretch; 5 degrees backstretch.
Length of frontstretch: 699 feet.
Length of backstretch: 699 feet.

In November of 2000, Chicagoland Speedway, not to be confused with Chicago Motor Speedway some 30 miles away, ran its first test sessions. The asphalt had cured and cars took to the track for the first time. By all accounts, it is going to become one of the best new tracks in the country.

Although the Chicago Motor Speedway is new and exciting, it is a flat track and caters more to CART cars than Chicagoland, which is banked and will concentrate on stock cars.

The track is set up with the fan in mind, with the lowest seat some 12 feet above the racing surface and an infield complex that is lower in elevation than the surroundings so that every seat can see the entire track.

The place offers grandstand seating for 75,000 spectators, with an infield at 1,200 feet x 2,850 feet, large enough to accommodate four Soldier Fields. Parking for the facility accommodates over 70,000 vehicles on 930 acres.

The track is a cooperative effort between the Indianapolis Motor Speedway Corporation, International Speedway Corporation and the founding owners of Route 66 Raceway. And in fact the facility is located on the Route 66 Raceway—a 240-acre motorsports complex located in Joliet that includes one of the country's best drag strips, a 3/8ths-mile clay oval and a road-course test track. Dale Coyne, who previously served as chief operating officer of Route 66 Raceway, is president of Raceway Associates, the joint-venture company.

The Indianapolis Motor Speedway Corporation, which of course owns the famed Indianapolis Motor Speedway, has combined with International Speedway Corporation, a leading promoter of motorsports activities in the United States led by NASCAR Chairman Bill France Jr., to expand into the Chicago market. And you have to believe that with all their experience, the facility will be first-rate.

With everything going on in the Chicago area, lodging isn't a problem, but what follows is a listing of Joliet hotels and restaurants, just to make the trip easier. For hotels in the Joliet area, try the Days Inn at 19747 Frontage Rd at (815) 725-2180, the Crown Inn at 2219 West Jefferson St. (815) 744-1220, The Elks Motel, located on Routes 55 & 52nd in Joliet at (815) 725-0101, the Fairfield Inn, located at 1501 Riverboat Cntr Dr. Joliet, IL 60436, (815) 741-3499, or the North Fairfield Inn, located at 3239 Norman Ave. Joliet, Il 60435, (815) 436-6577. You can also try the Holiday Inn Express, located at 411 S. Larkin Ave in Joliet at (815) 729-2000. Red Roof Inns has a spot on 1750 Mc Donough St. In Jolliet, (815) 741-2304, a Super 8 Hotel, on 1730 McDonough St. (815) 439-3838. Ramada, located at 3231 Norman Ave. in Joliet, call (815) 439-4200.

In Joliet there's a Wal-Mart & Sams Club Shopping Complex, Wendy's, Pizza Hut Delivery, White Hen Pantry Convenience Store, Phillips(Union)-66 Gas Station, Taco Bell, A Steak & Shake Restaurant and a Club Foods Supermarket Food Store, all on Larkin Ave. If you take Larkin north, then take a left onto Jefferson Street, you can find: Boston Market Restaurant, Dominics Food Stores, Grandma's Old Fashioned Pancake House, Heroes & Legends Sports Bar, and the Wilderness Mall, which features: Montgomery Wards, Old County Buffet restaurant, and Menards Home Improvement Center.

Darlington Raceway

P.O. Box 500
Dalrlington, SC 29540
Highways 151 & 34
Darlington, SC 29532
PH: (843) 395-8499
Degree of banking in corners One and Two: 25 degrees.
Degree of banking in corners Three and Four: 23 degrees.
Degree of banking on the straight: 2 degrees.
Length of frontstretch: 1,229 feet.
Length of backstretch: 1,229 feet.
Track record: qualifying—Ward Burton (Pontiac), March 22, 1996, 173.797 mph; race—Dale Earnhardt (Chevrolet), March 28, 1993, 139.958 mph.
Location: Northeast South Carolina, just west of Darlington, on Highways 34-151, six miles north of Interstate I-95. From I-95, take US 52 North at Exit 164, then west on Highway 151-34.
Circuit: 1.366 mile paved oval.
Major races: NASCAR Winston Cup Series Championship (two events); NASCAR Busch Grand National (two events).

Nicknamed the "Lady in Black," Darlington Raceway has punished many Winston Cup drivers who dared to push her to the limit. Darlington has the distinction of being the first super-speedway in the U.S.. Opened for business in 1950, Darlington now has a blend of old and new, which both elicits images of past days of stock car racing, and offers a glimpse of the technology in the series now which makes it one of the toughest in the world to dominate.

This is yet another International Speedway Corporation track, under the wings of the France family, and it has the same allure about it as Talladega or Daytona.

The "Darlington stripe" is one of the interesting aspects of Darlington. The stripe was formed as someone realized long ago that the fastest way around Darlington's quick 1.366 miles was to tap the right rear quarter-panel into the wall outside turn four. To run 400 perfect laps, drivers needed to tap the wall 400 times. The practice carried on through the '60s and early '70s, when track resurfacing changed the racing line.

Originally built as a 1.25 mile oval, it was repaved and altered slightly in 1953 to its present con-figuration of 1.366 miles. The slight changes affected only one end of the circuit, so the banking and turn geometry is different on each side—which is a nightmare for car set up.

Although originally planned as a true oval, the land owner, Harold Brasington, wanted to preserve a nearby pond, so it was changed to accommodate his wishes. Turns one and two are banked at 23 degrees, and turns three and four are banked at 25 degrees, making chassis tuning a compromise, at best. In addition, the high banks—which are 60 feet wide— only allow a true racing surface of 30 feet or so, allowing only a one-car groove in the turns—and tight racing for those who chose to try to make it a two-car groove.

The old Darlington is infield madness and tin-roofed grandstands; the new circuit is upgraded access roads, seating, and rejuvenated spectator facilities. As previously mentioned, start/finish has been moved to the oppo-site side of the track in front, essentially making the old Turn 3 the new Turn 1 to make room for more grand-

Darlington (continued)

stands. No one mastered Darlington quite like David Pearson, who won a record 11 times. The Pearson tower outside turn 4, which holds 12,000 fans, was built in his honor.

Camping in the infield is permitted provided the vehicles are self contained. The spaces are sold on a first-come first-serve basis or as a two-weekend package at the track. There are commercial camping facilities about 20 miles from the track for those who wish to pitch a tent.

Rooms are not overly abundant in the Darlington area. There are about 3,000 in the area—obviously far short of what's needed during a NASCAR weekend. Myrtle Beach and Columbia are good choices, if a 75 mile drive doesn't scare you, and Charlotte is also worth a look—at about the same distance.

While you're there for the race, be sure and stop at the NMPA Stock Car Hall of Fame/Joe Weatherly Museum, which is right there on the premises. For the Darlington Chamber of Commerce, call (803) 393-2641 and for the Florence area, call (803) 665-0515.

Daytona International Speedway

1801 Speedway Blvd,
Daytona Beach, FL 32914
P.O. Box 2801
Daytona Beach, FL 32120
PH: (904) 253-7223 (RACE)
FAX: (904) 947-6791
Degree of banking in the corners: 31 degrees.
Degree of banking on the backstretch: 3 degrees.
Degree of banking on the tri-oval: 18 degrees.
Length of tri-oval: 1,900 feet.
Length of backstretch: 3,000 feet.
Track record: qualifying—Bill Elliott (Ford) February 9, 1987, 210.364 mph; race—Buddy Baker (Oldsmobile), Feb 17, 1980 177.602.
Location: Central Florida, on the Atlantic coast, approximately 200 miles north of Miami.
From Miami, take I-95/Florida Turnpike to Daytona Beach, then east on U.S. 92.
Circuit: 2.5 mile tri-oval/3.4 mile road course.
Major races: NASCAR Winston Cup Series Championship (two races); Busch Grand National Series; Craftsman Truck, ARCA Championship.

The Indy 500 may be America's oldest motor race, but the Daytona 500 has nearly as much tradition behind it. Daytona International Speedway is at least as dear to American racers. But, while the Indy 500 only happens once a year, Daytona hosts an eclectic handful of world-class events throughout the season.

Daytona Beach is the kind of place that would have become famous for something sooner or later—racing just happened to be there first. Sunny or cool, the tropical air and the long stretches of beach—which are only minutes from the racetrack—make even the worst race weekend enjoyable.

Daytona has several major oval track dates—the most impressive being the NASCAR Winston Cup Daytona 500 in February, the season opener and the Winston Cup Superbowl.

And of course, refitted with state-of-the art lighting, the track now hosts a night race as well—that being the Pepsi 400, held in July.

Although rooms are plentiful for the smaller races, the Daytona 500 and the Pepsi 400 will be tough to book. Come the 500 mid-February, you won't find anything available—or if you do, rooms will be expensive. And although Daytona now seats 150,000 fans, tickets should be sorted out months in advance. You can frequently get single-day tickets for Sunday the day of the race from scalpers, but they will certainly be expensive.

Once you've sorted through all the headaches of rooms and tickets, getting to the track can be easy if you do it right. If you're flying in for the day, Daytona Regional Airport actually borders the speedway on the south-east side. If you're staying the weekend you'll probably want to get to your hotel upon arrival, but if not, the airport is literally within walking distance (flying in and out in one day is not a bad idea). AMTRAK trains also service the Daytona area)

DOTS (Daytona Orlando Transit Service) transports passengers from the Daytona airport to their hotels and back, or to and from Orlando International and Daytona Regional Airports (800) 223-1965); VOTRAN, the

Bob Fairman photo

Volusia County Transit Authority provides a good network of bus systems throughout Daytona Beach area. To get from Daytona Beach Shores, or from Ocean Shore or Atlantic Blvds, take the #10, or #17A, #17B, which become #10 buses as they turn toward the track. For other bus information call VOTRAN at (904) 761-7700.

If you drive, and you like to sleep late, be prepared for a traffic delay in the immediate track area during the days surrounding the races. There are really only two main ways into the track; the infield entrance, via Bill France Blvd; and the Hwy 92 entrance, which then splits into the different grandstand areas. On raceday, the unreserved Backstretch Grandstands are opened, and parking in that area is available—but only on race day. Once you buy tickets, simply follow the signs to the parking area closest to your seats.

Infield parking and admission is done on a first-come, first-serve basis. Once in the infield, overnight parking is allowed—but only on Saturday night during the Daytona 500 or Saturday night during the 24 hours—the remainder of the season the infield is cleared every evening. There is also RV parking available for overnight stays outside the track at the west end of the facility.

The general ticket information number can reserve spots in advance, and they are available beginning in February and going through the end of the August. Although the Speedway continues adding seats (there are now more than 140,000 permanent seats) they keep selling out as soon as they are completed.

The beach itself is an attraction far greater than the track, and the unique tradition of allowing autos on the beach for 10 MPH cruises up and down the coast on the sand still exists. Restaurants are plentiful, in both the inexpensive and fine dining versions, and discos and clubs are also sprinkled along the main streets—typically on Atlantic Ave. But be sure to visit "Daytona USA," called "The Ultimate Motorsports Attraction," which is also located at the speedway and is open daily.

Destination Daytona!, the Daytona Beach visitors bureau, is one of the most comprehensive tourist bureaus of any in the nation and will happily brief you on any happenings, or help you in any way they can. The national toll-free number is (800) 854-1234, and they can give you a complete rundown of hotel and motel accommodations, as well as a few private residences available for rent (usually on long-term basis only).

Dover Downs International Speedway

1131 North Dupont Highway
Dover, DE 19901
P.O. Box 843
Dover, DE 19903
PH: (800) 441-7223
FAX: (302) 734-3124
Degree of banking in the corners: 24 degrees.
Degree of banking on the straight: 9 degrees.
Length of frontstretch: 1,076 feet.
Length of backstretch: 1,076 feet.
Track record: qualifying—Rusty Wallace (Ford), September 25, 1999, 159.964 mph; race—Bill Elliott (Ford), September 16, 1990, 125.945 mph.
Location: Central Delaware, between Philadelphia and Salisbury, MD. From Washington, take U.S. Highway 50/301 East to 302 Delaware to Route 8, turning onto 13 North after going through the center of town—the track is approximately one mile past city-center, across from the Delaware State University campus.
Circuit: 1.0 mile paved oval.
Major races: NASCAR Winston Cup Series Championship; Busch Grand National; Craftsman Truck.

During competition weekends there is so much else to do at Dover Downs that racing is almost anti-climactic. Dover promoters deliver a complete range of entertainment over the three-day NASCAR event. The result: great races and good times.

The "Monster Mile" is one of the best tracks for ardent fans. From any grandstand seat the track is completely visible, and any pass or lead change is observable. The track is less than half the physical size of Talladega, but holds essentially the same amount of seated fans.

The track is used mainly as a harness track for standard-bred horse racing, running about 50 race nights per year. Dover's air-conditioned enclosed grandstand area on the backstretch is actually the main grandstands for harness racing. During the Winston Cup racing it's converted to backstretch seating and into a stage on Friday night (admission is free) for a live special edition of MRN's "NASCAR Live," with driver appearances and other entertainment. NASCAR certainly highlights Dover's season.

Dover, which was built in 1969, was constructed neither as a horse track or a race track, but as a dual-purpose sports facility for both horse racing and auto racing. Its first motorsports event was a NASCAR Grand National held on July 6, 1969 (and won by Richard Petty), and the first harness race ran November 10, 1969.

From that first season, the track has continued expanding and upgrading so that it has become one of the best tracks in the country. It has become the first facility to use concrete as a racing surface on a track at least one mile long, and seating continues to expand. As of 1999, the total for reserved seating was approximately 107,000.

In addition, Dover Downs Slots put a new area in the facility which features 1,000 slot machines on the premises. The slot machines operate 363 days a year (closed Christmas and Easter) and are available daily from 8 A.M. to 2 A.M.

Dover is a popular race, and tickets sell out earlier each year—even with the added seats. Sunday's tickets are reserved so order early. Infield tickets are sold at the gate, and self-contained vehicles (those with permanent toilets) are allowed into the infield area at 5:30 P.M. Saturday evening (there is a shuttle bus to the movie and back). Sunday at 6:00 A.M. the infield gates open to cars, pickups and vans. Note: no walk-ons are permitted into the infield, and each person must enter in a vehicle. For those who arrive earlier in the week, there is camping available outside the facility. For hotels and motels call the Chambers of Commerce Central Delaware: (302) 734-7513.

Homestead-Miami Motorsports Complex

One Speedway Blvd.
Homestead, FL 33035-1501
PH: (305) 230-RACE
Office: (305) 230-5000
Degree of banking in the corners: 9.25 degrees.
Degree of banking on the straights: 2.5 degrees.
Length of frontstretch: 1,265 feet.
Length of backstretch: 1,265 feet.
Track record: qualifying—David Green (Pontiac), November 12, 1999, 155.759 mph; race—Tony Stewart (Pontiac), November 14, 1999, 140.335 mph.
http://www.racemiami.com/
Location/Directions: In South Florida, near Miami off the Florida Turnpike at Speedway Blvd. (Exit 6), three miles to main entrance.
Circuit: One mile paved oval; slightly banked.
Major races: NASCAR Winston Cup; Busch Series Grand National Division; NASCAR Craftsman Truck.

In 1995, NASCAR racing debuted in the Miami area to a sellout crowd of 60,000. The Homestead track hosted its first race as the season finale for the 1995 NASCAR Busch Series Grand National Division season, and has become a popular place to race.

The track has a South Florida look and feel, with pastel colors and palm trees everywhere.

Fans here tend to stay out of the seats until the last minute, preferring instead to engage in one of many interactive areas (like a rock climbing wall or remote control car track, for example). TV monitors are scattered around the venue, so even if you aren't in the seats, you'll still be close to the action.

Floridians seem to like it as well. Track estimates set the annual impact on the local economy at $100 million dollars, drawing more than 300,000 fans and drivers each year. And that was prior to the Winston Cup race, which made its debut in 1999.

In fact, the facility has brought in fans from all over the country, but has also been successful in attracting non-traditional fans with the non-traditional format. Currently attracting some 40,000–45,000 for the Busch race and 70,000 for the Winston Cup race, the track still expects major growth.

Although there is some overlap, most of the people who attend this Winston Cup are a completely new crowd from those who attend Daytona. In fact, many are tourists who want to see South Florida and a race at the same time. Not only is the track a half-hour from Miami, it's also a half-hour from the Florida Keys. Fans can definitely combine racing with some quality vacation time.

The track now hosts a NASCAR Craftsman Truck Series race and a PPG Indy Car World Series race, as well as Spring Training for CART cars. What attracts the drivers is simple: it is a start-of-the-art facility in sunny Florida, right next to a major metropolitan market.

Indianapolis Motor Speedway

4790 W. 16th St.
Speedway, IN 46222
PH: (317) 481-8500
Degree of banking in the corners: 9 degrees.
Length of frontstretch: 5/8ths mile.
Length of backstretch: 5/8ths mile.
Track record: qualifying—Jeff Gordon (Chevrolet), August 5, 1999, 179.612; race—Dale Earnhardt (Chevrolet) Aug 5, 1995, 155.206 mph.
Location: Central Indiana, on the west side of Indianapolis, off Georgetown and 16th St.
Circuit: 2.5 mile paved oval.
Major races: Brickyard 400; Indianapolis 500.

"The Speedway," as the drivers call it, is richer in history than any other racetrack in the world. Most of the prestige is associated with the most famous race in the world, the Indianapolis 500.

But not any more. NASCAR staged their first "Brickyard 400," a race that established itself immediately as one of the most coveted prizes on the circuit, occurred in 1994. Although there was a great deal of hoopla surrounding the event, most figured it couldn't be as big as the Indy 500, and it wasn't. But it surpassed most expectations, and has become a race that appears to have a long, long future at the Speedway.

The track itself is, of course, probably the most famous sports venue in the world. The small oval with constant radius corners—a circle, really—didn't seem to fit the plot of land for which it was originally designed, so the straights were elongated until Carl Fisher, the track founder, felt it was suitable to the land, making it a 2.5-mile oval. Paved in brick instead of built of wood, which most tracks at the time were, it was nicknamed The Brickyard. A name it still has. Of course, now the bricks are gone—all except a row across start/finish.

There are some 300,000 permanent seats for the race (Unofficially. The Speedway doesn't publish actual seating figures). The Indy 500 still sells out, but the Brickyard 400 is just short of that. But don't wait too long to get on the list. It will sell out eventually. But for now seats are not impossible to get.

You can also sit in the infield. If you are neither assertive nor wealthy, head to the infield. "The infield is the greatest deal in all of sports," says one veteran journalist. You may not see much action, but you can use the infield to park your car, even if your seat is outside in the grandstands; or park your car and sit on top and watch.

The nice thing about Indianapolis is that they know a lot about racing. And a lot about watching racing. Indianapolis City Center volunteers offer one of the most comprehensive tourist hotlines of anywhere in the county. Even Destination Daytona! is not as easy to use as this system. With a toll-free call (800/323 INDY) any visitor can find information on Indianapolis' activities on a given day or week, and can even book a room, all on the same toll-free hotline. The caller simply uses the Touch-Tone pad on the telephone.

After a series of cues, and choices of prices and locations, you'll be connected to the hotel of your

Indianapolis (continued)

choice at no charge. The system can be accessed at any time—although it's best to call during business hours, when the operators can tell you what rooms are available without you going through the hit-and-miss on the phone.

Although rooms for the Brickyard 400 are slightly easier to get than for the Indy 500, there are still only 15,000 rooms in the city. If you haven't made reservations, and can't find a room in the immediate area, be prepared for a long drive and a long race day. The outskirts of Indianapolis fill up quickly, so all along the I-74, I-65, I-70, I-69 and 465 highways will be completely full. You'll really have a ways to go. Terre Haute, 75 miles west, will likely be filled, as will Columbus and Bloomington.

Cincinnati will probably be your best bet, which is some 110 miles southeast, or try Louisville. A two-hour drive in any direction will easily yield someplace to sleep. Two hours is a long drive, but sleeping in the car is not a lot of fun, either.

If you drive, you'll obviously have to park. There are several options. The Coca-Cola Parking lot, between 25th and 30th on Georgetown Rd. is probably your best choice, and is easiest to find a way out following the race (unbelievably, it never fills up). There are lots all along Georgetown Rd., between 30th and 38th, and several on 34th between Lafayette Rd. and Moller Rd. The two biggest parking areas are the infield and the North Forty Parking. Or you can park your car at the airport or downtown and take a shuttle to the track.

The Metro 500 Express takes passengers to and from the track during race weekends. Busses leave from three downtown areas: the first is on the east side of the Hoosier Dome, off Capitol Ave.; the second is outside the Pan Am Plaza off Georgia St.; and the last one is on Illinois St., between Market and Washington. The service begins at 8:00 and leaves every hour, on the hour. Returns from the speedway are on the half-hour. The service runs as long as there are passengers.

In addition, there is a shuttle from the airport—located at the main terminal's lower level—which begins at 6:30 A.M., and continues all day until the service is no longer necessary for outbound passengers. The service is only available on the first Saturday of qualifying and then again during the race.

Tickets for the shuttle are available in advance, through Metro 500 Express Tickets, P.O. Box 2383, Indianapolis, IN 46206 (317 635-3344). They cost $2.00 one-way on the first and second qualifying weekends; Sunday's tickets are $7.00 one way or $12.00 round-trip. The busses will let you off in front of the main gate on 16th (the front stretch, where the majority of the grandstands and the pits are, actually parallels Georgetown Rd.).

Las Vegas Motor Speedway

7000 Las Vegas Blvd. North
Las Vegas NV 89115
PH: (702) 644-4443
Office: (702) 632-8266
Degree of banking in the corners: 12 degrees.
Degree of banking on the frontstretch: 9 degrees
Degree of banking on the backstretch: 3 degrees.
Length of frontstretch: 2,275 feet.
Length of backstretch: 1,572 feet.
Track record: qualifying—Bobby Labonte (Pontiac), March 5, 1999, 170.643 mph; race—Mark Martin (Ford) March 1, 1998, 146.554 mph.
Circuit: 1.5-mile paved slightly banked oval (also has a 2.5-mile road circuit, quarter-mile dragstrip, paved as well as a half-mile dirt, go-kart track, motocross circuit and stadium truck racing track).
Location/Directions: North of the Las Vegas Strip, off I-15 north at Speedway, at Exit 54.
Major race: NASCAR Winston Cup; NASCAR Busch Grand National; NASCAR Craftsman Truck Series; Pennzoil World of Outlaws.

Las Vegas Motor Speedway PR people like to say that LVMS is a "diamond in the desert." Located 17 miles northeast of Vegas' famous "Strip," the facility picks up where off-roading in Nevada left off. It's pretty easy: fly in from anywhere and drive straight to the track.

Vegas has always been a motorsports town, but for the most part that was relegated to off-roading. The Mint 400 and a series of other off-road events were hugely successful.

In fact, one of the reasons there is so little off-roading in Nevada now is due to that success. Off-road races did a great deal of damage to the landscape and environmentalists complained. So off-roading is fading out. But stock car racing is moving in.

Construction began on LVMS in 1995 and finished in 1996 at a cost of $200 million. The superspeedway holds 107,000 fans, including 102 suites. The facility covers 1,600 acres, with room for motorhomes in the infield of the superspeedway, as well as more motorhome parking outside. There is enough parking for 60,000 cars. The track is banked 12 degrees in turns, 3 degrees in back straight and 9 degrees on the front stretch. More than just the newness of the track and grandstands, landscaping has never been neglected. The track planted 6,000 palm trees

The first major race was the Las Vegas 400, which Mark Martin won. The day before, Jimmy Spencer took victory at the Sam's Town 300 NASCAR Busch Series race.

The new track is located right across from Nellis AFB—a perfect neighbor to have for a racetrack. Sitting in the stands on a typical non-race day, fans will see an air show all day long, with planes coming and going fre-

Las Vegas (continued)

quently. Noise for the neighbors isn't ever going to be a concern. They're just as noisy. By the way, Nellis is also home of the famous Thunderbirds.

Staying in Vegas is obviously not a problem. Catering to visitors as Vegas does, rooms are abundant. But you still have to call ahead to make sure you have one. Remember, there is always something else going on in Las Vegas. Don't believe the only show in town will be the Winston Cup race, or the truck race, or whatever. But still, the track says that 82 percent of people who showed up the first year were from out of town, so this is not just a local interest event.

Speaking of which, during the winter SEMA show, the track has one of its two World of Outlaws races, with shuttles taking people directly from the convention center to the track. The dirt track is located just a couple hundred yards north of the superspeedway. It has its own stands, amenities and so forth, with a 12,000-fan capacity. It is a modern first-class dirt track.

If you like the idea of betting on your favorite driver, this is the one place you can do it. Most of the major casinos will give you a book on the game.

Getting in and out is very easy. The track is located off I-15. But during race days you'll have some delays, which are to be expected. A nice alternative is to stay in Mesquite, some 75 miles north. There are several motels, built originally for off-roaders. Since you're going the opposite direction of the traffic, you can get there in almost the same amount of time. Two of the Mesquite motels (with casinos) are the Casa Blanca and Virgin River.

You can try the speedway for information on rooms by going through the website at LVMS.com. Or the track suggests you try the Las Vegas Tourist Bureau at (800) 777-1977, or at LVTB.com. Many racers have been staying at the Monte Carlo and at the Excaliber, but with all the rooms available in Las Vegas, you can take your pick.

Lowes Motor Speedway

Highway 29 South
Concord, NC 28026
P.O. Box 600
Concord, NC 28026
PH: (704) 455-3200
Office: (704) 455-3209
Degree of banking in the corners: 24 degrees.
Degree of banking on the straight: 5 degrees.
Length of frontstretch: 1,952.8 feet.
Length of backstretch: 1,360 feet.
Track record: qualifying—Ward Burton (Chevrolet), October 5, 1994, 185.759 mph; race—Jeff Gordon (Chevrolet), October 11, 1999, 160.306 mph.
Location/Directions: Southern central North Carolina, 12 miles north of Charlotte, in Concord. From Charlotte, take Interstate I-85 to 49 Speedway Blvd. to Highway 29 North to the Speedway. Circuit: 1.5 mile paved, banked oval.
Major races: NASCAR Coca-Cola 600 Winston Cup; Mello-Yello 500 NASCAR Winston Cup.

From a fan's point of view, Lowes Motor Speedway—for decades known as "Charlotte"—is one of the most colorful and entertaining tracks on the NASCAR's Winston Cup calendar. If Talladega has a corner on the fastest NASCAR track, and Daytona has the distinction of being the oldest, Charlotte is definitely the loudest.

"Humpy" Wheeler's, Charlotte's General Manager (the track is owned by Bruton Smith), idea of racing was right along the lines of what Bill France saw as the essence of NASCAR: a good race and a great show. The Indy 500 used to be the most popular racing event on Memorial Day, but the Coca-Cola 600 is now a close second in popularity. Serious race fans can have it both ways, because the Indy race is run on Sunday, while the 600 is run on Monday.

Charlotte has built more on marketing than any other track in the U.S.—and the attendance suggests it has been worth the effort. To this day, it's still run like a last-ditch effort at survivability—even though it is much more permanent than any other NASCAR venue.

The land, described by CMS Public Relations people as "the worst piece of real estate in Charlotte," was transformed into a racetrack following some heroic construction. The first event was a disaster, as the uncured track broke up so badly during the first race that the cars were brought in for bolt-on metal windscreens to keep asphalt chunks from flying through the windshields. The next two years were not too great either, and the original owners were forced into bankruptcy. During that time, Wheeler was hired

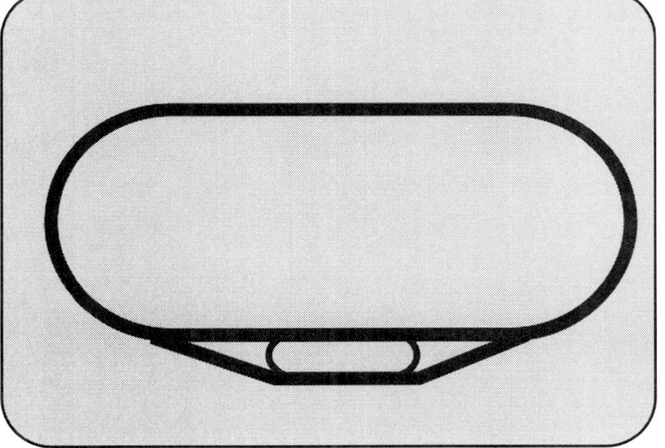

for PR. When the dust had settled, only one of the original owners remained, and the track relied upon Wheeler's shrewd marketing for spectators—a relic of those days that has remained and helps in the allure of Charlotte.

A feud between Bill Elliott and Dale Earnhardt in 1988 inspired one of the most clever campaigns in NASCAR history. To keep interest going, the media folks at the speedway sent out press releases—along with bent Coor's cans and broken wrenches (signifying the possibility of a crunch duel between the aptly sponsored stock cars).

Entertainment in recent years included: motorcycle stuntmen who jumped a football field's worth of junk cars; a 100-foot-tall robot that eats cars; and a reenactment of the U.S invasion of Panama—complete with helicopters and troops! To just say Charlotte is exciting racing is to have missed the point completely.

The track boasts an incredible 107,000 Grandstand seats, plus VIP and other suite seating, allowing

Lowes (continued)

better than 170,000 viewers. Remember that Winston Cup happens twice a year—with one of those events held in the early evening illuminated by a state-of-the-art lighting system.

As one could imagine, getting into Charlotte can be a zoo. Track officials allow three hour's time to finally clear the facility following a race. There are nine gates, and on race day there's a rear entrance for backstretch grandstands.

Infield tickets can be reserved. The infield tickets offer decent viewing, and are great if you can get close to the fence. The best spots are in turns 3-4, where you can see most of the track, including start/finish.

You can buy a two-day ticket to park in the infield, but the area is cleared following Saturday's final qualifying, and you must wait in line again for Sunday. By the way, vehicles begin lining up Saturday evening.

Getting into and out of the area is easy from Interstate I-85. Travelling to the track is simple, and there are four exits each way, which will take you north of Charlotte to Highway 29—all are well-marked. The track is two miles off highway 29. Unfortunately, there are no busses to the track, so you must find a ride somehow. There is plenty of parking.

Hotel and motel rooms in the Charlotte area are plentiful. Most teams are based here, so rooms normally booked for other races are available in Charlotte—so even late arrivals should have no problem finding something. For more information call: Charlotte Convention and Visitors Bureau at (800) 321-4636, or the Charlotte Chamber of Commerce: (704) 378-1332. Note: In the photo above, Bruton Smith, the longtime owner of Lowes Motor Speedway, chats with Jerry Jones, owner of the Dallas Cowboys, and then-Texas Governor George Bush (both at left), at the Texas Motor Speedway, a track he also owns.

Martinsville Speedway

U.S. Route 220 Business South
Martinsville, VA 24112
P.O. Box 3311
Martinsville, VA 24115
PH: (540) 956-3151
FAX: (540) 956-2820
Degree of banking in the corners: 12 degrees.
Degree of banking on the straights: none.
Length of frontstretch: 800 feet.
Length of backstretch: 800 feet.
Track record: qualifying—Tony Stewart (Pontiac), April 16, 1999, 95.275 mph; race—Jeff Gordon (Chevrolet) September 22, 1996, 82.233 mph.
Location: southern Virginia, 10 miles north of the North Carolina border, 50 miles north of Greensboro. From Greensboro, take Route 220 north into Virginia, toward Martinsville, taking the 220 south Business Loop to the track.
Circuit: Half-mile paved oval.
Major races: NASCAR Winston Cup (two races); NASCAR Busch Grand National (two races); Craftsman Truck.

The shortest track on the Winston Cup calendar, Martinsville Speedway's roots are obvious: the dual set of pits—one on either side of the oval— shows the dirt track history of the circuit.

The .526-mile asphalt speedway was originally built as a dirt oval in 1955, and has grown into one of the most popular races of the year for fans. For drivers, the track is a tough outing. With such small quarters, cars exchange paint and drivers bump and tap one another regularly.

Martinsville now seats more than 77,000 people, and this great little facility has all the big VIP hospitality areas in turns 1 and 2, leaving the grandstands pretty much left open to race fans.

The place is relatively flat (12 degrees in the turns) so the lower seats won't see directly across onto the backstretch. But because of the mostly level playing surfaces there's plenty of slipping and sliding, which makes for exciting racing.

Martinsville (continued)

It's a popular short track with the Charlotte crowd, many of whom travel three hours to Martinsville for the racing. It's an easy place to get into and out of, and because of the physical limitations of a half-mile track, the crowds are not gigantic.

Therefore, tickets for Martinsville will be a problem, and you'll have to book far in advance. There's no infield viewing, so that option won't be open to you on race day. There's an unreserved section for folks who show up late, but seats there are obviously limited.

Martinsville is a small city, but has a good amount of rooms. With the size of the track, it's possible to find lodging here if you book at the same time you buy tickets. You may have to drive a bit to either Roanoke, or Winston-Salem, where you'll be sure to find a room. There is some camping outside the track.

A word to the wise: Watch out for the Virginia Police. You can't use radar detectors in Virginia, and if caught with one in operation it will be confiscated and you'll be fined. Keep it in the trunk while you're there.

Call the track for hotel information, or the Virginia State Chamber of Commerce for more information at (800) VISIT VA.

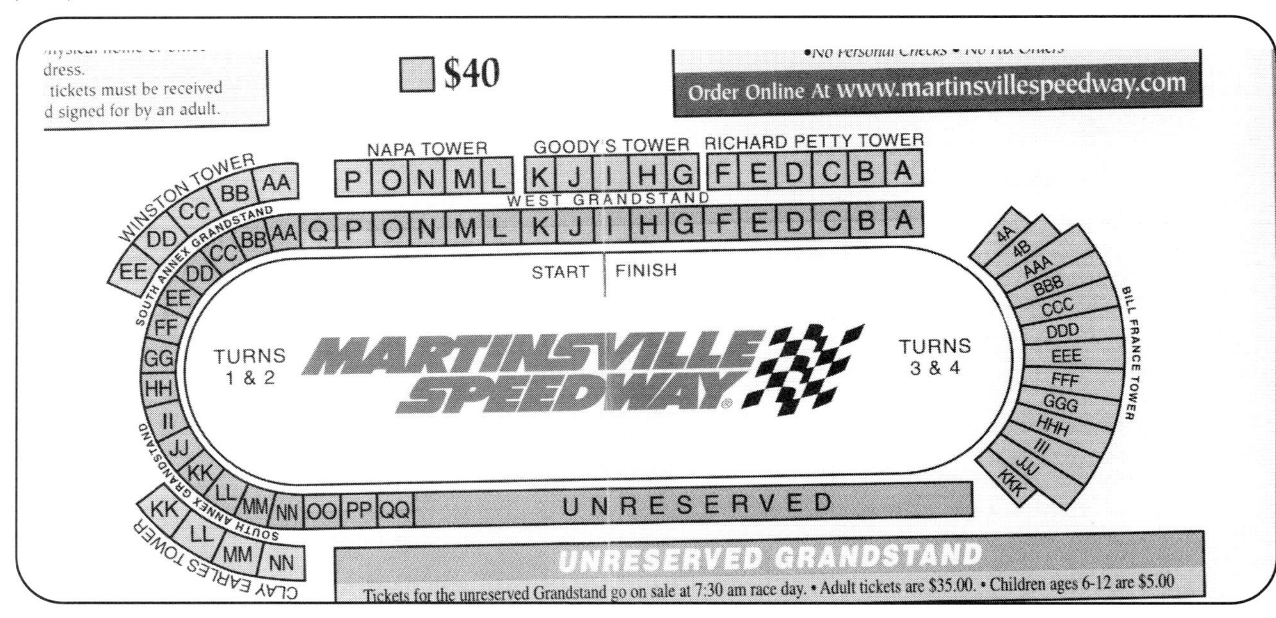

Michigan International Speedway

12626 U.S. Hwy 12
Brooklyn, MI 49203
PH: (800) 354-1010
Office: (517) 592-1208
FAX: (517) 592-3848
Degree of banking in the corners: 18 degrees.
Degree of banking on the backstretch: 12 degrees.
Degree of banking on the frontstretch: 5 degrees.
Length of frontstretch: 3,600 feet.
Length of backstretch: 2,242 feet.
Track record: qualifying—Ward Burton (Pontiac), August 20, 1999, 188.843 mph; race—Dale Jarrett (Ford), June 13, 1999, 173.997 mph.
Location: southeastern Michigan, in the Irish Hills area. One mile west on U.S. 12 from the intersection of M-50.
Circuit: 2.0 mile banked, paved oval.
Major races: NASCAR Winston Cup (two events); Craftsman Truck; International Race of Champions; ARCA Championship.

Michigan International Speedway is one of the finest ovals in the United States and one of the best circuits the Winston Cup boys race on, yet it is not usually mentioned in the company of Talladega Daytona, Charlotte, or Indy. MIS has to struggle for respect, although it is every bit the track any of the other four are.

The facility was designed by the same person who developed Daytona International Speedway, with the help of Grand Prix star Sterling Moss. Racing mogul Roger Penske bought the property in 1972 and began further upgrades, making it into a first-class racing facility known for wide open racing, where cars get three- and four-abreast regularly. With its steep banking, it is also one of the fastest.

The track is a great spectating venue, and you'll see almost the entire racing surface from anywhere in the stands. Although there is infield access, there is no entry into the infield Friday.

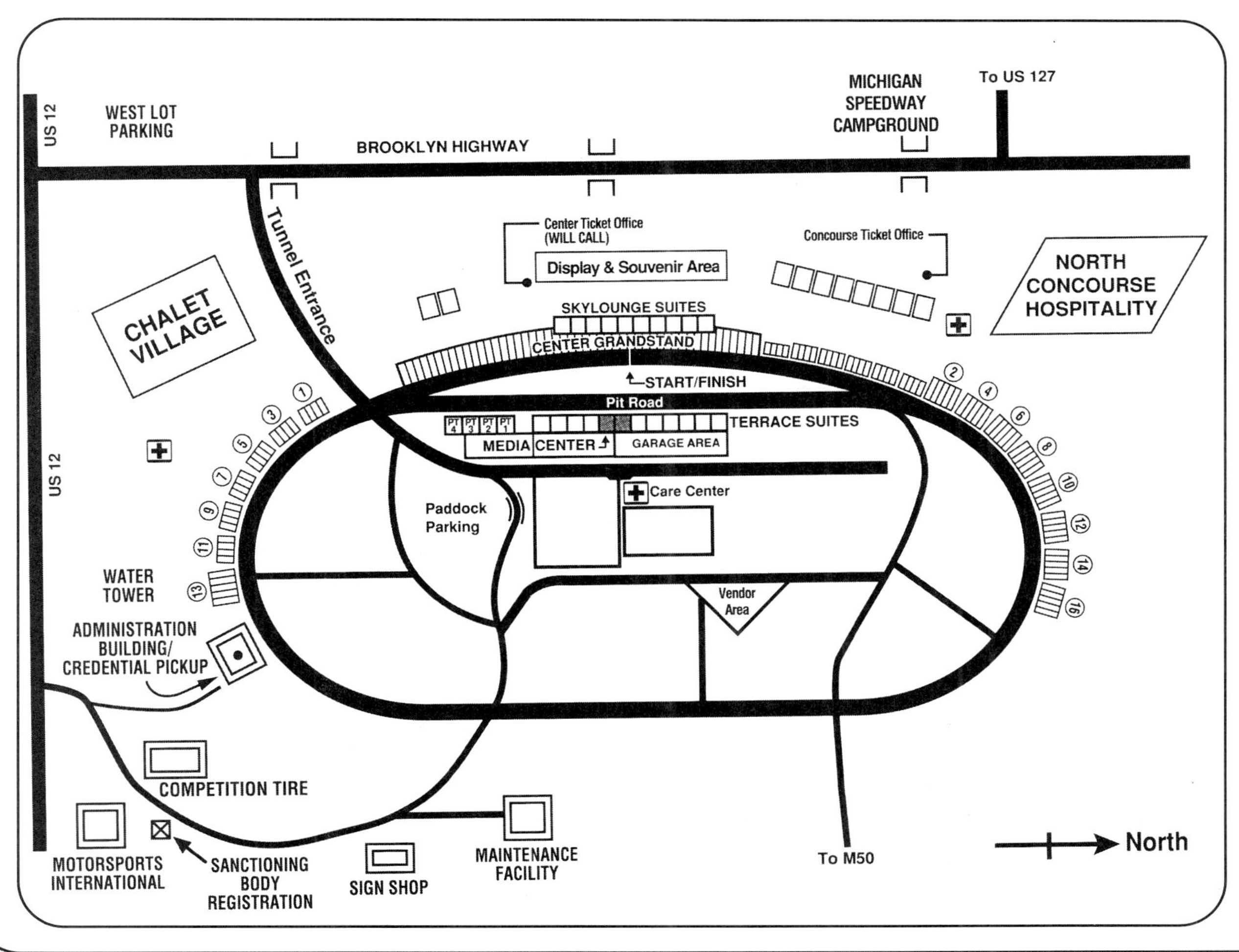

Michigan (continued)

Campers will have to find a room somewhere for Friday night or stay outside the track. The infield opens after practice. Camping is free outside, and you can pitch a tent directly across the track from main grandstands.

Located in Brooklyn, the area is not exactly a hotel mecca. It is 35 minutes from Ann Arbor, where there are lots of rooms available, even as late as Saturday. Brooklyn is a quaint little town—with nowhere to sleep. Jackson is larger, with 50,000 people, but there is little free there either, as the teams snatch those rooms up quickly.

There are several campgrounds in the Irish Hills area and there are lakes and lake cottages scattered about. There is also camping in the track's infield and outside the facility. For more information on lodging, call the Ann Arbor Area Convention and Visitors Bureau at (313) 995-7281; or call the track for more on ticket prices.

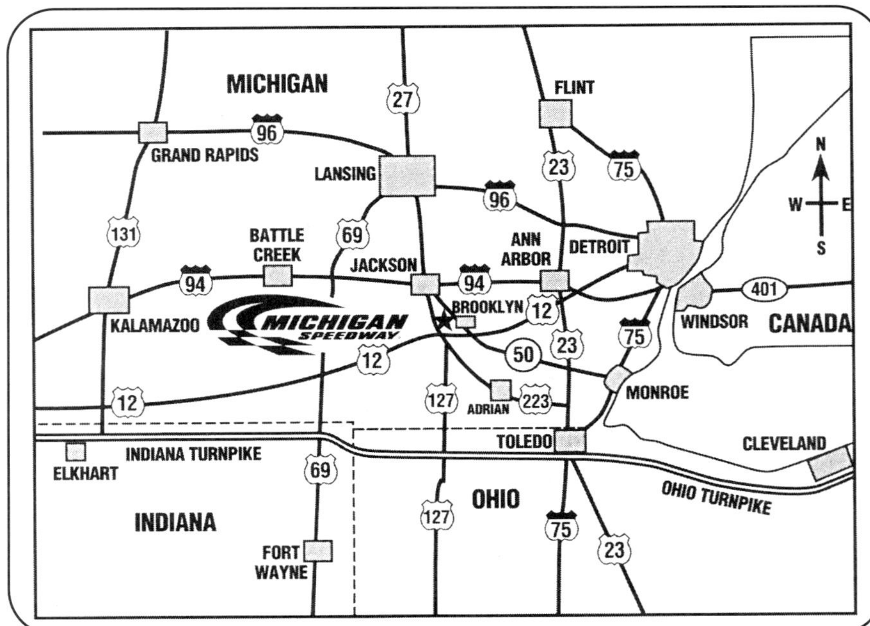

New Hampshire International Raceway

1102 Route 106 North
Louden, NH 03301
P.O. Box 7888
Louden, NH 03301
PH: (603) 783-4931
Degree of banking in the corners: 12 degrees.
Degree of banking on the straights: 2 degrees.
Length of frontstretch: 1,500 feet.
Length of backstretch: 1,500 feet.
Track record: qualifying—Jeff Gordon (Chevrolet), July 9, 1999, 131.171 mph; race—Jeff Burton (Ford), July 13, 1997, 117.134.
Circuit: 1.0 mile paved oval.
Location: Central New Hampshire, 10 miles north of Concord, 80 miles north of Boston, on Route 106. From I-93 in Concord, N.H., take I-393 to exit 3 (Route 106 North), 9 miles.
Major races: NASCAR Winston Cup; NASCAR Busch Grand National; NASCAR Craftsman Truck; NASCAR Busch North Series Grand National; NASCAR Featherlite Modified Tour.

New Hampshire International Speedway opened on May 26, 1990, with an inaugural SCCA race. Previously called Bryar Motorsports Park, owner Bob Bahre, who at one time owned Oxford Plains Speedway in Maine, completely leveled the old facility and started from scratch.

The facility is a top-notch oval, 80 feet wide and flat, except for the turns, which are banked at 12 degrees. The backstretch is elevated 6 feet enabling fans on the front straight to see all the action from their seats. There are 12 VIP suites, which can each accommodate 60 people. The lone grandstand seats 59,000 people, and the same grandstand also serves as the primary viewing area for the road course, which utilizes the same front straightaway and start/finish area.

NASCAR was slow to answer the call, so CART and then IRL raced here. Both attracted less than stellar crowds and moved on. But Winston Cup eventually showed up and, like everything NASCAR

New Hampshire (continued)

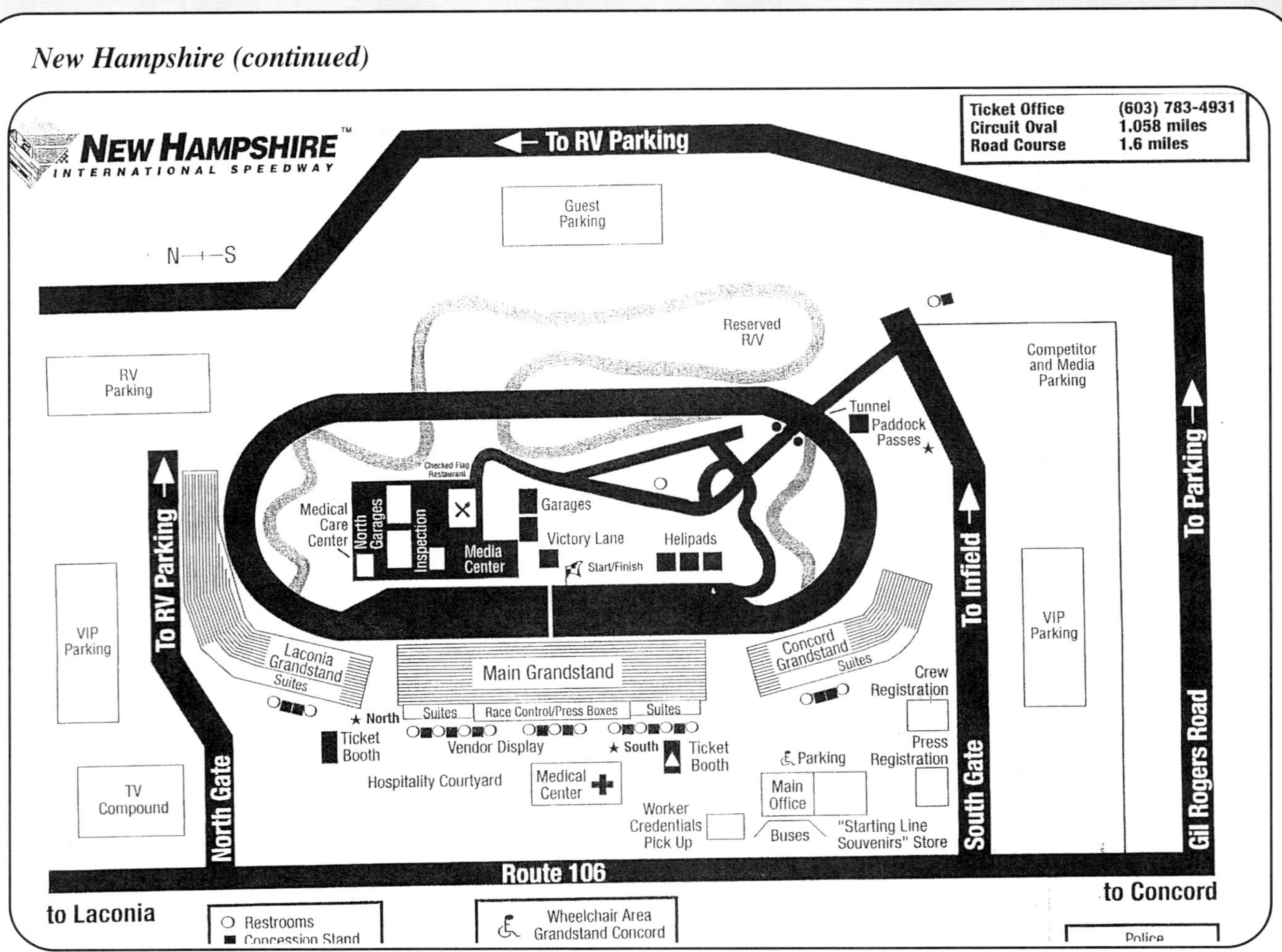

does, it was a roaring success.

Because of the Winston Cup, New Hampshire International Speedway has become New England's largest spectator sporting event with well over 80,000 in attendance in 1997.

Due to that success, the track management has continued to improve the speedway. They added 50 additional acres of parking and have continually upgraded the facilities.

Staying around Louden used to be a simple process. Now, with the interest in Winston Cup, it has become far more complicated. For more information on where to stay, call the Concord Vacation Information office of New Hampshire at (603) 271-2343, or better yet call the track.

North Carolina Motor Speedway

U.S. Highway 1 North
Rockingham, NC 28379
P.O. Box 500
Rockingham, NC 28380
PH: (910) 582-2861
FAX: (919) 582-3324
Degree of banking in corners One and Two: 22 degrees.
Degree of banking in corners Three and Four: 25 degrees.
Degree of banking on the straight: 9 degrees.
Length of frontstretch: 1,300 feet.
Length of backstretch: 1,367 feet.
Track record: qualifying—Mark Martin (Ford), February 21, 1997, 157.885 mph; race—Jeff Burton (Ford), October 24, 1999, 131.103 mph.
Location: southern central North Carolina, fifteen miles from the South Carolina border, at the junction of Highway 74 and U.S. Highway 1.
Circuit: 1.07 mile paved oval/ quarter mile dragstrip.
Major races: NASCAR Winston Cup Championship (two races); NASCAR Busch Grand National Series Championship (two races); NHRA Winston Invitational.

Rockingham is not just famous for racing, It's also one of the country's foremost golf resort areas. Located in the middle of what is essentially a golf mecca, the track is the clubhouse in a 10,000 hole greenery. The entire area is surrounded by country clubs, with such notable golf resorts as Pinehurst just up the road from the track.

For those who play golf, race week at Rockingham will be perfect—play a few rounds and watch a few laps. If, however, you aren't a golfer you won't understand why it costs so much to stay near a course. And won't have much choice when trying to find a room close to the track.

You either pray for a Motel 6 near the track, or you get stuck paying for a country club room. The teams avoid the hassle by commuting back and fourth from Charlotte, where most of them are based. It is, likewise, about two hours from Darlington (and teams also drive from there as well).

Florence is the best bet when booking early, but is a bit small, and can't handle all the traffic. New hotels have been built in Southern Pines, and a few in Cheraw, S.C., and the drive to each is not bad. Many people—including almost all the drivers—fly in, using Rockingham's dragstrip/airport to land.

As far as the track itself, Rockingham's wide, high-banked one-mile is one of the best. It was repaved in 1994 and renovated a year later. "The Rock," as it is known, traditionally hosts the first and last NASCAR Winston Cup Series events in the Carolinas each year.

Pits on both sides at "The Rock" make either side of the track good for viewing. But you'll want a view of turn two. As cars come out of turn-two the surface rises slightly. But as it begins to flattens out there is small lip in the last foot of pavement next to the wall. In qualifying, the faster cars use the

North Carolina Speedway (continued)

whole racetrack, and get spectacularly loose there as they try to keep the unsprung suspension settled with some full-fledged drifts.

Tickets are difficult to get for Rockingham. The VIP suites are above the main grandstands, which limits the seating on the front straight. The new L. G. Dewitt Grandstand is located in turn two and will give 1,800 people another view of the place. To secure tickets to any of the stands you should book far in advance. There's always the infield if you get there late, but it's better to watch from a real seat.

Call the track for ticket information. For Rockingham chamber of Commerce call (919) 895-9058; for the Darlington Chamber of Commerce, call (803) 393-2641; and for the Florence area, call (803) 665-0515.

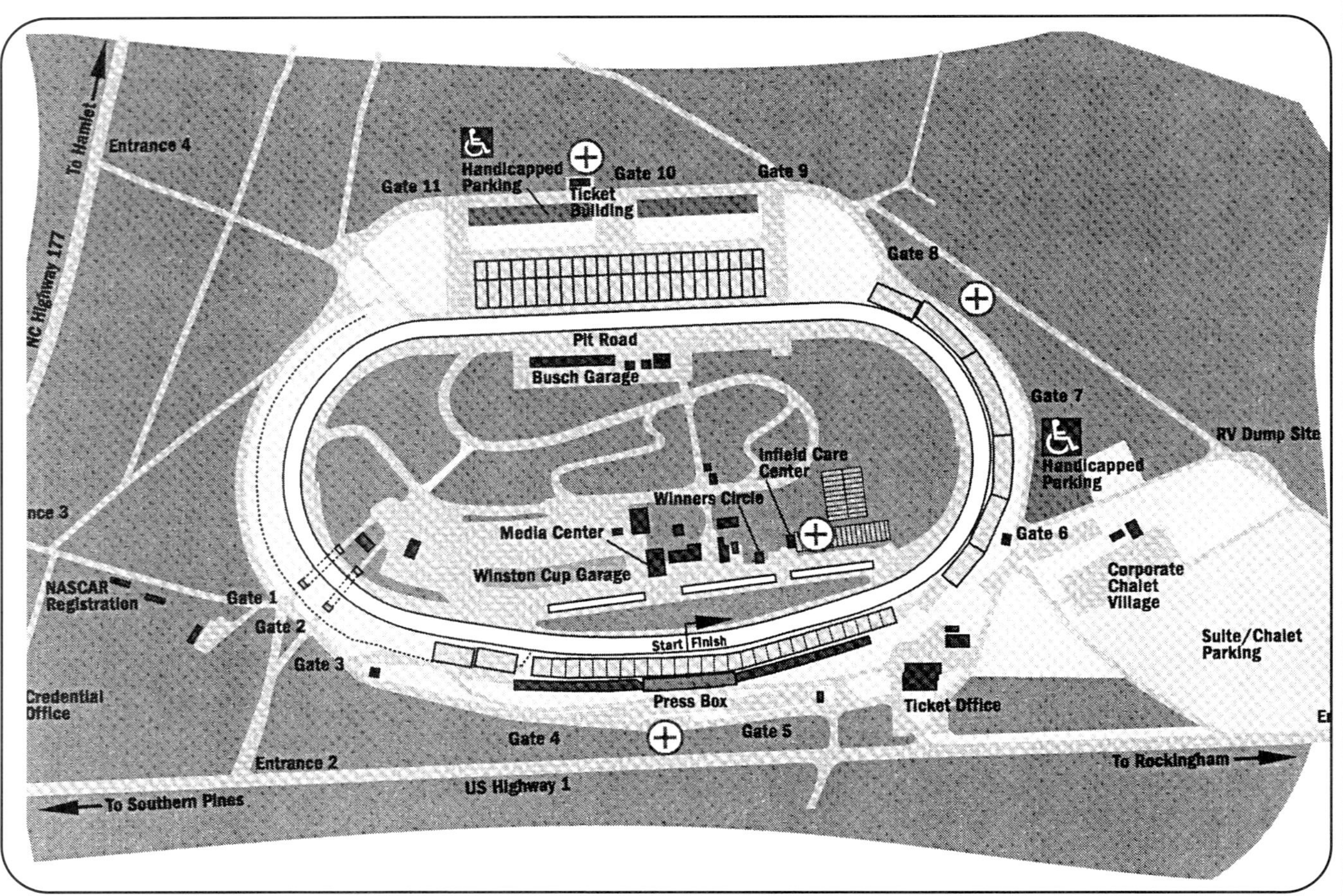

Phoenix International Raceway

**7602 S. 115th Ave
Avondale, AZ 85353
1313 N. 2nd St #1300
Phoenix, AZ 85004
PH: (602) 252-2227
(602) 252-3833
FAX: (602) 254-4622
Degree of banking in corners 1-2: 11 degrees.
Degree of banking in corners 3-4: 9 degrees.
Degree of banking on the straights: none.
Length of frontstretch: 1,179 feet.
Length of backstretch: 1,551 feet.
Track record: qualifying—John Andretti (Ford), November 5, 1999, 132.714 mph; race—Tony Stewart (Pontiac), November 7, 1999, 118.132 mph.
Location: southern Arizona, on the western edge of Phoenix, in Tolleson. From Phoenix, take Interstate 10 West to the 115th Ave. exit, turning left at the stop. Follow the 115th six miles; from Los Angeles, take I-10 through Arizona, exiting 115th just before the Phoenix city limits.
Circuit: 1.0 mile tri-oval.
Major races: NASCAR Winston Cup; Busch Series; Craftsman Truck.**

During the racing season, Phoenix International Raceway is easy to find; just follow traffic into the facility. But during the week, no matter what you read or see while looking for the circuit, you'll swear you're going the wrong way.

First, PIR is not in Phoenix proper, but far enough out in the desert so that you feel like you're on Mars. If you like Arizona scenery, with its saguaro cactus, you'll love PIR. If not, then it'll likely look like one big vacant lot with a circular road stuck in the middle of it.

But fewer facilities could change so much with a crowd.

It transforms from a dusty, barren place into a world of activity. And, as with anything that happens in Arizona, weather is a major factor in its success. For those who like the desert scenery, you'll have to come to grips with the climate—probably even liking it somewhat. If, however, you retreat when the mercury climbs

past 75 degrees, you'll find it hard to take.

November, in any other state means the beginning of winter. In Phoenix, it means the end of summer, and there is nowhere on earth with an Indian summer like Phoenix. It can, and generally does, get very hot.

But PIR really is one of the better places to watch a race. PIR first opened its gates in 1964, and has been consistently repaved and

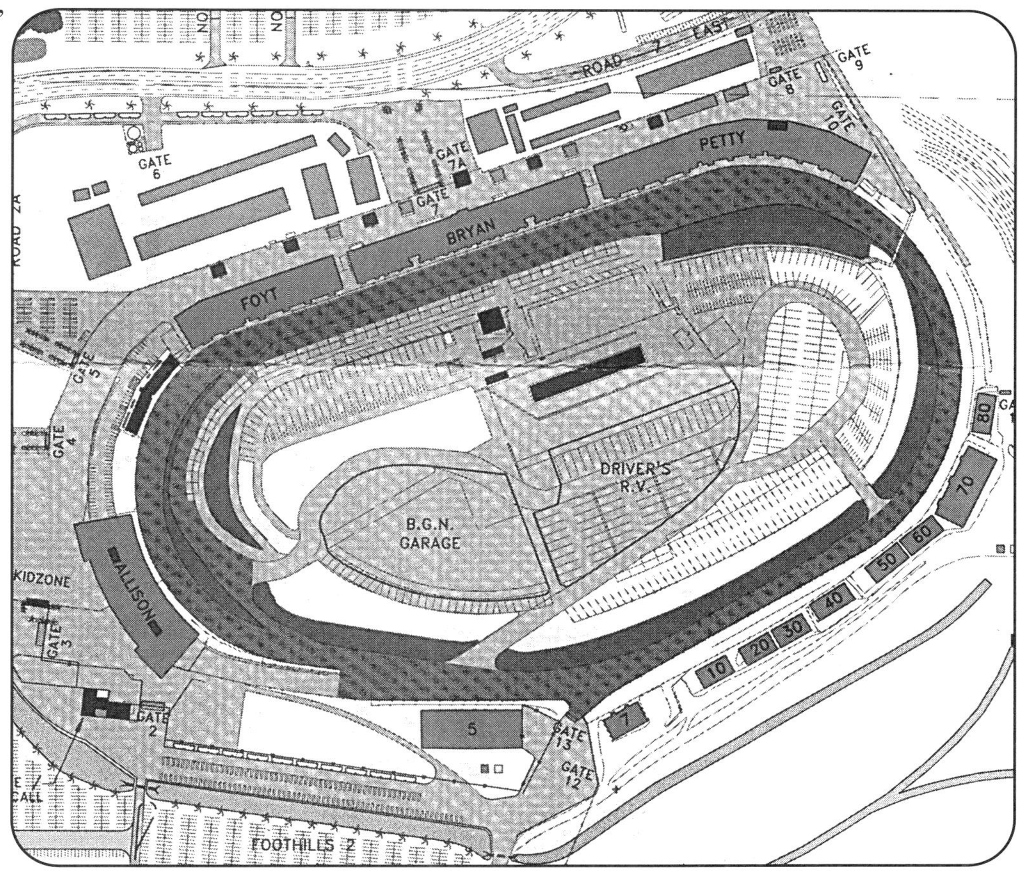

Phoenix International Raceway (continued)

upgraded since. In 1993 the track was again repaved and 10,000 more grandstand seats were added in 1995.

Phoenix itself is geared toward tourism probably like no other city in the continental U.S., so when the action on the oval gets dull, discover the delights of the desert. There are at least 75 golf courses in the Phoenix area. If it's hot, and you don't approve of the heat, just cool off in your hotel pool. Besides, as they say in Arizona, "It's a dry heat". . .

If you're staying in Phoenix proper, the track is 15 minutes or so to the west. Busses are non-existent, but there are a few shuttle services from the handful of hotels and motels affiliated with the track. Call the track for more information on those. Cars are best for travelling to the track, and there is a good

amount of parking outside the racetrack. There is no camping, but if you have a self-contained motorhome you can park it in the track lot for the duration of the weekend.

Once inside the facility, you'll need a seat unless it's race day. There's a general admission area on the hillside to the east of the tri-oval between turns 3 and 4, but it's only available Sunday. The best seats are the reserved grandstands overlooking start/finish, and there are several levels of quality there. In addition, seats are available on the back straight and third and fourth turns. Seats are best reserved ahead of time, especially for the NASCAR race.

There's infield parking for self-contained vehicles through the weekend, and there are almost 500 of those available on an advance basis. Friday, for Winston Cup, a general admission ticket is available in the infield. There's also a three-day infield package available—call the track for details.

It would be surprising to find yourself without a room in this city, considering its tourist-oriented economy, but you'll still want to book ahead of time. For more info call: Phoenix Metropolitan Chamber of Commerce at (602) 254-5521; or the Phoenix and Valley of the Sun Convention and Visitors Bureau at (602) 254-6500.

Pocono Raceway

Long Pond Rd.
Long Pond, PA 18334
P.O. Box 500
Long Pond, PA 18334
PH: (800) RACEWAY
(717) 646-2300
Degree of banking in corner One: 14 degrees.
Degree of banking in corner Two: 8 degrees.
Degree of banking in corner Three: 6 degrees.
Length of frontstretch: 3,740 feet.
Length of Long Pond Straight: 3,055 feet.
Length of North Straight: 1,780 feet.
Track record: qualifying—Sterling Marlin (Chevrolet), June 18, 1999, 170.506 mph; race—Rusty Wallace (Ford), July 21, 1996, 144.892 mph.
Location: eastern Pennsylvania, in the Pocono Mountains, 20 miles from the Delaware River, and New Jersey. From Newark/New York City, take 280/95 to Interstate I-80 West into Pennsylvania, following I-80 to Exit #43 to Route 115, and to Hulman Rd. into the speedway.
Circuit: 2.5 mile tri-oval.
Major races: NASCAR Winston Cup (two events).

Pocono's unique 2.5-mile tri-oval makes watching racing a different experience at this true triangular track. It is unique in that it has three distinct corners with different degrees of banking for each ending on three different-sized straights. It seems to work just fine, with close racing in the corners and good tight bumping and jockeying on the straights.

There is little in the Pocono Mountains in terms of large hotels so pre-planning for this one is essential. The roads are fairly narrow, so even the drive to the track requires some forethought. The track issues instructions for travelling to and from the area. For speedier entry, track officials suggest avoiding the standard I-80 to 115 route, instead coming from the south or east into Route 115 and Hulman Rd. For the complete list of suggested alternatives, call or write the track.

Tickets for Pocono's NASCAR Winston Cup races are usually available up until Thursday of the race weekend, making it one of the easiest races to attend at the spur of the moment. If you manage to miss the opportunity for tickets at Pocono, you can always watch from the infield. There is no general admission grandstand.

You can stay at the track if you have a self-contained vehicle—but only on Saturday night. On Sunday the infield is open to any vehicle. Spots are available in advance and are cheaper when purchased ahead of time. For infield parking, you must proceed through the tunnel, which is located east of the main entrance, on Long Pond Rd. Information for lodging is available by calling (800) 762-6667.

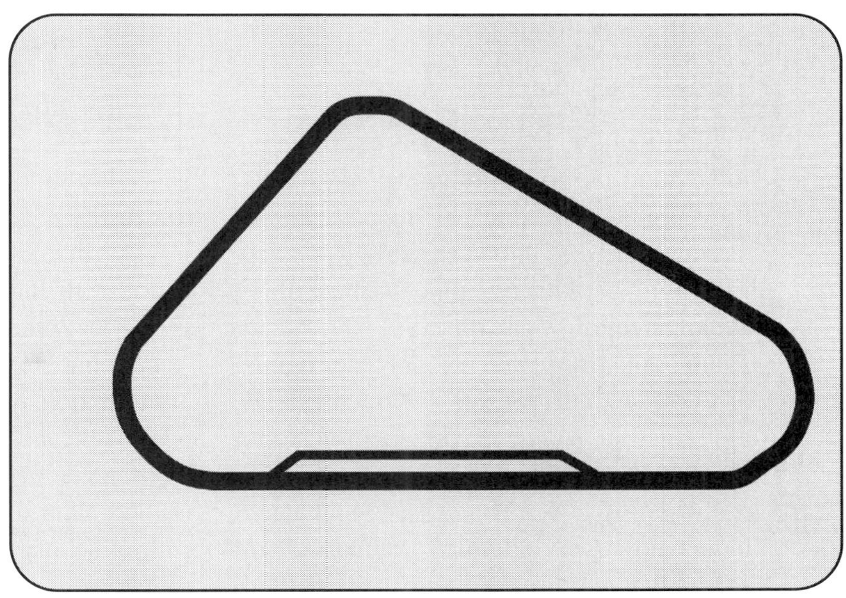

Richmond International Raceway

602 E. Labumum Ave.
Richmond, VA 23222
P.O. Box 9257
Richmond, VA 23227
PH: (804) 345-7223
FAX: (804) 329-5029
Degree of banking in the corners: 14 degrees.
Degree of banking on the backstretch: 2 degrees.
Degree of banking on the frontstretch: 8 degrees.
Length of frontstretch: 860 feet.
Length of backstretch: 920 feet.
Track record: qualifying—Jeff Gordon (Chevrolet), May 13, 1999, 126.499 mph; race—Dale Jarrett, September 6, 1997, 109.047 mph.
Location: North Richmond, at 600 E. Laburnum Ave, between I-64 and I-95, on Strawberry Hill, at the Virginia State Fairgrounds.
Circuit: .75 mile paved, banked oval.
Major races: NASCAR Winston Cup (2 races); NASCAR Busch Grand National Series; Craftsman Truck.

Richmond International Raceway is one of the easiest races on the Winston Cup circuit to attend. Richmond's large metro area makes finding a room an easy proposition—even if arriving late.

Although Richmond used to be the first race after Daytona and then again later in the season, it now hosts two races in the middle of summer—and it tends to be hot here for both events.

The track is located on the Virginia State Fairgrounds and was once called the Richmond Fairgrounds Speedway. The land upon which it stood was purchased by Paul Sawyer, who renamed the facility Richmond International Raceway—with the intention of divorcing the track from the image associated with being a fairgrounds event. He probably didn't need to worry—it is far from a fairgrounds race.

It has been a part of NASCAR's premier series since 1953 when Lee Petty won the inaugural race. The original track was a half-mile dirt track, which first saw auto races in the 1940s, then paved in 1968. It was enlarged to its present length in 1988 and has over 83,000 seats, giving fans a feel for the short track with the width and speed of a bigger facility.

The tri-oval is a fantastic spectating venue—with a wide, smooth surface, giving the drivers room to race. There's also not a bad seat in the house. Its brevity gives fans an intimate look at the racing, but it's fast enough that it makes for quick laps; it is slightly banked, so fans at each end can see the action on the far side easily; the pits wind around at each end, so you can actually see some of the pits from 75 percent of the seats. The grandstands are continually being upgraded, and eventually the entire place will be encompassed by seats.

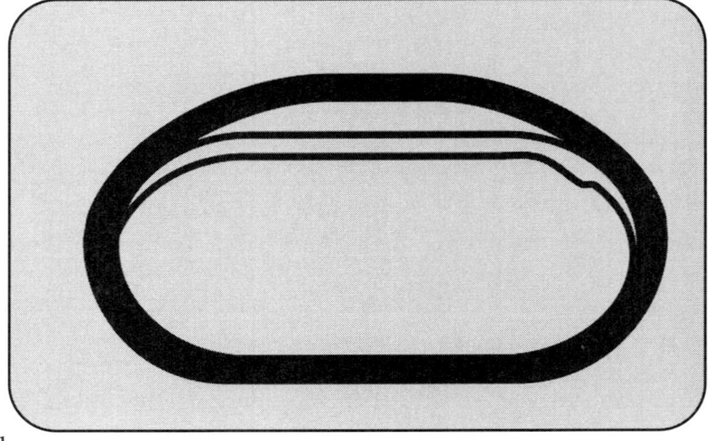

Staying in Richmond is a breeze. There are plenty of hotels within a few minutes of the raceway, and even the more distant accommodations are easy to get to and from during a race. There is also some camping outside the track. Call the track or the Virginia State Chamber of Commerce for more information at (800) VISIT VA.

Sears Point Raceway

Highways 37 & 121
Sonoma, CA 95476
(800) 870RACE
Track record: qualifying—J. Gordon, 98.711, 1:11.080, June 29, 1998;
race—E. Irvan, 81.412, June 7, 1992.
Craftsman Truck: D. Rezendes, 67.001, Oct. 5, 1996.
Location: from Sacramento; I-80 to Hwy. 12 to 29. North to 121, then West
on 121. Note: For quick access, avoid using Hwy. 37 westbound from
Vallejo to 121.
From East Bay Cities: I-580 West across the San Rafael Bridge to Hwy.
101, then North to Hwy. 37, and East to 121.
Circuit: 1.949 mile, 11-turn road course.
Major races: NASCAR Winston Cup, NASCAR Featherlite Mods.

Long the jewel of Northern California road racing, Sears Point Raceway is about to upgrade the already popular facility into a world-class racetrack. Sears will transform itself with a multi-million dollar renovation that will include new entrances and exits, new garages, new seats and a general facelift.

Already known as one of the premier road racing venues in the country, and one of just two on the NASCAR Winston Cup Series circuit. The facility first opened in 1968 and serves as the gateway to the beautiful and scenic Sonoma Valley, which is one of the top wine-producing regions in the world.

Sears Point Raceway will offer one of the most diverse schedules in its history in its fourth decade of racing, highlighted by the second decade of competition by the NASCAR Winston Cup Series with the Save Mart/Kragen 350. In addition, Sears Point will host the NASCAR Featherlite Modified Series events.

In addition to hosting the best in motorsports entertainment, Sears Point is also the North America headquarters of the Russell Racing School. The facility is also home to 75 on-site businesses and is in operation 50 weekends and 340 days a year, making it the country's busiest motorsports industrial park.

The track was modified in 1999 with the addition of a 890-ft. segment connecting what was turn 4 to turn 7, essentially eliminating two tricky corners. The new section, called "the Chute," was a dismal failure. Instead of creating an additional passing area at the entrance of the corner, it rounded it out, eliminating the braking areas into turn 7 and turn 4. With a lot of feedback from drivers—notably Jeff Gordon—the Chute was once again modified to create more overtaking opportunities.

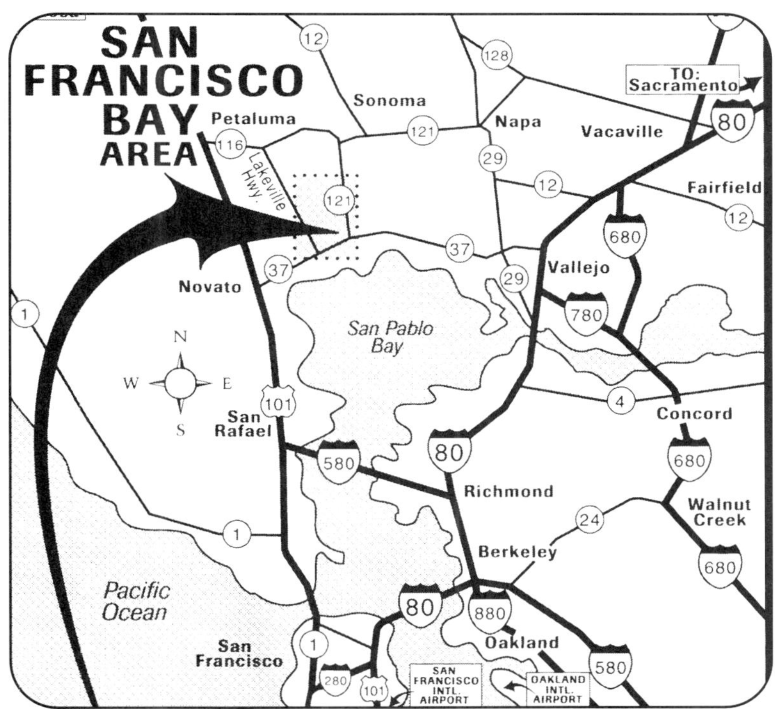

The modification planned for the 2000 season, including increased grandstand seating compacity and luxury suites, will cement the facility as the top road-racing venue in the country. And if you'd like to add a little sightseeing to your stay, San Francisco, one of the top destination hot-spots in the world, is a short 30-minute drive away. Sears Point Raceway took a giant step in its growth in 1996 when it was purchased by Speedway Motorsports, Inc.

Talladega Superspeedway

4000 Speedway Blvd.
Talladega, AL 35160
P.O. Box 777
Talladega, AL 35161
PH: (256) 362-7223
(256) 761-4705
Degree of banking in the corners: 33 degrees.
Degree of banking on the tri-oval: 18 degrees.
Degree of banking on the backstretch: 2 degrees.
Length of tri-oval: 4,300 feet.
Length of backstretch: 4,000 feet.
Track record: qualifying—Bill Elliott (Ford), April 30, 1987, 212.809 mph; race—Mark Martin (Ford), May 10, 1997, 188.354 mph.
Location: north central Alabama, between Birmingham, and Atlanta just off Interstate I-20. From Atlanta, take Interstate 20 west toward Birmingham, exiting in Talladega at exit 168; from Birmingham, take 20 East, exit same.
Circuit: 2.66 mile paved tri-oval; high-banked.
Major races: NASCAR Winston 500; ARCA.

Built by NASCAR's Bill France Sr. as the ultimate speedway, Talladega Superspeedway is an impressive place. Constructed as the longest speedway in the United States at 2.66 miles (Indianapolis and Daytona are 2.5 miles), it's the fastest stock car track in America (holding stock car speed records of 212 MPH, set by Bill Elliott in 1987 in his Ford Thunderbird; which will likely stand as long as there are restrictor plates). It's the widest, with four lanes of racing and a good-sized apron. It has 33-degree banking in the turns—which is four stories tall—and a 4,000 foot backstretch. In all, it is truly a magnificent race track.

Talladega Superspeedway is set on the western outskirts of the Talladega National Forest. Like most of the region, the area is green and alluring during the summer, providing a quiet lazy charm during the humid days. Unlike most tracks, which become desolate when abandoned between races, Talladega blends back into the country and almost looks like a natural part of the landscape.

Talladega, geographically, is the hub of the south. A day away from most major Southern cities including, New Orleans, Daytona Beach, Louisville, Charlotte, Memphis, and Atlanta, the speedway has 20,000,000 people living within a 300-mile radius, making it one of the most accessible speedways in America.

Entering the facility is all done via Speedway Blvd., or "thirty lane"—the huge complex of painted lines that point race fans in the direction of their seats and the infield. Once inside you'll be awed at the size of the place, quickly realizing the significance of the motto, "The Worlds Fastest Superspeedway." After the initial amazement, you'll want to find your seats. Hopefully you'll have reserved tickets. The best view is from tower seats where you can see all of the track.

Although Talladega has expanded, adding permanent seats every year for the last ten, it still only seats 180,000 fans, so tickets are still tough to get.

If unable to get reserved grandstand seats, the infield is a place for entertainment, if you're not as picky

about seeing serious racing. Do try, however, to get as close to the track as possible—the circuit is so large that the incredible speeds seem less impressive at a distance, and up-close at least you'll be able to get some feel for the racing.

Also make sure you check out the Motorsports Hall of Fame and Museum, which is open daily and is adjacent to the track.

You can camp, but the tickets are available on a first-come, first-serve basis and go quickly. Once you get into the infield, you can't take your vehicle back outside until the end of the event. Camping is free outside the track, but there are no electrical hookups.

Although the Talladega Municipal Airport bounds the speedway to the east (just like Daytona, its sister track), it's a small facility that only allows small non-commercial flights. For those who fly their own planes, there's a shuttle from the airport to the track. Birmingham and Atlanta International airports will be the best way to do a weekend if you don't own a plane, which covers most of us.

Talladega itself has very few hotels and the crews usually book those more than a year in advance. In fact, the entire area has less hotel rooms than it needs. Birmingham or Atlanta are probably easiest for the late-comer; and for those who reserve early, Anniston is a quiet Southern city within 20 minutes of the track that may have rooms if you call early.

For Birmingham Hotel information call (205) 252-9825; for Atlanta Chamber of Commerce (404) 586-8403; Atlanta Convention and Visitors Bureau (404) 521-6688; and for Calvin County Chamber of Commerce (Anniston) (205) 237-3536; Pell City (205) 338 3377; Talladega Chamber of Commerce (205) 362-9075.

Texas Motor Speedway

3601 Hwy 114
Justin, TX 76247
P.O. Box 500
Fort Worth, TX 76101
PH: (817) 215-8500
Office: (817) 215-8520
Degree of banking in the corners: 24 degrees.
Degree of banking on the straight: 5 degrees.
Length of frontstretch: 2,250 feet.
Length of backstretch: 1,330 feet.
Track record: qualifying—Kenny Irwin, March 26, 1999, 190.154 mph; race—Terry Labonte (Chevrolet), March 28, 1999, 144.276 mph.
Circuit: 1.5-mile banked, paved oval.
Location/Directions: In north Fort Worth, at the junction of Highway 114 and I-35W.
Major races: NASCAR Winston Cup; NASCAR Busch Grand National; NASCAR Craftsman Truck.

What Texans have known for a while, NASCAR—as well as CART and the NHRA—is only now figuring out: that Texas is motorsports crazy.

The inaugural NASCAR Winston Cup race sold out at the speedway, as did the second, as well as the Busch Grand National race. Even the IRL race did well. Although a great deal of the news related to TMS has been surrounding the races it didn't get (the lobbying effort to bring a second Winston Cup race to the speedway failed), its popularity can only get better.

And as everything is in Texas, it is big. How big? According to officials, the track is the second-largest sports facility in the country, and the third-largest in the world. Texas size. It has grandstand seats for more than 150,000 fans and room for 53,000 more in the

infield. Most of the seats are right on the front straight, with some 120,000 seats in the Texas-sized grandstand.

The track is owned and operated by Speedway Motorsports and Bruton Smith, the owner and operator of Atlanta Motor Speedway, Bristol, Charlotte, Las Vegas and Sears Point. So everything you'd expect to see at a first-class facility is included here at Texas Motor Speedway.

Groundbreaking for the circuit began in April of 1995 and the first race was run on April 5, 1997. Mark Martin won the Coca-Cola 300 BGN race, followed by a victory by Jeff Burton winning the first Winston Cup the next day. The following season, Dale Earnhardt Jr.

recorded his first ever BGN win before capturing the series title.

Unfortunately, during the 1998 event, the track surface somehow began seeping water, which affected qualifying. The race was run, but the track had to excavate and resurface that portion of the track that was affected. The repair (as well as some banking reduction) cost $4 million dollars. It was completed in just over a month's time.

The track now has a smaller facility inside the larger one. Named Lil' Texas Motor Speedway, the track is a fifth-mile banked oval that hosts Legends racing and other local races. The regular show for the small oval is called the Thursday Night Stampede and features Legends racing and Bandolero. There is also a quarter-mile oval, which utilizes the front straightaway.

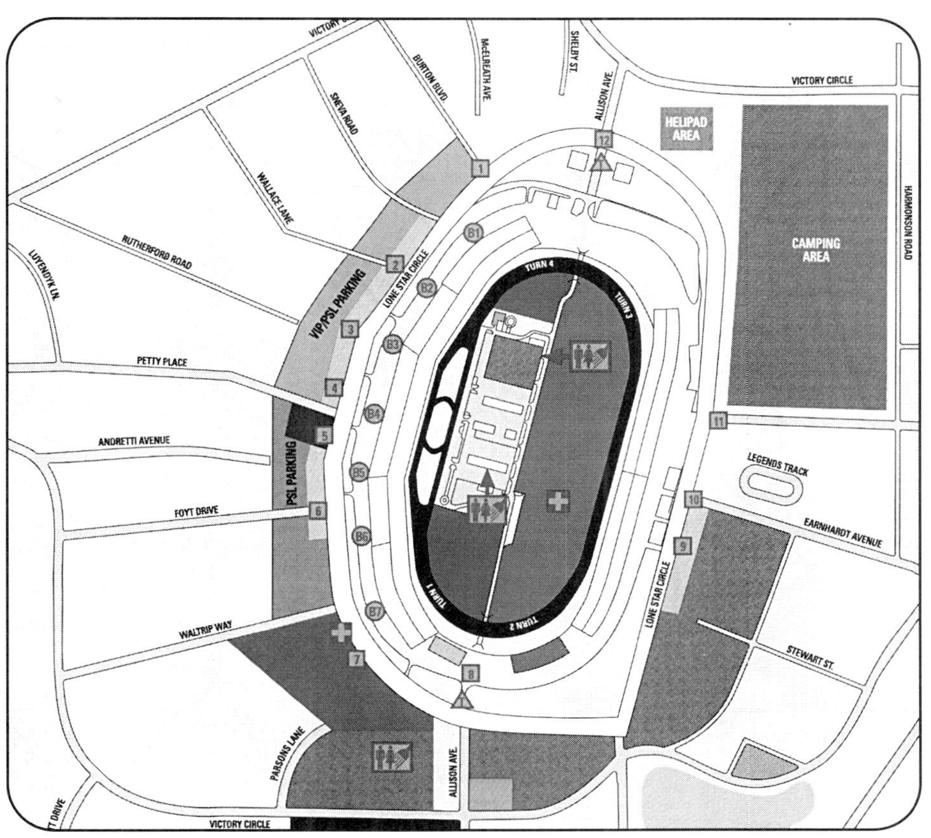

Staying for the race is easy enough, but prepare for a drive. There are quite a few rooms in the area, but there are also quite a few more people who want them. The best way to find a room is to call the Forth Worth Convention and Visitors Bureau at (800) 433-5747, the Dallas Convention and Visitors Bureau at (800) 2DALLAS, or the Denton Convention and Visitors Bureau at (888) 381-1818.

Camping is available at the track. There are 6,000 spaces available just outside the track, with a 5,100 square foot restroom facility, including 44 showers. So camping here is really not roughing it. Call the track for information and reservations at (817) 215-8500.

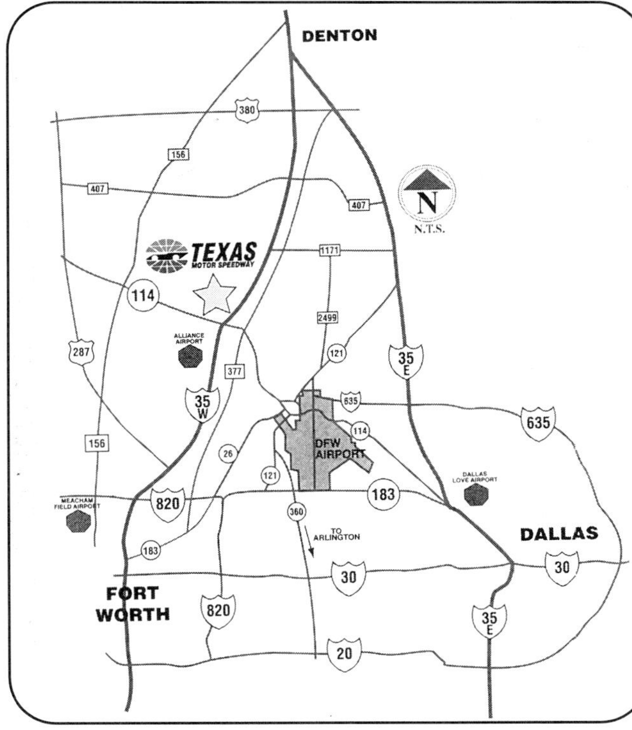

Watkins Glen International

P.O. 500 T
Watkins Glen International, NY
607/535-2481
Track record: qualifying, Winston Cup, D. Earnhardt, 120.733, 73.05, Aug. 9, 1996 Busch Series Qualifying Record, D. Green, 115.995, 76.038, June 29, 1996 Craftsman Truck Series, R. Fellows, 117.476, 75.079, May 29, 1998; race—Winston Cup, M. Martin, 103.030, Aug. 13, 1995 Busch, T. Labonte, 84.186, June 30, 1996.
Circuit: 2.45 mile road course.
Location/Directions: fifteen miles north of Elmira on Route 14, 18 miles northeast of Corning on Route 414, 40 miles south of Geneva on Route 14. Once in Watkins Glen International, take Route 414 to County Route 16, turn right and go two miles to the track. From Rochester and Interstate 390, take exit 42 (Cooper's Plains) off Route 17 and proceed east to the race track.
Major races: NASCAR Winston Cup; NASCAR Busch Grand National; NASCAR Craftsman Truck.

Watkins Glen International today continues a road-racing tradition that dates back to 1948—when sports cars competed on the streets of the village at the southern tip of scenic Lake Seneca.

The tradition began when a law student named Cameron Argetsinger had the vision to open a challenging course encompassing asphalt, cement and dirt roads in and around Watkins Glen. His dream was realized 50 years ago and the circuit has grown to become one of the most respected facilities in the northeast.

In 1998, as NASCAR celebrated its 50th anniversary, Watkins Glen did too. The track honored its 50 years of road racing by adding reserved camping and over 3,000 additional reserved grandstand seats.

NASCAR made its first appearance at the Glen in 1957, and the "Bud at the Glen" as it is now known, has anchored the track's schedule since 1986.

One of only two road courses on the NASCAR Winston Cup Series circuit, Watkins Glen features the unusual distinction of having seven right-hand turns within its eleven corners. The

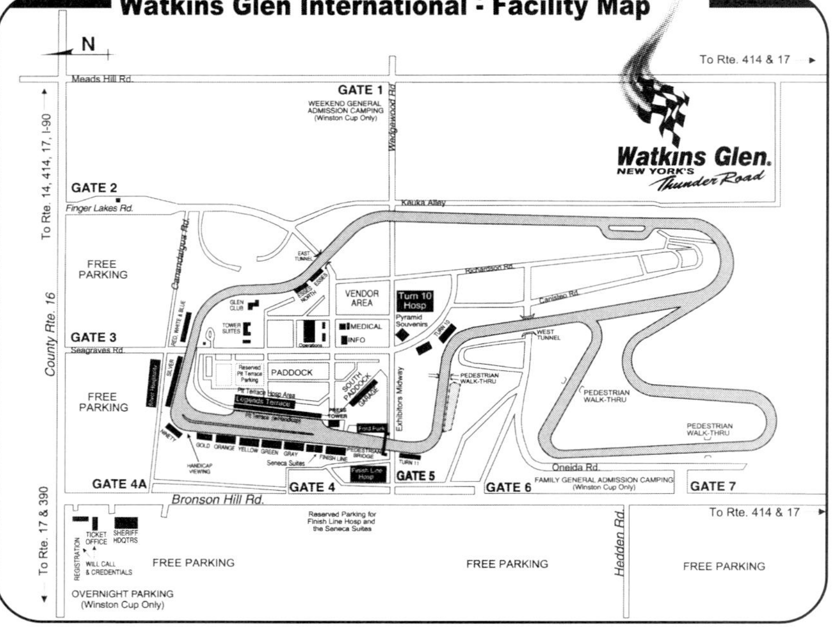

combination always challenges drivers' road-racing skills. It is also regarded as one of the finest spectator tracks on the NASCAR circuit.

NASCAR
BUSCH SERIES,
GRAND NATIONAL
DIVISION

3

THE BUSCH SERIES

The Busch Grand National Series appears to be an almost parallel series to Winston Cup. The cars are almost identical, some of the drivers are the same ones who compete in Winston Cup, the purses are big, the stands are packed and the racing is great.

But the Busch Grand National has not always enjoyed this kind of success. It was originally created as a series to serve as a training ground for new talent, both drivers and crew members. To a certain extent, it still serves this purpose today.

The series was originally created in the '50s as a cheap and competitive way to race. Although Winston Cup races, then called the "Sportsman Division," were supposed to be contended in inexpensive cars, those cars typically were still out of reach for most young racers (just like today). So NASCAR developed the "Late Model Sportsman

Division Stock Division," which was supposed to have been contended in less expensive late model cars with even fewer modifications allowed. And that was the way it worked for many years. In 1968, the name was changed to "Grand National," and then when Budweiser came along, it was the "NASCAR Budweiser Late Model Sportsman Series," and then "Busch Grand National" after the Anheuser-Busch sponsorship. It kept that moniker until 1995 when it was changed again to its current name, the NASCAR Busch Series, Grand National Division. But it's still known as BGN or Busch racing.

In any of those incarnations, the series enjoyed the talent of a lot of very good race car drivers. The names Dale Earnhardt and Ralph Earnhardt, Ned Jarrett and Dale Jarrett, Mark Martin, Harry Gant, Darrell

Waltrip and Jeff Gordon all had roots in Busch Grand National.

Today's Grand National is a far cry from the old days when the series would race some 60 races a year in small tracks throughout the South and northeast. The series was long on drivers and short on organization—short on interest, too, as a matter of fact. The Busch races of ten or fifteen years ago were almost non-existent in fan's minds

But with the big-bucks Busch sponsorship, the series began to take on a new look. Previously, with so many races run, the series was far from a series. Many drivers in the same championship never raced each other because of the sheer number of events and distance involved in getting to them. Nobody could make them all, so the idea was to do well in your own neighborhood. The new Busch Series, by limiting the amount of races to around 30, made it possible for all drivers to make all races.

In addition, Anheuser-Busch saw the wisdom in having the races at the same tracks as the big boys in Winston Cup. That was probably the main reason for the series success. Putting the race on the same track with the Winston Cup gave the series exposure because fans were there anyway, and it also gave the series exposure in another way: Winston Cup drivers constantly entered the Busch races to get in some practice for their own race. This helped make the rivalry better, and it also gave Busch regulars a chance to "train" with some of the big superstars, gaining invaluable experience. Fans loved it and began paying attention. But Busch has now grown to the point where it is almost as popular as Winston Cup, and it is now almost as difficult to get started here. The BGN of today spotlights drivers as soon as they hit the track. It is almost as difficult here as in Winston Cup.

There are now several races televised live on major network TV, not to mention the races televised on cable. And the purses,

Not only does the Busch series train drivers, but pit crews as well. Pit stops are conducted the same way.

which were once quite small, have grown accordingly. In 1982, when Anheuser-Busch began first sponsoring the series, the series points fund was a total of $50,000; in 1998, it was $650,000—and most pundits felt that was too cheap.

By the same token, the total attendance for all races in 1982 was less than 300,000; now it's almost over 2,000,000. And it keeps on growing in amazing increments. The Busch series is no longer a minor-league series, it has hit the majors. That probably isn't what the France family had in mind, but it hasn't hurt the NASCAR image any. Drivers in the regional series used to say they wanted to get to the Grand National Division. Nowadays that's almost too high a goal. They now say they want to go truck racing (which we'll cover in a just a moment).

Obviously, competition is intense in the

A Busch car runs a V8, but the compression ratio is lower, at 9.5:1 vs. 12.5:1 for the Cup car. This means a drop in horsepower by as much as 30 percent.

engine compartment. Busch Series cars run a 9.5:1 compression ratio V8s with a minimum of 350 and a maximum of 358 cubic inches, where Winston Cup cars run the same 350 minimum, 358 maximum with—here's the major difference— a 12.5:1 compression ratio. That usually drops the horsepower of the Busch car some 30 percent to the Cup car. That makes a big difference.

THE RACES

The Busch series is often the support race for Winston Cup, and therefore races on the day before the Cup race—even if they aren't racing at the same track on the same weekend. That is, if Winston Cup is racing somewhere else in the country, Busch Grand National will race the preceding day. That usually means Saturday. At races where Winston Cup races Saturday night, Busch races occur on Friday. If there are no Winston Cup races on that particular weekend, then the Busch series can step up to the spotlight and run a Sunday race, with qualifying on Friday and Saturday.

But normally, as the Winston Cup teams are gearing up for their first practices, Busch teams are gearing up for the first run at the pole position. Qualifying is done the same as Winston Cup: cars make one-lap qualifying runs and the fastest time gets the Bud Pole Award, and is slated to start in the number-one spot no matter what the second day qualifiers run. Likewise, the first 25 starters are locked in for the race. The remainder have to requalify the next day—usually Friday—to get the remaining spots.

The schedules throughout the weekend are similar to Winston Cup, except that they are a day earlier. The idea is that you never want to have the minors detract from the majors .

The practice and qualifying are essentially the same, just one day earlier in the week.

series. Sometimes, in fact, it is more intense that in Winston Cup itself. You don't have so many serious feuds in Winston Cup as you do in Busch racing, and you don't see as many impetuous and hotheaded mistakes. Again, that's what the series was designed for, to let these guys blow off steam and get reprimanded before they make it to Winston Cup.

The major difference, of course, is in the

Points

Points are slightly different from Winston Cup as well, with a little more credit given

the winner of the race. In Busch racing the winner gets 180 points, where second place gets 170 points, a ten point difference (in Winston Cup it's only five points between first and second). From second spot back to sixth, the points distribution drops by five points. Seventh gets 146; sixth gets 142 and so on, dropping four points back to 11th; then it drops in three point increments to the last place, usually 44th spot. Obviously, the driver with the most points at the end of the season wins the Busch Series title.

Awards

The Bud Pole Award is probably the most recognized, where, just as in the Winston Cup series, the fastest qualifier gets a cash award (currently only $800), and gets a trophy. The winner of the most Bud Pole Awards in a season wins an additional amount of money (currently $8,000).

The Gatorade Frontrunner award gives points that accumulate as the season goes on. The only caveat is that the points are awarded at the halfway mark, not at the finish line.

It shows who's fast and who may be hampered by poor mechanical reliability. The Goody's Headache Powder Award is the opposite, giving money to the driver with the worst luck. In fact, if the driver is in the top 35 in point standings he is not eligible.

The MCI Fast Pace award goes to the leader of the race who sets the fastest lap; the NASCAR Winston Cup Scene Most Popular Driver Award is based on voting for the guy with the best image; and the Raybestos Rookie of the Year Award is open to any driver in his first full year of competition, based on his performance against his peers.

In addition to the title itself, there are (like Winston Cup) eight different awards available. The AE Clevite Engine Builder Award goes to the engine builder with the most points at the end of the season (set on a different scale from championship points). Another related to the machine is the Bill France Performance Cup, which is awarded to the leading auto manufacturer.

Busch drivers run on many of the same tracks as the Cup cars.

4

BUSCH SERIES TRACKS

As mentioned previously, the Busch series frequently runs with the Winston Cup series on the same weekend—and sometimes at the same track. On other occasions, the Busch cars run at Winston Cup tracks at different times. The list of tracks when both Busch and Winston Cup run will not be repeated here. So Daytona, North Carolina, Las Vegas, Darlington, Bristol, Texas, Talladega, New Hampshire, Richmond, Lowes, Dover Downs, California, Michigan, Chicago and Atlanta Motor Speedway, which each run both a Cup race as well as a BGN race, are listed already in Chapter 3 on Winston Cup tracks. What follows is a listing of tracks exclusive to BGN and lesser series.

Gateway International Raceway

700 Raceway Blvd.
Madison, IL 62060-0200
PH: (618) 482-2400
Length of frontstretch: 1922 feet.
Length of backstretch: 1976 feet.
Circuit: 1.25-mile paved oval; 1.6-mile road course; quarter-mile dragstrip.
Location/Directions: just outside St. Louis, at the intersection of Interstate 70 and Interstate 55 in Madison, IL.
Major Races: NASCAR Busch Grand National Series; NASCAR Craftsman Truck Series.

Within sight of the Gateway Arch, Gateway International Raceway is yet another new major racetrack in a major metropolitan area. The raceway is located in Illinois, in Madison, but the famous concrete arch is visible from the track.

Oddly, the track—or some version of it—has been here since 1967. It was originally an eighth-mile dragstrip called St. Louis Raceway Park. In 1971, it was expanded to become a quarter-mile dragstrip and renamed St. Louis International Raceway. In 1985, the previous owners added a 2.6-mile road course. Two years later the name changed to Gateway International. And in 1995, ownership changed hands and the facility became a property of the Grand Prix Association of Long Beach. In 1996, the oval was added, a general upgrading commenced and racing resumed in 1997.

The new track, like all new tracks, is

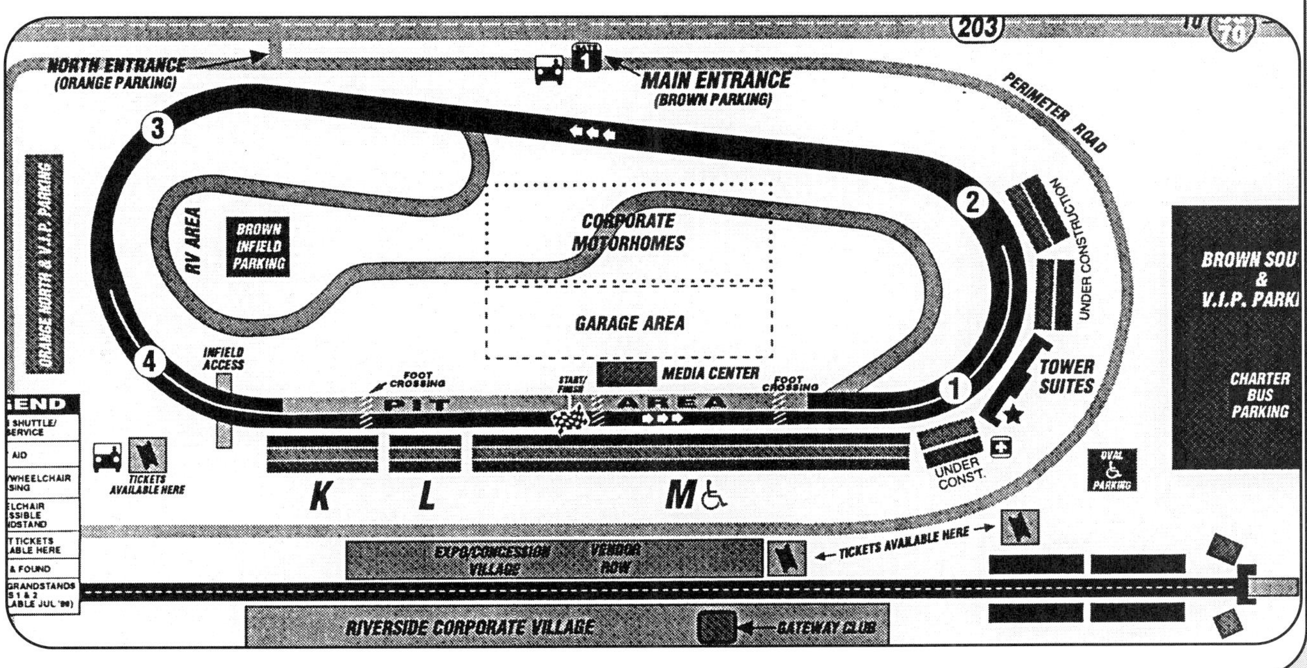

clean and modern. It's 150 acres of the state-of-the-art facilities, with 70,000 seats along the oval, and plans for more. There are private suites along the oval, and different stands and suites for the dragstrip, which is located outside the oval, directly in front of the start/finish grandstands.

The track itself is something of an enigma to drivers. It is similar to Darlington in that it is an egg-shaped oval, which plays havoc on race setup. The north end of the track is the bigger end, with turns three and four at a length of 856 and 871 respectively. Turns one and two are 657 and 620 feet long. Banking is different at each end too, with turns one and two banked at 11 degrees and turns three and four set at 9 degrees.

The track first saw use on May 24, 1997 with the CART/FedEx series. The inaugural NASCAR Busch Series Grand National race was held on October 17, and Dale Earnhardt Jr. took the checkered flag en route to the BGN Championship. There are currently two NASCAR weekends, the Gateway 250, a night race for Busch Grand Nationals, now held in July, and a Craftsman Truck Series race, held in August.

Staying in St Louis is no problem. You can try the St. Louis Visitors Center at America's Center, 7th & Washington Ave., 63101, (800) 916-0092, or call the St. Louis Convention & Visitors Commission, One Metropolitan Square, Ste. 1100, 63102, at (800) 916-0092. Or following is a list of hotels in downtown St. Louis: Marriott Courtyard, 2340 Market Street (800) 321-2211; Embassy Suites Hotel, Radisson Downtown/ Riverfront, 200 N. Fourth Street (800) 925-1395; Holiday Inn Select/Convention Center 811 N. Ninth Street, (800) 289-8338; Hyatt Regency (800) 233-1234; Ramada Inn at the Arch, 333 Washington Avenue, (800) 329-7466; St. Louis Marriott Pavilion Hotel, One Broadway, (800) 228-9290.

Indianapolis Raceway Park

10267 East U.S. Hwy. 136
Indianapolis, IN 46234
P.O. Box 34300
Indianapolis, IN 46234
Track location: 10267 East U.S. Highway 136
Indianapolis, IN 46234
PH: (800) 884-6472
FAX: (317) 291-4220
Degree of banking in the corners: 12 degrees.
Degree of banking on the straight: 12 degrees.
Length of frontstretch: 699 feet.
Length of backstretch: 699 feet.
Location/Directions: central Indiana, about five miles west of the Indianapolis Motor Speedway, one mile west of Clermont on U.S. Highway 136.
Circuit: .686 mile paved oval/quarter-mile dragstrip/2.5 mile road course; 14 turns.
Major races: NHRA U.S. Nationals; NASCAR Busch Grand National Series; USAC Silver Crown, Sprint, and Midget Championships; SCCA National Road Racing Championships.

Indianapolis Raceway Park is known not only for its oval track and its sprint car racing, but also for the NHRA's U.S. Nationals, the largest and most prestigious drag race in the world.

Three facilities on 300 acres make up IRP. The two-and-a-half mile road course, which is not used for any major series, runs local club racing and minor pro series. The .686-mile oval hosts NASCAR's Busch Grand National series and USAC Midget and Silver Crowns. The Budweiser "Night Before the 500" is one of the best USAC shows in the country. There is also a Skoal Classic on Indy Pole Night, which often attracts drivers from the 500.

The oval track has been the cornerstone of the popular ESPN "Thunder" series, which has an average of 1.1 million viewers per show, making IRP the most televised short track in motorsports.

The oval alone holds 20,000—which is full for special events like the Busch GN. The first race on the IRP paved oval was in 1961. A young Texan named AJ Foyt won that first IRP race—then promptly went to Indy the following day and won his first 500.

Rooms are easy to find unless there is a race here at the same time that the Indy 500 or Brickyard 400 are in town. Otherwise, the area around IRP will be easy enough to find rooms. See the Indianapolis track information on page 51, or call IRP for more information.

Kentucky Speedway

2418 Royal Dr.
Ft. Mitchell, KY 41017
(888) 652-RACE
(859) 578-2300
tickets@kentuckyspeedway.com
Track: 1.5 mile paved Tri-oval
Degree of banking in the corners: 14 degrees.
Degree of banking on the straight: 8 degrees frontstretch; 4 degrees backstretch.
Length of frontstretch: 681 feet.
Degree of banking, tri-oval: 10 degree of banking, 300 feet.
Length of backstretch: 1600 feet.
Location/directions: 35 miles south of Cincinnati in Sparta, Kentucky. From Cincinnati, take I-75 South to, I-71 South (Exit 173), get off at Sparta (Exit 57), turn right onto Highway 35 North into entrance 1–3 at the Kentucky Speedway. Or from Louisville, take I-71 North to Sparta (Exit 57), turn left into the Kentucky Speedway.

Kentucky Speedway's $152 million dollar state-of-the-art facility is a 1.5-mile tri-oval with 14-degree banking in the turns and lighting for night racing. As the first stage of construction ends, the facility will boast of some 65,989 grandstand seats, 50 luxury suites, a 210 seat, private, glass-enclosed restaurant and a 2,000-seat exterior club.

Opened in 2000, the second stage of development will enhance the paved oval to include a dirt track and drag-strip racing, plus it can expand the 1.5-mile venue to 120,000 seats with 120 luxury suites. The racing surface is nice and wide, some 70 feet wide, plus 12-foot shoulders.

You can camp at one of nine areas, including General James Taylor Park, in Newport, KY; Big Bone Lick State Park Florence, KY, Devou Park Covington, KY, Eagle Valley Camping Resort Sanders, KY, Frederick's Landing Wilder, KY, Florence Overnight RV Park Florence, KY, A. J. Jolly Park Alexandria, KY. The closest is Edge of Speedway Campground Sparta, KY.

For real rooms, try the Days Inn Carrollton, KY (16 miles from the track), Port William Motel also Carrollton, General Butler State Resort Park, Carrollton, Holiday Inn Express, Carrollton, Blue Gables Court, Carrollton, Super 8 Motel, Carrollton, Sunset Motel, Carrollton, Holiday Inn, Carrollton, the Hampton Inn, Carrollton and the Carrollton Inn. In Walton, some 19 miles from the track, there is the Richwood Motel, the Holiday Inn Express and the Days Inn. And you can always find rooms in Cincinnati if needed.

As close to Cincinnati as the track is there are plenty of places to dine. Listed here are just some that the track recommends. Try the Amerasia, located at 1 Madison Ave., Covington, KY (859) 261-6121, or Applebee's at 7383 Turfway Rd. Florence, KY (859) 371-4141 or at 1 Madison Ave. Covington, KY (859) 431-0930. There's also a Cracker Barrel on Turfway Rd., a Fuddruckers on Hansel Ave., Florence, an Olive Garden at 7844 Mall Rd., Florence, an Outback Steakhouse at 2301 Buttermilk Crossing, Crescent Springs and a Red Lobster at 7921 Dream St., Florence.

Memphis Motorsports Park

5500 Taylor Forger Rd.,
Memphis, TN 38053
PH: (901) 358-7223
FAX: (901) 358-7274
Degree of banking in the corners: 11 degrees.
Degree of banking on the straight: 4 degrees.
Location/Directions: Southern Tennessee, in North Memphis. From Interstate I-240 North, take Warford/New Allen Rd. exit north to Ral-Mill Rd., then go three miles, heading left on Ral-Mill, then left on Fite and a half mile to the track.
   Circuit: Half-mile clay oval/eighth-mile midget track/quarter-mile dragstrip/2.0 mile road course; nine turns.
Major races: NASCAR Busch Series, Craftsman Truck, Winston Racing Series; NHRA Mid-South Nationals; SCCA Regional Road Racing Championships; WERA Motorcycle Racing Championships.

It all started in 1986 as a multi-track facility run by a group of investors headed by Ed Gatlin. Gatlin and his business partners dealt in a no nonsense business style that allowed Memphis Motorsports Park to survive the up-and-down Memphis sports market and become the model of perseverance among Mid-South sports entities.

Gatlin and his group went through some learning pains, but the group took their failures and setbacks and went to work, piece by piece, starting with what has become the area's signature race, now known as the Pennzoil Nationals presented by AutoZone.

Following the 1996 Pennzoil Nationals the Grand Prix Association of Long Beach, one of the major players in American motorsports, bought Memphis Motorsports Park from Gatlin's group.

In 24 years, the organization founded by Chris Pook has developed one of the major events in CART FedEx Indycar circuit—the Toyota Grand Prix of Long Beach. Now they have reached out to Mid-America in a big way.

Memphis Motorsports Park is currently under a $2.5 million improvement plan, which has seen improvements to the track, stands and suite areas on the drag strip/road course, as well as the brand new 3/4-mile paved tri-oval, which will be the sight of a Busch Series race, a NASCAR Craftsman Truck Series, and an ARCA and USAC event.

The purchase of Memphis Motorsports Park comes on the heels of Automotive Safety and Transportation Systems (ASTS), a subsidiary of GPALB, acquiring Gateway International Raceway in Madison, Ill., just outside St. Louis. Gateway is coming off a successful season in which it hosted a CART FedEx Indycar circuit race, as well as a NASCAR Busch Grand National event and an NHRA Winston Drag Racing event. Tennessee was in dire need of a facility like this, but for now the closest the big road race machines of the SCCA will get to racing here is testing, which they do on occasion.

NHRA's Mid-South Nationals is the biggest show of the MIMP year with attendance of nearly 80,000. Contact the Memphis Convention and Visitors Bureau at (901) 576-8181 for hotel information.

Milwaukee Mile

Wisconsin State Fair Park
7722 W. Greenfield Ave.
West Allis, WI 53214
PH: (414) 453-8277
(414) 453-5514
FAX: (414) 453-5217
Degree of banking in the corners: 9.25 degrees.
Degree of banking on the straight: 2.5 degrees.
Length of frontstretch: 1,265 feet.
Length of backstretch: 1,265 feet.
Location: Central Milwaukee, just off Interstate I-94, in the Milwaukee State Fairgrounds.
Circuit: One mile oval, slightly banked.
Major races: NASCAR Busch Series; ASA Championships.

Originally opened in 1933 for Indy Car racing, Milwaukee is now becoming known for NASCAR, but it has been around long enough to have been known for other things as well. The facility marked its 100th anniversary as a racing venue in 1991, with horses being the original competitors. Its first auto races began in 1903.

Milwaukee's first introduction to modern NASCAR racing was in 1984, when the venerable track hosted NASCAR Busch Grand National racing. Although the race was off the schedule until 1993, it became a permanent stop for BGN and now hosts a NASCAR Craftsman Truck Series race as well.

Almost like baseball's Wrigley field, the circuit is in the middle of the city—a place you rarely find a racetrack these days. The Interstate (I-94) bounds the north side of the speedway, and on the backstretch, 60 to 80 yards from the track, is a row of suburban Milwaukee houses. Due to its unique location it does not host a weekly show and only has racing an average of once a month.

Ten minutes from downtown Milwaukee, hotels are available, but Brookfield has more rooms, and is only five minutes away. The strip where Wisconsin Fair Park is located follows I-94 west which, by travelling either direction, will have plenty of hotels; 84th St. also has lots of hotels.

Although the circuit is located in a congested area, parking is not a problem. You can, however, take a bus to the entrance of the track on Greenfield Ave. if you like. For bus information on routing and times, call (414) 344-6711 for the Milwaukee County Transit System. For more information on lodging, call the Greater Milwaukee Convention and Visitor's Bureau at (414) 273-7222.

Nashville Speedway USA

Nashville TN 37204
PH: (615) 726-1818
FAX: (615) 726-0691
http://www.nashvillespeedway.com/
PO Box 40304
Degree of banking in the corners: 18 degrees.
Degree of banking on the straight: 3 degrees.
Length of frontstretch: 679 feet.
Length of backstretch: 665 feet.
Location: southern Nashville, off I-65 at exit 81 Wedgewood Ave. to the Tennessee State Fairgrounds.
Circuit: 5/8-mile paved oval.
Major races. NASCAR Busch Series; Craftsman Truck; Winston Racing Series.

Nashville Motor Raceway is located within the Tennessee State Fairgrounds, a few minutes from downtown Nashville. Regular racing is again a Saturday night NASCAR program after several seasons of being without. Racing runs from April through September in the warm Tennessee heat.

The track is one of the oldest in the country, with a rich stock car history dating back to 1904. In the fifties, it was one of NASCAR's premier tracks, with drivers such as Lee Petty, Fireball Roberts and Joe Weatherly all competing on a regular basis here. Now renamed and run with new management, the track has been repaved, renovated and seems to be back in the NASCAR fold.

Nashville has become increasingly tourist oriented in the past few years, and although there is no lodging within walking distance of the track, there are plenty of hotels in the area. For more information, call the Nashville Chamber of Commerce for reservation information at (615) 259-3900.

Nazareth Speedway

P. O. Drawer F
Hwy. 191
Nazareth, PA 18064
PH: (888) 629-7223
Degree of banking in corner One: 3 degrees.
Degree of banking in corner Two: 4 degrees.
Degree of banking in corners Three-Four: 6 degrees.
Degree of banking on the straights: 2.7 degrees.
Length of frontstretch: 800 feet.
Length of backstretch: 1,200 feet.
Location: eastern Pennsylvania, in the Lehigh Valley, eight miles from the New Jersey border, eighteen miles northeast of Allentown. From Newark, take I-78 to U.S. 22. From there, take U.S. 33 north, heading east at State Route 248. There are entrances on 248 and SR 191.
Circuit: One mile paved tri-oval.
Qualifying Records: Busch Series: E. Sadler, 129.674, 27.762, May 18, 1997.
Craftsman Truck Series M. Bliss, 128.315, 28.056, July 11, 1998.
Race Records: Busch Series, C. Bown, 104.772, May 11, 1991.
Craftsman Truck Series: J. Sprague, 99.252, June 30, 1992.
Major races: NASCAR Busch Series; Craftsman Truck; NASCAR Winston Modifieds.

Nazareth was a semi-banked, dirt, D-shaped, 1 1/8th-mile oval when it was built in 1966. Located in the beautiful Lehigh Valley area near Allentown, Pa., Nazareth Speedway hosts the Busch Series Grand National Division, as well as the NASCAR Craftsman Truck Series

The uniquely shaped track is a sister track to Michigan Speedway and is operated by Penske Speedways.

Nazareth Speedway was originally built in 1966 by the late Jerry Fried. Fried also operated the track, running weekly shows, night races, and championship events until 1971 for dirt, midget, sprint and stock cars. Mario Andretti, who grew up near the speedway and began his driving career at the track, won the last championship race held on the old track in 1969.

The track lay dormant for 10 years, until Lindy Vicari reopened the raceway in 1981 to run special events only, namely the USAC championship dirt cars. Kenny Brightbill won the last race at Nazareth Speedway under Vicari's ownership, a $50,000-to-win modified event in 1983. In 1985, the track went into bankruptcy.

Roger Penske purchased the 90-acre facility in September of 1986 from the Bank of Pennsylvania and immediately began an extensive renovations, including a complete repaving of the track.

Groundbreaking for "Pennsylvania International Raceway" began on October 16, 1986. Used in the construction and renovation were 41,000 tons of gravel, 22,000 tons of asphalt, six miles of fencing, and two miles of guard rail. Construction was completed by the next year in time to run the inaugural race on September 20, 1987.

In 1997, Nazareth Speedway underwent its most extensive renovation since the track opened in 1987. The grandstands on the frontstretch were replaced by state-of-the-art, high-rise grandstands with aluminum seats and backrests. The construction created a new "skyline" for Nazareth and 10,000 additional prime seats. While the bleachers were removed, construction crews replaced the retaining wall on the perimeter of the frontstretch. The remainder of the wall along the backstretch was replaced in time to open the 1998 season.

The Lehigh Valley area is old country Pennsylvania. And, although great for sightseeing, the remoteness makes it difficult to find places to stay. There is really almost nowhere to stay in Nazareth itself. Bethlehem and Allentown have a few rooms, but the crews usually rollover reservations to the following season in preparation for the next race, so finding a room there will not be easy either. Phillipsburg, NJ, or Clinton, NJ, which are just over the Delaware River, are other possibilities; or try Quakertown, or the Poconos, which are about an hour away.

Infield overnight parking is permitted following time trials—for Grand National events, that's Friday night. Although there is really no general admission ticket, anyone can enter the infield. Unfortunately, you'll have to pay the same price as someone who goes by car. In all cases, children 12 and under are admitted free with a paying adult.

The Allentown/Bethlehem/Eastman area does have an airport, named, aptly, ABE Municipal Airport. There are commercial flights, and 727's do land there. For the Chamber of Commerce of Nazareth, call (215) 759-9188; for Bethlehem, call (215) 867-3788; in Allentown (215) 437-9661. Or call the track and ask for a short list of the area's hotels.

Pikes Peak International Raceway

16650 Midway Ranch Rd.
Fountain, Colorado 80817-0430
P.O. Box 430
Fountain, Colorado 80817-0430
PH: (888) 306-RACE
Or: (719) 382-RACE
Fax: (719) 382-918
Degree of banking in the corners: 10 degrees.
Degree of banking on the straight: 10 degrees.
Circuit: one-mile D-shaped paved oval; 1.3 mile road course.
Location/Directions: Located 14 miles south of Colorado Springs and 90 miles from Denver. From Denver or Colorado Springs, take I25 south to exit 122 or 123.
Major races: Busch Grand National, Craftsman Trucks, Winston West, USAC Silver Crown.

Sitting at 5,300 feet above sea level, and at the base of the famous Pikes Peak, the relatively new Pikes Peak International Raceway is more than just another racetrack. It's a sporting facility in the middle of some of America's greatest scenery.

Only open since 1997, the facility expands big-time racing into yet another market. By 1999, the track had already hosted a BGN race, trucks, USAC Silver Crown, two IRL races per year and an American Motorcyclist Assocation Superbike race. Not bad for a new facility. It's biggest event of the lot is the Busch race— although the IRL also almost fills the 43,000 seat stands to capacity.

The track itself is regarded as a fine place to race by most drivers—either IRL or stock car drivers. The racing surface is very smooth and very fast. Pikes Peak is known as the fastest one-mile in the country. The record (at the time this guide was being prepared), was set by Scott Sharp in an Indy Car in 1998, with a speed of 176.116 mph.

Part of the speed comes from the banking. Since it is a D-shaped oval, the front straight—which, of course, isn't actually straight at all—is banked at 7 degrees. The turns are banked at 10 degrees and the back is banked 3. The banking, and the way the stands are elevated, makes it easy for fans in almost any seat to see the action on the track. The first row of grandstand seating is some 15 feet above the track, so even fans at the bottom can see most of the track. And the infield has only a two-story press facility, 36 garages (capacity for 72 racing vehicles) and an infield care center which could block your vision. Typically, you'll see everything there is to see from almost any seat.

So far there is no permanent school at the track, but the Richard Petty Driving Experience comes to town from time to time, so there is a reason to visit the track even when no racing is going on. The Fourth of July is a down weekend for the venue because of the world famous Pikes Peak Hillclimb—and many of the track personnel will be out there helping with that event.

Pikes Peak (continued)

    To stay for a race, the closest places will be Pueblo and Colorado Springs. Most teams stay at the Doubletree in Colorado Springs, or the Ramada in Pueblo, although there are many others. The track has a Fan Guide that's available by calling. It will give you an entire list of hotels in the area, as well as prices, plus KOA and other camping locations.

NASCAR CRAFTSMAN TRUCK SERIES

5

THE CRAFTSMAN TRUCK SERIES

The NASCAR Craftsman Truck Series has been a hit since the first race in 1995. The series was one of the few in U.S. racing history that opened to packed grandstands with full fields and a television deal that had every race on TV.

The Truck series has capitalized on what Americans buy most—trucks. When the series started, just over half of all vehicles sold in the United States were trucks. It seemed only natural that somebody would race them.

And leave it to NASCAR to make truck racing a success in its first year. Again, NASCAR was not just trying to establish a new series that would be attractive to fans, it was also trying to establish a new series that would serve as a training ground for drivers and crew, just like Busch Grand National.

Mike Skinner, the first Truck Champion, now drives a Winston Cup car. And Skinner didn't have to go to Busch first. It's proved to be a viable series on its own—and another steppingstone into the big leagues.

TRUCK SPECS

Both the Winston Cup car and the Craftsman truck run the 12:1 V8. They both run the same 358 cubic inch restriction and they use the same induction system, a

Truck racing has been immensely popular with crowds since its inception in 1995. It offers all the excitement and close racing of the Cup cars, but in a package many fans can easily identify with—their truck.

Holley 830 cfm 4-barrel carburetor. The horsepower is between 700 and 725 and torque is between 490 and 530. Transmissions are the same 4-speed manuals. Four-wheel discs stop the trucks, as they do the cars, and the suspensions are almost identical.

Of course, the similarities end there, because one is, afterall, a truck. The height of a Craftsman truck is 59 inches vs. 51 for a Winston Cup car. The nose is 27 inches high on the Cup car, where the Craftsman truck is 33 inches high. The width of the Craftsman truck at its fenders is 77 inches, vs. 74 on the Winston Cup car. The length of the nose on the Craftsman truck is stubbier, at 36 inches compared to the longer, more sculpted 44-inch Winston Cup nose. Right side weight can be as little as 45 percent on the Craftsman truck where the Winston Cup car needs at least 45 percent of its weight on the right side—frequently more. And the wheelbase is longer on the Craftsman truck, two inches longer compared to the Winston

Cup car.

The major factor that creates the speed difference is, of course, the shape of the body. The truck is like a brick in the air, where the Winston Cup car is more like a contoured brick. The height of the Craftsman truck hurts its top speed, but more than that the chopped off roof behind the cab really affects its handling.

The roof on a Winston Cup car slopes gradually back down to the deck lid and then is sculpted into the bumper. The wing is mounted to add downforce and reduce lift, but basically the design is fairly efficient for a streetable vehicle. At the front of the Winston Cup car, the hood moves up in a nice gradual sweep to the winsdhield, which is also raked for style and aerodynamics.

The Craftsman truck on the other hand is a truck body, which is aerodynamically one of the most inefficient vehicles on the road. Now it's on a race track.

Probably the worst thing about the truck is the roof. To start with, the roof is high, as

The trucks are plenty powerful, running the same compression as the Cup cars in the same V8, but their chunky aerodynamics keep speeds down.

mentioned earlier, it's eight inches taller. And then it simply ends, chopped off almost vertically. That 90-degree rear window causes a small tornado at speed, a vortex, that cannot be eliminated. The vortex can actually produce lift in some circumstances.

To get from the tall roof to the stubby nose, the windshield has very little rake or angle to it, which is not aerodynamically efficient. The stubby nose also hurts overall front-end downforce, since the hood also acts as a spoiler of sorts. The truck's hood is not just flat, it's short too. Unfortunately, it's very tall, so, once again, it hinder the overall ability of the truck to cut through the wind.

Truck racing is fast, furious and extremely tight.

Like Busch Grand National, Craftsman trucks are viewed as a great training ground for future Cup drivers and crew members.

POINTS SYSTEM

The points are identical to Winston Cup, with 175 going to the winner and dropping five points back to sixth, with seventh through 10th dropping four points, and the remainder dropping by three to 45th position.

Races are held at various tracks from the Walt Disney Speedway in Florida to Mesa Marin in California, and from short tracks to Watkins Glen and Sears Point. There were 24 events in 2000.

6

CRAFTSMAN TRUCK TRACKS

Craftsman Trucks run more road circuits than any other major NASCAR series. Trucks also run on the previously mentioned Nashville Speedway, Homestead-Miami Speedway, Phoenix International Raceway, Texas Motor Speedway, Bristol Motor Speedway, The Milwaukee Mile, Nazareth Speedway, California Speedway, Pikes Peak, Indianapolis Raceway Park, New Hampshire International Speedway, Martinsville Speedway, Las Vegas Motor Speedway and Richmond International Raceway, so turn to those tracks in the Winston Cup and Busch sections for information. What follows is a listing of tracks that currently only run Craftsman Truck, which amounts to just three: Evergreen, Mesa Marin and Portland.

Evergreen Speedway

P.O. Box 745
Monroe, WA 98272
PH: (360) 794-5917
FAX: (360) 794 7633
http://www.evergreenspeedway.com/
Degree of banking in the corners: 8 degrees.
Degree of banking on the straight: 4 degrees.
Length of frontstretch: 850 feet.
Length of backstretch: 850 feet.
Circuit: .646-mile paved oval.
Location/Directions: located 25 miles northeast of Seattle. Take I-5 north to Highway 2 east to Monroe.
Major races: NASCAR Craftsman Truck series.

Situated inside the Evergreen State Fairgrounds in Monroe, Washington, Evergreen Speedway has been in existence since 1952 as a versatile, all-around motorsports track. The track's unique design combines a 5/8-mile outer oval with a 3/8-mile inner oval, as well as a 1/5-mile oval (it also has a figure-eight track and an 1/8-mile drag strip).

The outer oval is the headliner, with NASCAR Craftsman Trucks' NAPACARD 250 run here, and Winston West, Northwest Tour and Southwest Tour all having an annual migration to the larger loop. The smaller ovals (and the figure-eight track) host the regular NASCAR Great West divisions.

A 7500-seat, covered grandstand and an additional 7500-seat temporary grandstand gives race fans a great view of all of the tracks.

The track's location near Seattle makes finding a hotel a simple task. What follows is a brief listing of the hotels closer to the track: Best Western Baron Inn, (360) 794-3111; Fairgrounds Inn (360) 794-5401; Inn at Snohomish (360) 568-2208; Embassy Suites (206) 775-2500; Best Western Landmark (206) 775-7447; the Silver Cloud (206) 775-7600; Holiday Inn (425) 337-2900; Marina Village Inn (425) 259-4040; Everett Quality Inn (425) 347-9099. For RV information, call the Evergreen State Fairgrounds Office at (360) 794-4344. For Camping, call (360) 458-2274.

Mesa Marin Raceway

P.O. Box 9518
Bakersfield, CA 93389.
PH: (805) 366-5711
FAX: (805) 366-5123
http://www.mesamarin.com
Degree of banking in the corners: 17 degrees.
Degree of banking on the straight: 7 degrees.
Length of frontstretch: 700 feet.
Length of backstretch: 700 feet.
Location/Directions: southern California, in Bakersfield, 10 miles east of U.S. Highway 99, south of State Highway 178.
Circuit: Half-mile paved oval.
Major races: NASCAR Craftsman Truck Series Championship; Winston West Championship; NASCAR Southwest Tour.

Mesa Marin reckons itself the fastest half-mile track west of the Mississippi. The facility has 7,000 seats, most of which are generally occupied when the Craftsman truck, Winston West or Southwest Tour cars come to the fast track. It is also becoming an oval which is successfully being attacked by road racers, with formula cars running here more and more often. The track is also often used for movie, television, and film production.

You'll be best suited by staying in downtown Bakersfield, or on the outskirts. The track lists the following as the closest lodgings: Best Western 800-424-4900; Days Inn (800) 329-7466; Quality Inn Airport (800) 221-2222; Rio Bravo Resort (888) 517-5500; Travel Lodge Hotel (800) 578-7878.

Portland International Raceway

1940 N. Victory Blvd.
Portland, Ore., 97217.
Or: Global Events Group.
P.O. Box 3024
Portland, OR 97208.
Tel. (503) 823-7223/(503) 232-3000
Circuit: 1.944-mile, 12-turn course.
Location/Directions: West Delta Park, seven miles north of downtown Portland, off I-5 at Exit 306B.

Racing at Portland International Raceway has been known mostly for sports cars and CART Indycars, but starting in 2000, NASCAR Trucks now run on the old West Delta Park road course. Owned and operated by the city of Portland through its bureau of Parks and Recreation, the raceway generates its own revenues and receives no general fund tax dollars. The raceway's varied, year round activities bring between 30 and 40 million dollars into the surrounding community each year.

Although the CART race is still the largest event of the season, the NASCAR Craftsman Truck races are well attended, with banging and bumping going on in the tight corners leading to a start-finish straight.

For lodging, try the Best Western/Inn at the Meadows 1-800-448-5544/(503) 286-9600. The Days Inn is also located near the track at (800) 833-1800/(503) 289-1800. Or try the Oxford Suites at (800) 548-7848/(503) 283-3030, the Courtyard Marriott (800)321-2211/(503) 735-1818; Double Tree/Jantzen Beach (503) 253-4488, Double Tree/Columbia River (503) 283-2111, and the Holiday Inn (800) 465-4329/(503) 283-8000.

Or, if you prefer downtown, try the Ramada Inn at (800) 472-9766/(503) 239-9900, the Double Tree Hotel/Lloyd Center at (800) 733-5466/(503) 281-6111, the Westin Benson (800) 228-3000/(503) 228-9611, the Portland Marriott (800) 228-9290/(503) 226-7600, the Portland Hilton (800) 445-8667/(503) 221-0450, the Alexis Hotel (800) 227-1333/(503) 228-3233, or the Embassy Suites at (800) 362-2779.

For restaurants, try Atwater's at 111 SW 5th Ave. 30th Floor for Greek food (220-3600). For French, try Brasserie Montmartre at 626 SW Park (224-5552). For Steaks and seafood try Bush Garden, located downtown at 900 SW Morrison (226-7181). For Chinese, try Chang's Yangtze located Downtown on 921 SW Morrison (241-0218). For seafood, try Digger O'Dell's located at 532 SE Grand (238-6996). For Cajun, the Harborside Restaurant is located on the waterfront at 309 SW Montgomery (220-1865).

NASCAR'S TOURING SERIES

7 TOURING SERIES & THEIR TRACKS

NASCAR also sanctions a "Tour" system, where drivers of certain types of cars and in certain areas can compete with more of a broad-based field of drivers. The concept started as a way to give drivers who traveled to tracks in their area—or sometimes out of their area—a championship on which to concentrate.

The Touring series varies in different regions based on whatever was the most popular form of racing when the Tour started. In the Midwest, the cars, although still stock cars, resemble Modifieds in their weight, setups and driving style. In the South there are both Modified classes and more of a pure stock car–based class.

What is similar in every instance is the level of competition in each series. This is certainly less prestigious than Winston Cup or Busch Grand National—and even the Truck series—but it is still serious competition and there is usually a good-sized purse at stake. What follows is a brief description of each of the seven "Tour" series with their respective tracks, as well as Winston West, which is not so much a Touring class as it is a regional class of NASCAR Winston Cup.

One important note: Because these series are so interrelated, there is a lot of crossover with the tracks. If you don't find the track you're looking for listed within one of the series, check the index at the back of the book. It may well be listed in another series.

NASCAR's Touring Series includes many different types of stock cars. Above is a Modified from the Featherlite Tour series. Modifieds like these run mainly in the Northeast. Courtesy Flemington Speedway.

BUSCH NORTH SERIES

The Busch North Series is a Northeastern touring championship contested on tracks in Pennsylvania, New York, Delaware, New Hampshire, Vermont, and Connecticut.

The cars used in the series are very similar to Busch Grand National Series cars in that they are current or late model (within two model-years old) American-made production passenger sedans. They must weigh not less than 3,100 pounds (which is 200 pounds less than the BGN cars) and have a wheelbase of 105 inches, with a track of 60 inches. The engines are limited to 358 cubic inch, 9.5:1 compression ratio V8s or 274ci V6s (compression on the V6s is unlimited). They cannot be fuel injected, but must run a lone four-barrel carburetor.

A partial listing of tracks includes: USA Speedway, Riverside Park Speedway, Thompson International Speedway, New Hampshire International Speedway, Nazareth Speedway, Holland International Speedway, Watkins Glen, Stafford Motor Speedway, Star Speedway, Jennerstown Speedway, Thunder Road International Speedbowl, and Beech Ridge Motor Speedway. Of course, the championship may add or subtract venues from the schedule, but the majority of these paved ovals (plus one road race at Watkins Glen) have been on the calendar since the series started in 1987. The series has been a steppingstone for some top drivers, notably Ricky Craven, Joe Bessey and Chuck Bown.

BUSCH NORTH TRACKS

Beech Ridge Motor Speedway

70 Holmes Road
Scarborough, ME 04074
PH: (207) 885-0111
24-Hour Automated Race Information Line: 207-885-5800
Fax: (207) 885-0110
http://www.beechridge.com/
Circuit: .33-mile paved oval.
Major Races/Regular divisions: NASCAR Late Model Sportsman, Super Sportsman, Limited Sportsman, Wildcats.
Location/Directions: Beech Ridge Motor Speedway is located approximately 1 1/2 miles from the Maine Turnpike, in Scarborough, Maine. From Portland, travel east toward Scarborough along Maine Mall Road until it becomes Payne Road, then straight on Payne Road to Holmes Road, right on Holmes Road one mile to the track.

Beech Ridge Motor Speedway's 1/3-mile, semi-banked paved oval boasts of being one of the top five short tracks in the U.S. Having seen drivers such as Joe Bessey, Steve Park, and Ricky Craven as drivers who competed regularly on it, that seems to be a pretty good indication of its status among competitors.

The Beech Ridge grandstands hold 6,500 on the front stretch and another 2,000 can be accommodated in the pits, making it an expansive short track indeed. NASCAR's Late Model Sportsman; Super Sportsman; Limited Sportsman; and Wildcats headline Saturday action. Accommodations: Days Inn—(207) 772-345; Coastline Inn—(207) 772-3838; Fairfield Inn—(207) 883-0300; Sheraton Tara Hotel—(207) 775-6161; Hampton Inn—(207) 773-4400; Marriott Hotel—(207) 871-8000.

Holland International Speedway

Glenwood Rd.,
Holland, NY 14080
PH: (716) 537-2272
FAX (716) 537-9749
www.hollandspeedway.com
Location/Directions: northeastern New York, 25 miles south of Buffalo, on State Route 16.
Circuit: 3/8-mile paved oval.
Major races: NASCAR Northeast Regional racing.

Holland International Speedway seats 6,000 amid the scenic rolling hills country of upstate New York. Annually, the biggest shows are Busch North and Featherlite Modified Tour, but racing happens here every Saturday night in front of up to 7,000 fans.

Constructed in 1960 as a 1/3-mile oval, it was expanded to its current 3/8-mile length in 1964, then paved in 1968. It became a member of NASCAR's Northeast Region Division more recently, which has attracted more attention. If you get tired of racing, the Speedway boasts of an amusement park, consisting of a Ferris wheel, small roller coaster, and other rides. If that isn't enough, Darien Lake Amusement Park is only 20 miles away.

There really isn't anywhere to stay in Holland, but you can stay in nearby Buffalo, South Wales, or Chaffee.

Jennerstown Speedway

P.O. Box 230 (Intersections of Rt. 30 and Rt. 985)
Jennerstown, PA 15547
PH: (814) 629-6677
FAX: (814) 629-7121
http://www.jennerstown.com/
Location/Directions: western Pennsylvania, 75 miles east of Pittsburgh, 15 miles off I-70, on U.S. Highway 30, at the intersection of Highway 30 and Rt 985 .
Circuit: 5/8-mile paved oval.
Major races: NASCAR Great Northern Region, Late Model, ProStock/Trucks, Grand American Modifieds, Street Stocks, Legacy Cars, and Chargers.

Located in the Laurel Mountains of western Pennsylvania in Somerset County, Jennerstown Speedway hosts a Modified Tour race as its seasonal feature event, but its main staple is the NASCAR Winston Racing Series.

The track is fast, at 5/8 of a mile, and a 6-degree banked 550 ft. frontstretch, and hosts some great racing on Saturday nights from May to September.

There are a few rooms in Jennerstown, or you can stay in Boswell. The Days Inn Somerset is the official hotel of Jennerstown Speedway, and for reservations you can call (800) 325-2525 or direct at (814) 445-9200. Or try: Holiday Inn Somerset, (814) 445-9611; Ramada Inn Somerset (814) 443-4646; Hampton Inn Somerset (800) 428-7866. For meals try: G. Whilliker's, the Grapevine or Hoss's Steak and Sea House.

Busch North Tracks, continued

Lee USA Speedway

**90 Hanover St.
Newbury, MA 01951-1127
PH: (978) 462-4252.
http://www.leeusaspeedway.com/
Circuit: 3/8-mile paved oval; semi-banked.
Major Races/Regular divisions: NASCAR Busch North Series; NASCAR Featherlite Modified Series; NASCAR Winston Racing Series.
Location/Directions: located on Rt. 125, in Lee, NH. From the east, take I-95 south to Portsmouth, and the Spaulding Turnpike north to Route 4 west and then Route 125 south.**

Readers of *Trackside* magazine call Lee USA Speedway their "favorite Friday night asphalt track in the northeast." The weekly Friday show features NASCAR Winston Racing Series Pro-Stock cars, with Winston Short Track Division, Street Stocks, Hobby Stocks, and Roadrunners also on the card. ISMA Supermodified race in August in the Lee Classic, The Downeast Drilling Pro Stock Nationals, a $10,000-to-win Pro Stock race that attracts over 70 of the best in the Northeast and Canada, and the Oktoberfest, run mid-October, marking the season's end at which ten divisions and over 400 cars appear. Call the track for information on lodging and dining.

Riverside Park Speedway

**P.O. Box 307
Agwam, MA 01001
PH: (413) 786-9300
www.riversideparkspeedway.com
Location/Directions: Connecticut/Massachusetts line, four miles north west of Springfield, in Agwam, MA, on State Route 159.
Circuit: 1/4-mile paved oval.
Major races: NASCAR Winston Racing Series, Northwest Region.**

Riverside Park Speedway can be found inside the grounds of the Six Flags Amusement Park. The amusement park is complete with roller coasters and several other thrill rides. The 8,500 seat facility hosts the Modified Tour and Busch Grand National North together at the end of August—which is the biggest race of the year. There is plenty of lodging in the area since Springfield is just 15 miles north of the track, and Hartford is close as well. Hotels can be found on Route 5, which is also known as Riverdale Rd.

Stafford Motor Speedway

P.O. Box 105
Stafford Springs, CT 06076
PH: (860) 684-2783
Location/Directions: northeastern Connecticut, 15 miles northeast of Hartford, on Routes 32 and 190.
Circuit: 1/2-mile oval.
Major races: NASCAR Winston Racing Series, Northeastern Region.

Located in mountainous, rural, northern Connecticut, Stafford Motor Speedway sits in a valley four miles off I 84. Crystal lake Recreation area, which is five miles from the track, supplies most of the entertainment when the track is not in use, but the area in general is sparsely populated and quiet.

The facility seats 11,500, and the biggest show of the racing year—the Modified Tour race—fills the stands. Racing runs from April to October, mostly on Friday nights. There's camping at the track, although there are no facilities. Rooms are available in Vernon, which is 20 miles distant; or call the track for more information.

Star Speedway

P.O. Box E
Epping, NH 03042
PH: (603) 679-5306
http://www.hudsonspeedway.com/
Location/Directions: southern New Hampshire, eight miles southeast of Brattleboro, in Epping, near the junction of Rt. 125 and Rt. 27. It can be approached from Rt. 125, Rt. 101, or Interstate 95. From I-95 (north or South): follow I-95 to exit #2 for Rt. 51, following Rt. 51 two miles west until it becomes Rt. 101, then right on Rt. 27 and one mile west to the track.
Circuit: 1/4-mile paved oval.
Major races: NASCAR Regional Series (New England Region).

Star Speedway's charming green countryside location is quiet most of the year. But when Star hosts racing during its 11 Saturday nights throughout the season, the area becomes a hotbed of activity. The biggest event is the Star Classic, run just after Labor day. The facility seats 6,000. Stay in Exeter, Seabrook, or Manchester. There is limited camping at the track, but there is a good deal of public camping less than an hour away.

Thompson International Speedway

P.O. Box 276
Thompson, CT 06277
PH: (860) 923-2280
Location/Directions: northeastern Connecticut, 15 miles west of Providence, RI, on Rural Route 193.
Circuit: 5/8-mile paved oval.
Major races: NASCAR Winston Racing Series, New England Region.

Thompson International Speedway sits in the northeast corner of Connecticut, bordering Massachusetts and Rhode Island. The rural section of Thompson where the track stands is in farmland country.

The track holds some 8,000 fans, and the biggest show of the year is the Labor Day's NASCAR show. Thompson Dam, just a few miles away, is good for camping—or fishing or hiking, for that matter. There are other campsites in the area as well. Hotels can be found in Webster and Putnam, and the area is one hour from Hartford, Boston, and Providence. Call the track for more information.

Busch North Tracks, continued

Thunder Road International Speedbowl

P.O. Box 296
Waterbury, VT 05676-0296
PH: (802) 479-2151
Office: (802) 244-6963
FAX: (802) 244-1616
Circuit: 1/4-mile high-banked paved oval.
Major Races/Regular divisions: NASCAR Busch North Series.
Location/Directions: In Barre, VT, on Quarry Hill Rd., two miles off I-89 Exit 6, head east to Route 14, turning left on RT. 14 to Quarry Hill Rd.

Thunder Road is a jewel of a racetrack located in the beautiful scenery of the Northeast. Set in scenic Vermont, the track hosts a regular Thursday night Late Model show most of the season, with occasional Sunday racing. The season highlights include the Busch Grand National North Series and a American-Canadian Tour series four times a year.

The grandstands seat 7000, which is usually mostly full, and sells out a few times a year. The venue, which is co-owned by motorsports announcer Ken Squire, attracts vacationers in the area who come for the scenery as well as the racing. The track is located on a hilltop and from the grandstands you have a view of green mountains in every direction.

Staying in the area is not a problem even during the Busch race. This is the Capital District of Vermont, so it is close to Barre and Montpielier. There is camping at the Lazy Lions a few miles up the road, and within 25 minutes are a pair of Gratten state parks.

FEATHERLITE MODIFIED SERIES

The Featherlite Modified Series, established in 1985, runs in a geographical area similar to the Busch North Series (Pennsylvania, New York, Delaware, New Hampshire and Connecticut), but the series also extends down to Virginia and New Jersey and has no races in Vermont. The difference between them is the sponsorship (the championship points fund in the Modified Series is established by the Featherlite Trailer Company as opposed to Anheuser Busch's North Series) and the cars are Modifieds, the only open-wheeled "Tour"

championship sanctioned by NASCAR.

The tracks in the championship are as follows: Riverside Park Speedway, in Agawam, MA, Thompson Speedway, in Thompson, CT, Martinsville Speedway, Martinsville, VA, Nazareth Speedway, Nazareth, PA, Stafford Motor Speedway, Stafford, CT, Watkins Glen, Watkins Glen, NY, Jennerstown Speedway, Jennerstown, PA, Riverhead Raceway, Riverhead, NY, New Hampshire International Speedway, Louden, NH, USA Speedway, Lee, NH, Holland International Speedway, Holland, NY, and Flemington Speedway, in Flemington, NJ. As with any series, tracks may be added or deleted from year to year.

The cars are current to 15-year-old American-made, production-based passenger sedans, although when they finally hit the track they look nothing at all like production cars. They must conform to a 2,600-pound weight restriction including the driver (no less than 2100 pounds), and run on a 107-inch wheelbase with a track of 84 inches or less.

The engines are limited to 350 cid and compression ratio of no more than 12:1 via a four-barrel carburetor; no fuel injection is allowed.

FEATHERLITE MODIFIED TRACKS

Flemington Speedway

P.O. Box 293
Flemington, NJ 08822
PH: (track) (201) 782-2413
Location/Directions: western New Jersey, approximately 35 miles from New York City, just north of Flemington, on State Route 31—the track is one mile northeast of U.S. 202 on State Route 31.
Circuit: .625-mile semi-banked paved oval.
Major races: Featherlite Modified, NASCAR Winston Racing Series Northeast Division.

Flemington Speedway is found in a rural area outside the city of Flemington. The regular show is a modified stock event, which takes place every Saturday from April through October.

The track used to be one of the country's premier dirt tracks, hosting one of the biggest World of Outlaws Sprint Car Championship Shootout and a USAC Silver Crown Championship and United Racing Club Sprints race when it was dirt. Now it has become a force as a paved short track with NASCAR as the staple.

The deviations from the standard program usually pack the 10,000 seat stands. A monster truck show brings in lots of spectators, but the Craftsman Truck racing is the biggest of the season. The best places to stay are in Clinton, where the Outlaws stay at the Holiday Inn during a race. There are also rooms available in Flemington.

Featherlite Modified Tracks, continued

Riverhead Raceway

1732 Great Neck Rd.
Copiague, NY 11726
PH: (631) 842-7223
http://www.riverheadraceway.com/
Location/Directions: coastal New York, eastern Long Island, off Highway 24.
Circuit: 1/4-mile semi-banked paved oval.
Major races: NASCAR Featherlite Modified Series; Winston Racing Series, Eastern Seaboard Region.

On the east end of Long Island in the Hamptons, just before Long Island splits into its famous north and south forks, Riverhead Raceway appeals to wayward race fans. The paved oval attracts the tourist crowd during peak season, and the NASCAR Winston Modified Tour race (usually held in the last week of July) generally fills the place to near capacity. The facility holds 5,000 spectators, including pit viewing. The track recently repaved the racing surface that had existed since 1951, and the pace of racing at Riverhead increased dramatically.

There is camping outside the track, although there are no services, nor are there hookups for RVs. If you want a room, there will be plenty in the area, but Riverhead has a few that will be the closest to the racing.

SLIM JIM ALL-PRO SERIES

The Slim Jim All-Pro Series contends its year-long championship in NASCAR's own neighborhood, with races run mostly in Florida, Georgia, North and South Carolina, Tennessee, Kentucky, and Virginia, with events in Missouri, Indiana, and Pennsylvania.

The tracks used in this series that were previously listed are: Homestead-Miami Motorsports Complex; Memphis Motorsports Park, in Memphis, TN; Nashville Speedway, in Nashville, TN; Nazareth Speedway.

The series is based on late model (one to five-year-old) American-made passenger sedans, with Pontiac Grand Prix, Buick LeSabre and Regal, Chevy Monte Carlo, Olds Cutlass, and Ford Taurus and Thunderbird. They conform to a 105-inch wheelbase (with a minimum of 101 inches) and a 63-inch track.

SLIM JIM ALL-PRO TRACKS

Greenville-Pickens Speedway

P.O. Box 5206
Greenville, SC 29606
Office: (864) 269-0852
Circuit: 1/2-mile paved oval
Major Races/Regular divisions: NASCAR Slim Jim All-Pro Series; NASCAR Goody's Dash; NASCAR Winston Racing Series.
Location/Directions: Located at the fairgrounds on Highway 123. Take I-85 to Exit 44, then north on Highway 25 to Highway 123 South.

Greenville-Pickens is as much a part of racing in the South as Darlington or Rockingham, it just isn't on any major schedules anymore. The track has been in existence since 1946, when it started as a dirt oval, then became asphalt in 1970. The facility used to run two Grand Nationals back when Winston Cup was called Grand National, so the Pettys, the Pearsons, the Yarboroughs, among others, all raced here.

Now, although purses are usually high, the track has to suffice with smaller series. The venue seats 8,000, and frequently sells out all seats. But the backstretch is tiered, like a drive-in movie, making it possible for you to watch from your car. And general admission there has never sold out.

The track is located six miles from Greenville and six miles from Easley. Motels in Easley, at the near edge of town, are three miles from the track. Teams stay in the Comfort Inn, which also serves as headquarters during the bigger races. The motel is located at 1804 Highway 123 South, Easley, SC 29640, and can be reached at (864) 859-7520. Regular fans eat at Applebee's or Fats Cafe in Easley.

Slim Jim All-Pro Tracks, continued

I-70 Speedway

Office at Lakeside Speedway
5615 Wolcott Dr.,
Kansas City, KS 66109
PH: (913) 299-2040
FAX: (913) 299-1105
Circuit: 1/2-mile paved oval.
Location/Directions: Located approximately 40 miles east of Kansas City. Take I-70 East to Lexington-Mayview exit (#41), then north to N. Outer Rd., to the track.
Major Races/Regular divisions: NASCAR Slim Jim All-Pro Series; ASA AC Delco Challenge Series; NASCAR Winston Racing Series.

I-70's biggest show of the season is the Craftsman Truck series race, which sells out all 10,000 seats in this renown half-mile. Plan ahead if attending because all seats on the front straight are reserved and the best seats will be hard to come by.

If you happen to come late, standing room is available on the hill behind the grandstands, which still offers a decent—if far-off—view of the track. The regular show runs from April through September and is held on Saturday nights. Built in 1968, the track has been upgraded consistently and has modern amenities. Call the track for some suggestions on lodging and dining.

Lanier National Speedway

One Raceway Drive
Braselton, GA 30517
PH: (770) 967-8600
FAX: (770) 967-4411
www.lanierspeedway.com
Location/Directions: 40 miles northeast of Atlanta, in Braselton, Georgia, on Highway 53, five minutes from either Exit 49 off Interstate 85, or Exit 4 off Interstate 985.
Circuit: 3/8-mile paved oval.
Location: across the street from Road Atlanta on Highway 53, Lanier Raceway—like Road Atlanta—is very hot and very humid during the season: mid-80s to high 90s.
Major races: NASCAR (Eastern Seaboard Region); USAC Midgets.

Lanier used to host a Busch Grand National—which was the biggest event of the season. The biggest now is the Budweiser Superbowl, at which all Lanier racing divisions get together on one date to run several endurance-style races.

Lanier seats 4,500 in the grandstands, but has trackside and tiered parking where families can sit and watch from their cars or from picnic areas. Camping is available—but not at trackside.

Lake Lanier Island, a 500-acre lake and recreation facility, is close by, and Six Flags over Georgia Amusement Park is 60 miles from the track. You can stay in Gainesville, which is 10 miles away; in Suwanee—where the Atlanta Falcons practice—which is 20 miles from the track; or in Oakwood, which is five-and-a-half miles distant.

Louisville Motor Speedway

P.O. Box 19678,
Louisville, KY. 40259
PH: (502) 966-2277
FAX: (502) 969 8582
http://www.louisvillespeedway.com/
Degree of banking in the corners: 12 degrees.
Degree of banking on the straight: 6 degrees.
Length of frontstretch: 350 feet.
Length of back curve: 2,000 feet.
Location/Directions: north central Kentucky, in Louisville, on Outer Loop Road, one mile west of I-65's Exit 127, five minutes from Louisville International Airport.
Circuit: 3/8-mile, D-shaped, paved oval (also a figure-eight track).
Major races: NASCAR Winston Racing Series Mid-America Region; USAC Midgets.

Louisville Motor Speedway is found four miles from Churchill Downs, Kentucky's famous horse racing track and the home of the Kentucky Derby. The Motor Speedway is set at the end of the Stanford Field Airport, a few miles from downtown Louisville. The track, which opened for business in 1987, seats 12,000 fans.

The facility runs some 50 to 60 events a year, including several non-racing shows. The biggest race is now the NASCAR Craftsman Truck Series race, followed by the Bluegrass 300, a set of three 100-lap events for late-model stocks. The next biggest is the Mid-South Figure 8 Championships; or the Granger's Race of Champions, another race that's beginning to gain in popularity with several name Winston Cup drivers competing in a match race.

There are 10 motels within two miles of the track, and accommodations, in general, are no problem. Call the track for the names and numbers of those inns, or call the Louisville Visitors' Bureau at (502) 582-3732 to make your own lodging arrangements. Or, Executive West Hotel (I-264 at Fairgrounds) is recommended by the track. (502) 367-2251. Camping is also available with track permission in designated areas. There are no hook-ups.

Myrtle Beach Speedway

4300 Highway 501
Myrtle Beach, 29577, SC
Rt. 2, P.O. Box 280
N. Myrtle Beach, SC 29582
PH: (843) 236-0500
Degree of banking in the corners: 13 degrees.
Degree of banking on the straight: 5 degrees.
Length of frontstretch: 780 feet.
Length of backstretch: 700 feet.
Location: coastal South Carolina, just west of Myrtle beach on U.S. Highway 501. From Interstate 95, take 501 west to Myrtle Beach.
Circuit: 1/2-mile paved oval.
Major races: NASCAR Busch Grand National Series Championship.

Myrtle Beach Speedway is five miles from the famous beach town of the same name. It has recently become a tennis and golf oasis, with new resort areas popping up each year. It is a quaint place to go spend a few summer days . . . and a

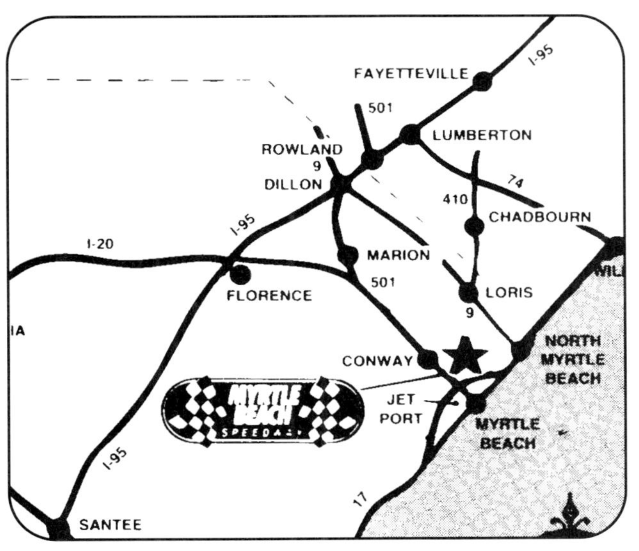

good place to watch racing.

The 14,000 seat racing facility fills up for the BGN, and the NASCAR Dash races are also very popular. There is open-wheeled Modified All-Pro racing here, as well as ASA Sportsman racing. Most of the competition, however, is limited to full-bodies NASCAR racing, which is normally here on

Slim Jim All-Pro Tracks, continued

Saturday nights. The track has gone from dirt to paved and back again four times—now running as a paved oval. Head down Highway 501 East for rooms at the Beach. Call the Myrtle Beach Chamber of Commerce at (800) 722-3224 (or 800 692-2472 in SC) for more information on accommodations.

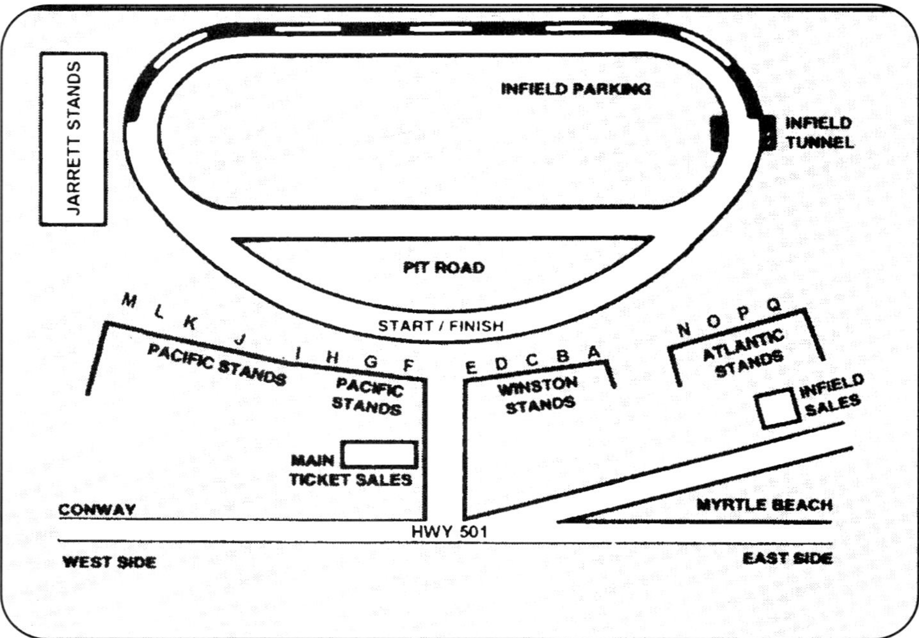

St. Augustine Speedway/Florida Speed Park

900 Big Oak Road
St. Augustine, Florida 32095
PH: (904) 825-2886
FAX: (904) 824-2889
http://www.st-augustine-speedway.com/
Location/Directions: northeastern Florida, approximately 40 miles north of Daytona, 35 miles south of Jacksonville, FL.
Circuit: 1/2-mile D-shaped paved oval.
Major races: NASCAR Winston Racing Series.

St Augustine's 14-degree banked D-shaped oval hosts racing every Saturday night through the racing season. The facility holds some 6,000 spectators and pulls in a nice crowd each weekend.

On weekdays, two racing schools teach would-be racers how to take advantage of the tricky track configuration. David Pearson Performance Programs (904) 788-3774 and Finish Line Racing School (904) 427-8522 are within a phone call.

To stay in St. Augustine, the track recommends a "St. Augustine Vacation Guide," which gives fans a comprehensive listing for hotels, motels, restaurants, and so forth. Call (904) 829-1711 for a copy.

South Boston Speedway

P.O. Box 759
South Boston, VA 24592
PH: (804) 572-4947
Degree of banking in the corners: 12 degrees.
Degree of banking on the straight: 7 degrees.
Length of frontstretch: 360 feet.
Length of backstretch: 360 feet.
Location: southern central Virginia, 10 miles from the North Carolina border, in South Boston, off Highways 501 and 58. From Highway 58 West, take 360 East two miles to the track.
Circuit: .40 mile paved oval.
Major races: NASCAR Busch Grand National Series; NASCAR Winston Racing Series, Mid-Atlantic Region.

South Boston Speedway is located just outside the city of South Boston. Halifax county has a population of 35,000 mostly die-hard racing.

South Boston used to be a Busch Grand National track, hosting races beginning in 1982, but it hasn't had one since 1998. The track also has regular weekly NASCAR Winston Racing Series racing plus NASCAR Slim Jim All-Pro Series racing.

The speedway, which was enlarged to .400-mile in 1994, up from .354 and was repaved in 1998. It can accommodate nearly 11,000 people—although the grandstands only hold 7,000. The remaining fans sit mostly in an area around turns 3 and 4. There's normally a very good crowd for regular shows, averaging 5,000 a week. There are only general admission tickets here, and nothing can be reserved, nor are there any advance ticket sales.

The biggest race is the mid-September 100-mile race for late-model stockers—which offers a purse of $20,000.

You can stay in South Boston, Danville, Clarksville, or Roxboro, NC. There is also camping available at Buggs Island Lake, which is a state park 25 miles away; or camp in Halifax at the Staunton River State Park. For more information on rooms, call the Virginia State Chamber of Commerce at (800) VISIT VA; or the North Carolina Travel and Tourism Division at (800) VISIT NC.

Southern National Speedway

PO Box 220
Kenly, NC 27542
PH: (919) 284-1114
Location/Directions: found in the heart of North Carolina, north of Goldsboro. Take I-95 to Exit 107, then north on Route 301 to Route 581, then right to Newsome Mill Road to the track.
Circuit: 4/10-mile paved oval.
Major races: NASCAR Winston Racing Series.

Southern National Speedway's 4/10-mile high-banked asphalt oval features a Saturday Night program that features NASCAR Late Model Stocks.

The track is banked at 17 degrees in the banks and seven degrees on the straights, with an average width of 70 feet. It was designed by Talladega designer Francis Tuttle and is well-lit in the infield as well as in the grandstands. Call the track for recommended accommodations.

Slim Jim All-Pro Tracks, continued

Volusia Speedway Park

1500 E. Highway 40
De Leon Springs, FL 32028
PH: (904) 255-2243
(904) 985-4402
http://www.volusiaspeedwaypark.com/
Location: in Barbersville, Florida, just north of central Daytona, Atlantic Coastal Florida.
Circuit: 1/2-mile clay oval.
Major races: NASCAR Winston Racing Series, Sunbelt Region.

Volusia Speedway runs its first major event in the first week of February, coinciding with the start of Daytona's Speedweeks. While Daytona gets ready for the Busch race, Volusia runs 11 straight nights of Modifieds.

Barberville itself is 30 minutes northwest of Daytona, in an extremely flat area. As one official put it, "it's not near anything—it's just flat." The area has the same humidity as Daytona, but it's in a wooded area and occasionally has cool weather. It's one hour from Orlando, or Disneyworld.

The facility seats 9,500, and probably the biggest show is the Slim Jim All-Pro race. The next biggest is the annual Winston Invitational Showdown—which is an invitational late-model race.

There is camping at the track, and showers are available, or stay in Deland or the Daytona/Ormond Beach area. Call the track for more information, or check the Daytona International Speedway listing in this guide.

Winchester Speedway

P.O. Box 31
Winchester, IN 47394
PH: (765) 584-9701
Location/Directions: central Indiana, 70 miles northeast of Indianapolis, off State Highway 32, just west of Winchester.
Circuit: 1/2-mile paved oval.
Major races: USAC Sprint Car and Midget Championships; ARCA Championship.

Winchester Speedway is the second oldest purpose-built facility in the country—only Indianapolis has a deeper history. The track boasts of 13 regular drivers who went on to win the Indy 500. The town of Winchester has a few rooms; or call the track for a better idea of where to stay.

GOODY'S DASH SERIES

The Goody's Dash Series is similar to the Slim Jim All-Pro Series in that it is run in roughly the same areas, Florida, Georgia, North and South Carolina, Tennessee, and Virginia. The difference, however, is the cars driven—and of course the sponsor.

The race cars in the Goody's Dash series are smaller cars, different from the Slim Jim series—and most other NASCAR Touring Car series—by virtue of their stock counterparts. These cars are compact and sub-compact bodied cars, like Chevrolet Cavaliers, Ford Escorts and Probes, Pontiac Sunfires and, yes, even a Toyota Celica or two.

The cars have a 100-inch wheelbase rule, with a weight restriction of 2,650-lb. minimum for four cylinder cars and 2,750 lb. for sixes. The engines are limited to 165 cubic inches, with 13:1 compression rations on the fours and 268 cubic inches, with 9:1 compression ratios for the V6s.

Goody's Dash Series boasts some of the best alumni of all NASCAR grassroots series. Davey Allison, Rob Moroso, Larry Pearson and Phil Parsons all cut their teeth on this series, and Michael Waltrip and Hut Stricklin are past champions.

The tracks are as follows: Daytona International Speedway; Hickory Motor Speedway; Caraway Speedway; Lowes Motor Speedway; Tri-County Motor Speedway; Lanier National Speedway; Bristol Motor Speedway; Summerville Speedway; Greenville-Pickens Speedway, in Greenville, SC; Orange County Speedway; Southern National Speedway; Myrtle Beach Speedway; Concord Motorsport Park; Langley Speedway; St. Augustine Speedway; and Homestead-Miami Motorsports Complex; and Volusia County Speedway.

GOODY'S DASH SERIES TRACKS

Hickory Motor Speedway

3130 Hwy. 70 SE
Newton, North Carolina, 28602
PH: (704) 464-3655
Location/Directions: central western North Carolina, in Hickory, just off Interstate 40.
Circuit: 2/5-mile paved oval.
Major races: NASCAR Busch Grand National.

Hickory Motor Speedway lays claim to some of the best NASCAR racing history of the region.

Junior Johnson began his career on the red clay banks of Hickory. So did Ned Jarrett, Ralph Earnhardt, and Harry Gant. Of the newer breed, Dale Jarrett, Dale Earnhardt, and Morgan Shepherd began racing careers at Hickory—which was finally paved in 1969 after opening in 1951 as a dirt oval. The track is the second oldest NASCAR track in existence.

Located in the Piedmont Foothills, the area is famous for its furniture and textile industries. Just one hour away from the Blue Ridge Mountains, the track is also central to the majors of NASCAR racing (Charlotte, Darlington, Rockingham, North Wilkesboro, Martinsville, and Bristol). Rooms are available in Hickory, but you must book early. Call the Catawba County Chamber of Commerce at (704) 324-0754. If not Hickory, Charlotte will have plenty of space.

The Days Inn, at 1607 Fairgrove Church Road, Conover, NC 28613, (800) 824-0427 or (704) 465-1100, is recommended by the track.

Goody's Dash Series Tracks, continued

Langley Speedway

3165 North Armistead Ave.
Hampton, VA 23666
PH: (757) 865-1100
PH (track): (703) 865-1992
Fax: (757) 865-1147
Office: 3200 W. Moore St.
Richmond, VA 23230
www.langleyspeedway.com
Location/Directions: in CIA country, outside Langley AFB in northeastern Virginia, on the Potomac, located on N. Armistead Ave. in Hampton, VA, just across from the NASA wind tunnel. From I-64 East, exit at 261B, Follow NASA signs, heading left just before NASA gate, and proceeding a quarter mile to the track.
Circuit: 2/5-mile paved oval.
Major races: Goody's Dash, NASCAR Interseries (Mid-Atlantic Region).

Langley Raceway takes its name from the famous air force base—and the infamous CIA headquarters. The track hosts a Saturday evening full-bodied show, and occasionally hosts a NASCAR Goody's Dash. Langley Speedway's 4 1/2-degree banked, .395-mile hosts Winston Racing Series events on Saturday nights through the spring and summer. Langley has only a few rooms, but there are rooms in the area, heading across the Potomac to Bethesda.

Summerville Speedway

330 Robin St.
Moncks Corner, SC 29461
PH: (843) 873-3438
(843) 871-8331
http://www.summervillespeedway.com/
Location/Directions: eastern South Carolina, 25 miles northwest of Charleston, two miles from the southern end of Lake Moultrie.
Circuit: 2/5-mile paved oval.
Major races: Bud NASCAR Winston Racing Series, Eastern Seaboard Region.

Summerville Speedway hosts the NASCAR Winston Racing Series on Saturday night for a regular racing card. The big show is the Budweiser NASCAR Dash, which is held mid-July in conjunction with the regular five Summerville racing divisions. There are a few hotels around Lake Moultree, and rooms should not be a major problem.

USA International Speedway

3401 Old Polk City Rd.
Lakeland, FL 33809
Mailing: P.O. Box 1500
Polk City, FL 33868
PH: (800) 984-7223
Track: (941) 984-3173
Circuit: 3/4-mile high-banked paved oval.
Location/Directions: halfway between Orlando and Tampa, at Exit 20 off I-4, then north a half-mile on SR 33 to the track.
Major races: NASCAR Goody's Dash Series; Hooters Pro Cup.

USA International hosts only a few special events per season. Owned by the Hooter Restaurant chain, the most prestigious events for the track are, of course, the four annual Hooters Pro Series races, run with older Busch Grand National–style cars. The other three to four races are NASCAR Goody's Dash or other selected high-visibility local series races. The venue holds an impressive 10,000 seats, and they actually sell out frequently.

Lakeland Host Motel, (941) 858-3851, is the headquarters during race weekends, or try the Lakeland Motor Lodge in Lakeland.

BUSCH ALL-STAR SERIES

The Busch All-Star Series has been tailored to Midwestern drivers who may wish to go on into either sprint cars or in Winston Cup someday. The series is dedicated to dirt track racing and the cars are set up to reflect that single-minded purpose.

The tracks are located in South Dakota, Nebraska, Iowa, Illinois and also Tennessee, and range in length from three-eighths miles to half-mile dirt ovals—always dirt.

The tracks are as follows: Crawford County Speedway; Davenport Speedway in; Sunset Speedway; West Liberty Raceway; Adams County Speedway; Freeport Raceway Park; Farley Speedway; Park Jefferson Speedway; Tri-City Speedway; Butler County Speedway.

The cars are more like sprint cars than standard stock cars. They are very light, weighing 2,400 to 2,650 pounds (including the driver and full tanks), and use 358 cid V8s. The cars are built to slide around the track, with grooved tires mandatory. That means they basically slide around the corners as opposed to turning left into them. Other differences between the standard stock car format is that in the All-Star Tour, the field is broken up into two qualifying races, a consolation race and the feature, which is the points-paying race.

BUSCH ALL-STAR SERIES TRACKS

Adams County Speedway

P.O. Box 8
Nodaway, IA 50857
PH: (515) 322-4184
Location: Southwest Iowa, 90 miles south east of Omaha, on Hwys. 34 and 148.
Circuit: 1/2-mile clay oval.
Major races: Busch All-Star; NASCAR Winston Racing Series (Midwest Region).

Adams County Speedway is located at the Adams County Fairgrounds in the northeast section of Corning. Adams is the smallest county in the state, and the track is set in the largest residential area of mostly rural Corning. The county seat is only 2,000 strong.

The facilities were recently upgraded with new lighting, and can accommodate 2,500 spectators. Once a horse racing track, it was modified, banked and has been used as a motor racing track for 40 years. It joined the Winston Racing Series in 1984. Staying here is not the easiest thing to do. There are a few rooms in Nodaway, but there is no Hilton.

Butler County Speedway

Allison, IA
Office: HJ Promotions
P.O. Box 338
Webster City IA 50595
PH: (515) 832-6043
Circuit: 1/2-mile high-banked paved oval.
Location/Directions: Llocated 30–40 minutes from Waterloo and Cedar Fall, in the Butler County Fairgrounds, just off Highway 3.
Major races: NASCAR All-Star Tour; Winston Racing Series.

Butler County Speedway, run by the same people who operate Crawford County Speedway, runs a regular Saturday night show (Crawford's show is Friday night) with Late Models, Modifieds and 360 Sprint cars. The track is one of the newest members of NASCAR's Winston Racing Series.

You can stay in Allison, or try Cedar Fall or Waterloo. For more information, call the track.

Crawford County Speedway

Highway 39 North
Denison, IA
P.O. Box 338
Webster City, IA 50595-0338
PH: (712) 263-8221
Office: (515) 832-3713
Circuit: 1/2-mile high-banked dirt oval.
Location/Directions: located at the Crawford County Fairgrounds, five miles north of U.S. 59 on SR 39.
Major races: NASCAR Busch All-Star Series; NASCAR Winston Racing Series.

Crawford County's regular show is a Friday night NASCAR program featuring Late Models, Modifieds, Pro-Stocks, Hobby Stocks and Econo Stocks. The track is run by the same folks who operate Butler county, which is why the program is a Friday affair; Butler runs Saturday night.

You can stay in Denison, at the Best Western, (712) 263-5081; or the Days Inn, (712) 263-2500; or the Park Motel, (712) 263-4144.

Davenport Speedway

2815 West Locust
Davenport, IA 52804
PH: (319) 326-5338
Location/Directions: located in Davenport, IA, at the County Fairgrounds off 280 at Locust St. Exit 4, then east approximately three miles.
Circuit: 1/2-mile banked dirt oval.
Major races: NASCAR Busch All-Star Series; Hav-A-Tampa Dirt Racing Series; NASCAR Winston Racing Series.

Davenport's regular show is Friday night, with occasional IMCA sprint car races on Wednesday nights. The biggest race of the year is the Hav-A-Tampa series, usually held in June, but the Busch All-Star races, usually two, held in April and September do well also. The facility seats 5,500 and it sells out for the Hava-A-Tamps race and the bigger races. The average weekly fan count averages 3,000.

The track is located south of the fairgrounds, behind the grandstands. There are accommodations all around the area, but the track suggests the Heartland Inn in Davenport IA, or the Budgetel or Ramada. The place to eat is the Iowa Machine Shed off 80 and W30. The facility is also just five miles away from the Riverboat Casinos.

Dubuque Fairgrounds Speedway

14583 Old Highway Rd
Dubuque, IA 52011
PH: (319) 588-1406
Location/Directions: west Iowa, seven miles from the border of Illinois, 220 miles from Chicago. From Dubuque, take Highway 20 to Old Highway 20, or 416 to the track entrance.
Circuit: 3/8-mile clay oval.
Major races: Busch All-Star Series; NASCAR Midwest Region

Just a few short miles west of the Mississippi River—in the same area where river boat gambling is starting to explode, Dubuque Fairgrounds Speedway is located. Already five miles from the dog track, it is certainly about to see a boom in interest with the explosion of gamblers coming through the area. Who knows? By the end of the decade you may be able to get odds on Steve Kinser.

Built in 1966, the oval has seats for 10,000 and fills most of them with a good series of weekly shows. You can camp at the fairgrounds, and there are a handful of hookups. For real beds, call (319) 557-9545.

Farley Speedway

**2044 Washington Ave
Cedar Rapids, IA 52403
P.O. Box 220
Swisher, IA 52338
PH: (319) 744-3620
Location/Directions: northeastern Iowa, 20 miles from Dubuque, on Highway 20.
Circuit: 1/2-mile high banked clay oval.
Major races: NASCAR Busch All-Star; NASCAR Winston Racing Series, Midwest Region.**

Farley Speedway boasts of a 5,000 seat facility. Some 20 miles from Dubuque, 60 miles from Cedar Rapids, the track is in the heart of farming country. The oval itself is a high banked clay racetrack just on the edge of town.

Racing is contested Friday, with Late Models, Modified Pro Stock, Outlaw Stock Cars, and two annual Busch All-Star NASCAR races filling the card. There is camping at the facility. And just up the road, the Mississippi River is surrounded by campgrounds. Call the track and they'll give you more info.

Freeport Raceway Park

**1910 South Walnut St.
Freeport, IL 61032
Office: (815) 233-0202
PH: (815) 233-0390
Location/Directions: south of US 20 on SR 26. South West Ave.) From Rockford take SR 20 to town and Walnut St., then down the hill to the track.
Circuit: 1/2-mile clay oval; slightly banked/1/4-mile clay.
Major races: NASCAR Busch All-Star Series; NASCAR Winston Racing Series.**

Freeport Raceway Park is located in a wooded area outside Freeport, Illinois, a few miles from Rockford. The regular program happens on Saturday nights from April to the end of September, with Late Models, Modifieds, Sportsman, Hobby Stocks and Pure Stock as regular classes. The biggest race of the year is the Busch All-Star Tour, or the USMS, which stops here for one race per season. The venue seats 4,000. Pits are located on the outside of the track.

You can stay at the Ramada Inn (815) 235-3121, County Inn Suites (815) 233-3300, Best Western (815) 233-0300, Super 8 at (815) 232-8880. Dining can be found at the Country Kitchen, Snitzles or Diamond Dave, Memories Bar and Grill, Peaches and Applebees all on South Street or West Street. Everything listed above is within a half mile of the track.

Park Jefferson Speedway

**Office: P.O. Box 508
Sioux City, IA 51102-0508
PH: (605) 966-5517
Office: (402) 494-4166
Circuit: 1/2-mile semi-banked dirt oval.
Location/Directions: just north of Sioux City, Iowa. From Sioux City, take I-29 north to McCook Lake, Exit #4, then north on SD105 2 miles.
Major races: NASCAR Busch All-Star Series; NASCAR Winston Racing Series.**

In existence since 1985, Park Jefferson is a former horse track turned racetrack that has flourished under NASCAR sanctioning—which it has had since 1986. The track hosts a regular Saturday night show with NASCAR Late Models, Modifieds, All-American Street Stocks, Chargers and Super Trucks. The special shows are NCRA Sprint cars and a Busch All-Star Tour race, which usually fill to capacity. The facility holds 4,000 in the bleachers and a few more in the suites and outside. You can stay in Sioux City, Iowa or Sioux City, South Dakota at the Comfort Inn, North Sioux City, SD (605) 232-3366; Super 8, North Sioux City, SD (605) 232-4716; Apple Inn, North Sioux City, SD (605) 232-9600; or the Holiday Inn, Sioux City, IA (712) 277-3211. Restaurants on the Iowa side of Sioux City include Applebees, Horizon Family Restaurant and Perkins Family Restaurant.

Busch All-Star Series Tracks, continued

Sunset Speedway

6201 N. 132nd St.
Omaha, NE 68164
PH: (402) 493-5491
(402) 493-5271
http://www.sunsetspeedway.com/
Location/Directions: eastern Nebraska, in Omaha, two miles off I-680 at Exit 6.
Circuit: 3/8mile clay oval.
Major races: Busch All-Star; NASCAR Winston Racing Series, Midwest Region.

Sunset Speedway is located on the outskirts of north east Omaha, in the Nebraska farmland that bounds the city. The facility seats 5,000 in all-new grandstands. Racing is scheduled for Sunday nights, with a few special events dotting the calendar.

The biggest crowds appear near the end of the season as several NASCAR Winston Racing specials are held in conjunction with three other tracks in the area. Sunset also holds some special sprints races—but no WoO racing. Hotels are plentiful in the Omaha area, but call the track for the nearest inns.

Tri- City Speedway

P.O. Box 3305
Springfield, IL 62708
Track: (618) 931-7836
Office: (217) 753-1619
Location/Directions: Southwestern Illinois near the border of Illinois and Missouri, 20 miles from St. Louis. From northern St Louis, take I-270 East to Exit 203 south, following SR 203 about a half-mile to the track.
Circuit: 1/2-mile clay oval; semi-banked/quarter-mile clay oval.
Major races: Busch All-Star; World of Outlaws Sprint Car Championship; USAC Sprint Cars.

Tri-City Speedway's 31 acres can accommodate 5,000 people on the larger of the facility's two tracks. The facility is open twice a month, and each track is used once a month. On the half-mile oval, the World of Outlaws, USAC Midgets and Late Model full-bodied cars run, while the Econo Late Models and Street Stocks use the quarter-mile track.

The best place to stay while in the area is Edwardsville, which is just three miles from the track—where the WoO have their headquarters when they come to town.

West Liberty Raceway

Office: P.O. Box 220
Swisher, IA 52338-0229
PH: (319) 627-2414
Circuit: 1/2-mile semi-banked dirt oval.
Location/Directions: eastern Iowa, 40 miles southeast of Cedar Rapids, five miles south of I-80, at the West Liberty exit. Track is two blocks west of downtown West Liberty, at the fairgrounds on Calhoun St.
Major Races: NASCAR Busch All-Star Series; NASCAR Winston Racing Series.

West Liberty Raceway is located in the town of West Liberty, at the Muscatine County Fairgrounds. The grassy rolling hills around the facility belie the fairgrounds layout, which, like most, is completely level. The biggest race of the year is the Spring Championships for late model cars, but the regular show is a Saturday night NASCAR WRS with Late Models, Modifieds, Sportsman, Bombers and Pro Stock. There are campgrounds in the area, although nothing is available at the fair. Call the track for more information on where to stay.

RAYBESTOS BRAKES NORTHWEST SERIES

The Raybestos Brakes Northwest Series is contested mainly in the Pacific Northwest, but also out as far east as Montana and Idaho.

Tracks include: Evergreen Speedway; Portland Speedway; Yakima Speedway; South Sound Speedway; Tri-City; Portland International Raceway; and Magic Valley Speedway. The tracks are as small as a quarter-mile oval to the nearly two-mile road course of PIR.

The rules regarding the series are almost identical to the All-Pro Series and the Southwest Tour Series, with smaller, lighter versions of Winston Cup cars. They are late model (three years old or newer) American-made, passenger sedans, with aftermarket fiberglass bodies for the race cars. The car models themselves are the exact same as those in Winston Cup: Chevy Monte Carlos, Ford Tauruses, and so on. The cars weigh at least 2,900 pounds, with a wheelbase no less than 101 and no more than 105 inches, and powered by a 358ci V8 with a maximum of 9.5:1 compression ratio. This series, like the Southwest Tour, is the main steppingstone for the Winston West series.

RAYBESTOS BRAKES NORTHWEST SERIES TRACKS

Magic Valley Speedway

Office: 355 S. Locust St.
Twin Falls, Idaho
PH: (208) 734-3700
Circuit: 1/3-mile semi-banked paved oval.
Location/Directions: approximately nine miles southeast of U.S. 30 on E2800, a mile west of Twin Falls Regional Airport on Grandview Dr. in Twin Falls, ID.
Major Races: NASCAR Raybestos Northwest Series; NASCAR Winston Racing Series.

Magic Valley Speedway's regular show is held Saturday nights and features the NASCAR Winston Racing series. The biggest race of the season is the NASCAR Northwest Tour race, usually held in September. Another good-sized event is the American Indycar Series race, usually held in July. Both races typically sell out. The facility holds 2,999 seats—all reserved. The track has been in operation since 1986 and was paved in 1988.

You can stay in Twin Falls, and the track recommends the Super 8 Motel (208) 734-5801. Try dining at Perkins or Gerdie's Oven Cookery.

Raybestos Brakes Northwest Series Tracks, continued

South Sound Speedway

Office: 3730 183rd Ave. SW
Rochester, WA 98579
PH: (360) 273-6420
Office: (360) 273-7456
Location/Directions: located off of I-5, at Exit 88-A, turning east approximately three miles to the track.
Circuit: 3/8-mile semi-banked paved oval.
Major races: NASCAR Raybestos Northwest Series; NASCAR Winston Racing Series.

South Sound runs a regular Saturday night NASCAR Winston Racing Series Late Model show, with Modifieds, Sportsmen, Streets, Figure 8s and occasional Bombers. The stands hold 5,000 spectators, but usually there's room, even for the Northwest Tour race.

You can stay in Centralia; try either the King Oscar or the Ferrymans Motel. And the track recommends The Red Barn or the Lucky Eagle Casino.

Yakima Speedway

1600 Pacific Ave.
Yakima, WA
Mailing: 19232 90th Ave NE.
Bothell, WA 98011
PH: (509) 248-0647
Office: (360) 794-9839
Location/Directions: east Yakima, I-90 to I-82 to Knob Hill exit. Track is approximately one mile from the Knob Hill exit.
Circuit: 1/2-mile semi-banked paved oval.
Major races: NASCAR Raybestos Northwest Series ; NASCAR Winston Racing Series.

Yakima's Saturday night program is highlighted by a pair of Northwest Series races and the GM Goodwrench Fall Classic, a popular Street Superstock and Late Model Tour show, which attracts some 250 race car drivers. The biggest shows sell out all 4,000 seats. Typically, however, the NASCAR Winston Racing Series Late Models, Street Stocks and Bombers make up the weekly racing.

The track has been in existence for 50 years, originally born as a dirt track, but being converted in the late 50s to half-mile asphalt. It was repaved in '92 and has a great reputation on the West Coast for good racing.

You can stay at the Sun Country Inn, or any of the small hotels in Yakima. For more information, call the Visitors and Convention Bureau at (800) 221-0751.

FEATHERLITE SOUTHWEST TOUR SERIES

As good as it is, the Featherlite Southwest Series is really something of a feeder class for the bigger and more prestigious Winston West series.

As mentioned above, four series use similar rules: the All-Pro Series, Raybestos Brakes Northwest, and the Southwest Tour Series. They are essentially smaller, lighter versions of Winston Cup cars. These late-model cars (three years old or newer) are American-made, passenger sedans, with aftermarket fiberglass bodies for the race cars. The car models themselves are the exact same as those in Winston Cup; Chevy Monte Carlos, Ford Taurus, and so on.

The cars weigh at least 2,900 pounds, with a wheelbase no less than 101 and no more than 105 inches, and powered by a 358 cid V8 with a maximum of 9.5:1 compression ratio.

The races are held in the West, from California east through Nevada, Utah, Arizona and Colorado.

Some of the tracks are: Phoenix International Raceway; Las Vegas Motor Speedway; Mesa Marin Raceway; Colorado National Speedway; Sears Point Raceway; and Cajon Speedway. If these tracks are not listed in the next few pages, check the index for their listings.

FEATHERLITE SOUTHWEST TOUR SERIES TRACKS

Cajon Speedway

P.O. Box 7
El Cajon, CA 92022
PH: (619) 448-8900
www.cajonspeedway.com
Location/Directions: in El Cajon, 15 miles east of San Diego, off I-8 on Highway 67, at Bradley Exit, next to Gillespie Airport on Wing St.
Circuit: 3/8-mile paved oval.
Major races: NASCAR Southwest Tour, Sportsman, Grand American Modifieds.

Although the area is about as American as you'll find, Cajon Speedway might as well be in Mexico. The terrain is Baja-California dry.

The Southwest Tour or Supermodified show is the biggest of the year, although the facility usually gets close to selling out its 5,500 seats during regular Saturday night shows. There is no camping at the track, but El Cajon has plenty of inexpensive rooms.

In operation since 1961, former baseball player Earle Brucker Jr. was hoping to turn his vacant plot of land into a baseball stadium. But a change in tax laws changed his mind. It ended up being a football field, which was used mostly by local high school players, and eventually ringed by a motorcycle track, which was paved later when the track began attracting full-time racers. It was enlarged from 1/4 mile to 3/8 mile for the 1964 season and paved in 1966.

Track stats have more than 3 million fans passing through the gates of Cajon Speedway in the last 35 years, making it one of the longest running race tracks on the West Coast.

Colorado National Speedway

Office: 2009 Market Street
Denver, CO 80205
PH: (303) 665-4173
Office: (970) 867-2101
www.coloradospeedway.com.
Circuit: 3/8-mile paved oval.
Location/Directions: located 20 miles north of Denver, Colorado. Take I-25 north to the Erie exit, #232 and north on Frontage road to the Speedway, on the left.
Major races: NASCAR Craftsman Truck Series; NASCAR Featherlite Southwest Series; NASCAR Winston Racing Series.

Colorado Speedway's Saturday night racing program is highlighted by a Truck race and a couple of major tour shows, namely the Southwest Tour and Winston West. The regular show features six NASCAR Winston Racing Series divisions, with Late Models, Grand American Modifieds, Super Stocks, Figure-8s, Pro Trucks and Trains as staples.

The speedway opened in 1964 as a half-mile dirt track, but was paved a few years later, becoming what track officials say is one of the top ten short track facilities in the United States. The seating capacity is an impressive 15,000 with the possibility of expanding that to 18,000 with temporary seating. The track can give you information on lodging and dining.

RE/MAX CHALLENGE SERIES

This is the Midwest region for the NASCAR Tour series, with rules and car regulations similar to the Busch All-Star, Slim Jim, Featherlite and Raybestos Northwest Tour. RE/Max joined the Tour series in 1998. It is the newest series in NASCAR's Touring Division.

As with those series, the cars are essentially smaller, lighter versions of Winston Cup cars. These late-model cars (three years old or newer) are American-made, passenger sedans, with aftermarket fiberglass bodies. The car models themselves are the exact same as those in Winston Cup: Chevy Monte Carlo, Ford Taurus, Pontiac Grand Prix.

The cars weigh at least 2,900 pounds, with a wheelbase no less than 101 and no more than 105 inches, and powered by a 358 cid V8 with a maximum of 9.5:1 compression ratio.

Some of the tracks include: Rockford Speedway, Gateway International, Madison International Speedway, Wisconsin International Speedway, Colorodo National Speedway, LaCrosse Fairgrounds Speedway, Lake Geneva Speedway, 1-70 Speedway, Pikes Peak Raceway, Chicago Motor Speedway, and Lebanon I-44 Speedway. If you don't find the tracks in the pages that follow, check the index for the listing elsewhere.

RE/MAX CHALLENGE SERIES TRACKS

I-94 Speedway

Fergus Falls Speedway
Office: 62824 250th St.
Litchfield, MN 56355
PH: (218) 739-5205
PH: (320) 352-5263
Office: (320) 251-9497
FAX: (320) 352-5479
http://www.i94speedway.com/
Location/Directions: take I-94 to SR 210 (exit 54), then approximately one mile east to North Tower Rd. to the stop sign, then left for about a half-mile.
Circuit: 3/8-mile paved oval.
Major races: RE/Max Challenge; NASCAR Winston Racing Series.

I-94 Speedway is part of a two-track racing group located in Fergus Falls and Sauk Centre Minnesota. I-94 sits on Interstate 94, in Sauk Centre, Minnesota, hosting NASCAR Late Models, NASCAR Modifieds, NASCAR Trucks, NASCAR Pro IV Mods, and NASCAR U-Cars. Racing is every Friday Evening starting at 8 P.M. Fergus Falls Speedway sits in Fergus Falls and hosts Late Models, Modifieds, Trucks, Pro IV Mods, U-Cars, and Legends. Racing is every Saturday Evening starting at 7:30 P.M. Call the track of your choice for accommodation and dining suggestions.

LaCrosse Fairgrounds Speedway

W. Salem, WI
P.O. Box 853
West Salem, WI 54669
PH: (608) 786-1525
FAX: (608) 786-1524
http://www.lacrossespeedway.com/
Location/Directions: located at the La Crosse Fairgrounds in West Salem, WI, at the intersection of U.S. Hwy 16 and County Rd. M. From the west, take I-90 to the Onalaska / West Salem exit, then head east five miles, turning left at the next stop light to the fairgrounds.
Circuit: .546-mile paved oval/1/4-mile paved oval.
Major races: RE/Max Challenge; NASCAR Winston Racing Series.

LaCrosse Fairgrounds boasts a large track with "2 1/2 grooves" of racing, which are used weekly by the NASCAR Late Models and the Grand National Sportsman classes. United Auto Supply Thunderstox also race on the quarter-mile oval, located inside the bigger track. The regular show is Saturday night, with practice and qualifying at 6 P.M. and racing at 7:30 P.M.

In addition to the regular programs, LaCrosse also hosts a handful of very unique shows—like the Trailer Race of Destruction, which has drivers pulling boat and trailers and campers in a race with no rules! Or how about "The Midnight Ride," where drivers turn on their headlights and race in complete darkness. Or the "Spin To Win," where the drivers must do a 360° spin down the front straight during the race. Or the "Outhouse Race," where drivers race to an outhouse, stop their cars, go inside the outhouse to pick off some toilet paper, then go back and race.

RE/Max Challenge Series Tracks, continued

Lake Geneva Raceway

1015 Bloomfield Rd.,
Lake Geneva WI 53147
PH: (262) 248-8566
FAX: (262) 248-6434
www.racingonline.com/lgr
Location/Directions: located about an hour from either Madison or Milwaukee. Track is located west of I-43; take Highway 50 to Lake Geneva and the track.
Circuit: 1/3-mile paved oval.
Major races: NASCAR Re/Max Challenge; Super Late Models and Super Stocks.

Lake Geneva Raceway's is a 100-acre complex encompasses not only the paved oval, but an off-road track and motocross track, where major off-road and Stadium Motocross events occur on a regular basis.

But the regular show is on Saturday evening and held on the pavement, with as many as 20 different racing divisions competing regularly. The track is open from April through October

Lodging can be found in Lake Geneva. For meals, try: Culver's (414) 248-6730; Hunter Country Club (815) 678-3000; Richard's White Oaks (414) 539-2323; or the Stein Steakhouse (414) 248-7997.

Lebanon Valley Speedway

Box 9, Route 20
W. Lebanon, NY 12195
PH: (518) 794-9606
(518) 794-9965
Location/Directions: central eastern New York State, eighteen miles southeast of Albany on U.S. 20.
Circuit: 1/2-mile clay oval; high banked.
Major races: RE/Max Challenge; World of Outlaws Sprint Car Championship Shootout.

Lebanon Valley Speedway is basically a series of dragstrips: a paved quarter-mile strip that acts as a true dragstrip; and two dirt stretches that comprise each of the main straightways of the oval. The clay at Lebanon is very quick, and the turns are a tad tighter than normal, giving it an appearance of having gigantic frontstretches and backstretches.

The track is located in a green secluded area, and gives the often dusty world of dirt racing a bit more class than one might expect to see. The oval portion seats some 20,000 so it's a noteworthy facility in that respect alone.

The dragstrip, on the outside of the oval, also is set up to seat some 10,000, and the drag racing show—although not hosting an NHRA National event—does have some excellent nitro-methane, and jet-powered car shows. For a brief list of nearby hotels, call the track, or call the Department of Economic Development Division of Tourism at (800) 225-5697.

Madison International Speedway

P.O. Box 6496
Madison, WI 53716-0496
PH: (608) 835-8305
Office: (608) 221-0119
www.racingonline.com/MIS
Location/Directions: located in Madison, on Sunrise Rd., just south of U.S. 138, between the towns of Stoughton and Oregon, Wisconsin.
Circuit: 1/2-mile paved oval; high-banked.
Major Races: NASCAR RE/MAX Challenge Series.

Madison International Speedway hosts a NASCAR RE/MAX Challenge Series race—two races, in fact—but does not host a regular NASCAR Winston Racing Series. The regular program is Late Model, Midwest Truck Series (similar to NASCAR Craftsman trucks), Limited Late Model, Midwest Modified and Sportsman. Racing takes place every Friday evening late April–early May through late September.

The track originally opened in the late 1968 as a paved, high banked 1/2-mile oval named Capitol Speedway, but in 1986 the track was covered over with clay. Then in 1992 the track was repaved and reopened as Madison International Speedway and has been operating under that name since. Several name drivers have competed here such as Dick Trickle, Matt Kenseth and Rich Bickle. The track can give you more details on where to stay.

Rockford Speedway

P.O. Box 1000
Rockford, IL 61105
PH: (815) 633-1500
http://www.rockfordspeedway.com/
Location: northern Illinois, north of Rockford.
Circuit: 1/4r-mile paved oval.
Major races: RE/Max Challenge; NASCAR Winston Racing Series, Heartland Region.

Located near Illinois' 2nd largest city, Rockford Speedway runs several programs on a weekly basis. Mainly a late-model track, Rockford also hosts a four-cylinder U.S stock division, Limited Sportsman, and Road Runners. But the facility's biggest show is the mid-September three-day Winston National Short Track Championship.

Actually located in the city of Love's Park, the privately owned track has only a few rooms in the immediate area. For the National Short track weekend you can camp on the grounds, but the County Health Department considers any area that allows more than six nights of camping a year as a campground; so don't count on camping there the rest of the season. Try 10 miles up the road in South Beloit, or on State St. in Rockford.

Wisconsin International Raceway

W 1460 Country Rd. KK
Kaukauna, WI 54130
PH: (920) 766-5577
Office: (414) 766-5575
www.racingonline.com/wir/
Location/Directions: located a half-mile east of Highway 55, on County Trunk KK in Kaukauna, WI.
Circuit: 1/2-mile paved D-shaped oval/1/4-mile paved oval/1/4-mile dragstrip.
Major races: NASCAR Winston Racing Series.

Wisconsin International Raceway's unique D-Shaped oval is the "Home of Thursday Night Thunder!" with five divisions of racing hosted Thursday nights during the season. The 1999 season marked the 25th consecutive year of weekly racing program at WIR, as presented by the sanctioning association, the Fox River Racing Club. The weekly show pulls in some 150 cars each Thursday on the track the Club calls "Little Daytona."

You can stay in Kaukauna, home of the famous cheese of the same name. Call the track for details on accommodations and dining.

NASCAR'S WINSTON WEST SERIES

NASCAR'S Winston West Series was originally supposed to have been the West Coast version of Winston Cup—although it never quite caught on like Winston Cup did.

The main problem was that the tracks were not really designed to host major-league circle track racing, and although the series has a good amount of prestige and a great amount of history (founded in 1954) it is not even close to the Southern-bred Winston Cup.

Winston West basically combines its appearances between tracks of the Southwest Tour and of the Northwest Series. The tracks vary in length and in configuration from three-eighths-mile ovals to two-mile ovals and road courses (plus two non-points races in Japan, both road courses).

The tracks they run at listed in this guide include: Las Vegas Motor Speedway; Phoenix International Raceway; California Speedway; and Portland Speedway. Winston West cars are almost identical to Winston Cup cars in that they have a wheelbase of 110 inches and a minimum weight of 3,400 pounds, which are propelled by 358 cubic inch V8. Compression is, however, 9.5:1, as opposed to the higher limit in Winston Cup.

NASCAR'S WINSTON RACING SERIES

The different local regional series championships, thirteen in all, have local racers looking for a way to pass their weekend nights, or perhaps a way up into the big leagues of Busch, or Winston Cup racing. One of the best ways to get there is through NASCAR's Winston Racing Series and up one one of the nearly 100 tracks throughout the country.

And in fact, Dale Earnhardt began his career in NASCAR's regional series. So did Darrell Waltrip and Richard Petty, and a bunch of others. To start a career, the best place to do it is at a local track with NASCAR and Winston backing.

Drivers can participate when and if they have the time, or they can race for championships. A title is a sure way to be noticed, and since it is a local title that can actually be translated nationally, it makes sense to run as many NASCAR tracks for NASCAR Winston points as possible.

The rules concerning the way points count toward the championships are a little bit confusing. The champions are not simply determined by who wins and who comes in second and so on. The champions are selected via a weighted points system. The points system takes into consideration average win percentage, number of cars and percent of available starts to produce a series champion.

Racers have to compete in at least 18 events by mid-September within their designated NASCAR Winston Racing Series region (in fact, at their designated "home" track) to be eligible for the Regional championship and divisional honors in the championships. A guy who wins 10 of 10 races, but only competes in 10-car fields will lose to a guy who competes in 20 races of 25-car fields and wins only six times.

There are currently 10 regions of NASCAR Winston Racing across the U.S. All regions are based strictly on location. The champions come from the local area, and the championships are held right there on the tracks in that area. In that way, local drivers compete against one another and do not have to endure any hardship to get to each race to ply their trade.

The idea, first and foremost, is to become the track champion. Of course, that championship should be based around conforming to the Winston Racing Series rules regarding regional and national championships. If you're already doing enough to win the track championship, then you're probably not too far from becoming regional. At that point, it's all based on statistics. What some drivers do to assure themselves of the regional championship is drive in the same class at different tracks, doing a Friday night race at one speedway, and a Saturday night race at another.

At any rate, there's a divisional champion from each division of each individual region, and a national champion chosen from each of the ten regional titlists. In other words, if a driver becomes track champ, then through the points system becomes regional champ, the next step is the National Championship, which is, again, based on a point system that already coincides with the other two titles. If the points add up right a lone driver will become National Champion. There is only one per year, and it isn't based on division status, but on success rate.

All successful racers—that is, all regional champions from each division, go to the NASCAR's Winston Racing Series Banquet in Nashville.

The racing divisions vary from region to region. Some divisions do not run at every track. What seems like a ridiculous series to one driver will be common to others. What follows is a list of names from the regions: Powder Puff, Rear Wheel Mini Stock, Front Wheel Drive Mini Stock, Super Late Model, Mighty Compacts, Pony Stock, Steelstock, Hobby Stock, Factory Stock, Pro Modified, Thunderstox, Shorttracker, Grand National, Road Runners, Winged Women on Wheels, Short Track Modified, Thundercar, Fun, Pr Stock, Pro IV, Pro Ams, Wildcar, Supersportsman, Blunderbusts, Late Model Charger, Strictly Stock, Daytona Late Model, Baby Grand, Super Mini Truck, Limited Stock, 4 Cylinder, Grand American Modified, Late Model, Pure Stock, Pure Sport, Mini Stock, Pro Mini, Charger, American Mini Stock, Great American Late Model, Figure 8, Rookie Figure 8, Bomber Figure 8, Street Stock, Winston Mini, Sportsman, Stadium Stock, Modified, Supersport, Limited Sportsman, Thunder And Lightning, Charger 4, Gran Stock, Four Cylinder Stock, Four Cylinder Modified, GA Modified, Pro Am, Flyers, Fam Sedan, Fastrucks, Pro Stock Trucks, Trucks, Mini Supertrucks, Speed Trucks, Modified Pony, Grand Am, Gulf Coast Modified, Hot Stock, and Spectator. All are from the 10 regional championships. All are from NASCAR tracks.

Frankly, most of these classes differ only in geographical location and title, not so much in actual technical differences. Tracks in each individual region will change divisional names depending on what track originated the name. If Track X comes up with a Big Red Car division and it becomes popular, Track Z, trying to capitalize on the full fields already cultivated by Track X, may have a Big Red Car division as well. So mostly the divisions are the same types of cars, if not in spirit, in name.

The Late Model class is by far the most prevalent national class. It is one of the fastest classes, and generally the closest to Winston Cup in level of competition—although they are not the same caliber of cars. Also known as the "Silhouette Class" since the car is almost identical in silhouette to their American passenger car brethren, these cars are full-blooded race cars. The Late Model class is limited to American-made passenger cars, such as Chevrolet Lumina and Ford Taurus, again, just like Winston Cup. Tires are restricted, as is engine displacement and compression ratio. The class is limited to between 2,900 and 3,150 pounds, with 110-inch wheelbase and 10-inch-wide tires.

Sportsman, Super Sportsman, or Street Stock classes, again, depending on where you are, are generally modified street cars. The bodies of the cars must remain, for the most part, stock, and the pieces are highly modified, but are still based on stock parts. The weight of these cars ranges from 3,100 to 3,450 pounds, depending on the engine size. This class uses eight-inch-wide tires, and engines are highly restricted, with only two-barrel carburetors allowed.

Classes that are also becoming popular—or that have always been popular—are Stock classes, which vary in intensity to true stock classes depending on where you are. True "Stock" classes are usually any 1955-current model American-made, steel-bodied passenger car. Usually, these cars are as close to actual street cars as possible, with safety modifications. This is not a division for the Winston Cup wannabes. There is very little at stake, very little to gain, and even less notoriety for a driver when he wins. This is generally a good jumping off point for people who want to know how racing feels, but to make a name, you need to move into something else.

Another up-and-coming series is based around trucks and the popularity of the Craftsman Truck series. There are several different divisions based on types of trucks and sizes of engines. In general, the bodies of the trucks must remain in the same silhouette as stock.

Those are just a few. They will change depending on where you are and what the name of your division is called. At any rate, tracks will run series based mostly on participation. If they have a big Grand American Modified class, they'll run those; if they have a lot of people trying to run Limited Sportsman, they'll have that class as a featured division. Usually you won't see all ten divisions racing at one track. It takes just way too much time to get all of it in on one night of racing.

Another reason is that not all tracks are alike. Each track has its own individual history and has its own following. By the same token, each track may not be the same in what can be run. In other words, NASCAR is still done on dirt and pavement alike. It is done on tracks of different length with and without banking and in great facilities and in not so great ones. It's done on egg-shaped ovals, round ovals, and, in some places, figure-8s. Like the country itself, NASCAR local racing changes depending on where you're located.

PACIFIC COAST REGION

The Pacific Coast Region. This is comprised of nine tracks in California and one in Nevada. Tracks are located from as far north as Stockton Speedway, just east of San Francisco, to as far south as Cajon Speedway in El Cajon, a few miles from the Mexican border. Six of the nine are asphalt and three are dirt. The tracks include, Cajon Speedway, Las Vegas Motor Speedway, Mesa Marin Raceway, Orange Show Speedway, San Jose Speedway, Stockton 99 Speedway, and Watsonville Speedway. See previous listings as needed.

PACIFIC COAST TRACKS

Orange Show Speedway

P.O. Box 5749
San Bernardino, CA
PH: (909) 888-6788
www.osspeedway.com
Location/Directions: southern California, near Riverside off I-210, and the Orange Show Rd. exit, then take E St. two blocks to the speedway.
Circuit: 1/4-mile paved oval.
Major races: NASCAR Winston Racing Series Pacific Coast Region; USAC full Midget series.

Orange Show Speedway boasts of being the largest of the smallest. The 10,000-seat stadium is one of the biggest in the state in terms of spectator room, but is one of the smallest paved ovals at a quarter-mile. Located in an ex-football stadium, the facility has several different shows, including Super Vs and a unique Model A Clash.

The area around the track is hot and dry during the summer. It's a good place to catch some California sun. For information regarding hotels in the Riverside area call the track, or Riverside Visitors Bureau at (619) 683-7100.

Stockton 99 Speedway

4105 N. Wilson Way
Stockton, CA 95205
PH: (209) 466-9999
www.stockton99speedway.com
Location/Directions: central California, off State Highway 99.
Circuit: 1/4-mile paved oval.
Major races: NASCAR Winston Racing Series, Pacific Coast Region.

Stockton 99 Speedway is another hot mid-California racetrack that offers great summer night racing.

The track seats 5,000, and the biggest event is the Fourth of July 100-lap main for Late Model stocks. Built in 1946, Stockton 99 Speedway's claim to fame is likely Ernie Irvan, who was a Late Model champion here, and who went on to become a competitive Winston Cup driver. The track is 10 miles from downtown Stockton, and rooms are easy to find there.

Watsonville Speedway

Watsonville, CA
Office: P.O. Box 6658
Scotts Valley, CA 95067
PH: (408) 438-3210
Office: (408) 728-4747
http://www.watsonville.com/speedway/
Location: central coastal California, in the Monterey Bay Area, off State Highway 1, at the Santa Cruz County Fairgrounds on Highway 152. From Monterey, take Highway 1 North to Riverside Exit, then East on Riverside to Blackburn, left on Blackburn to East Lake Ave. (Hwy 152) and right to the track.
Circuit: 1/4-mile clay oval.
Major races: NASCAR Winston Racing Series, Pacific Coast Region.

Watsonville Fairgrounds Speedway enters its 35th year of racing in 1992. Located at the Santa Cruz County Fairgrounds in Watsonville—two miles from the Pacific Ocean—the area is quiet and green. There is camping available at the fairgrounds, and Watsonville is 15 miles from Santa Cruz, where there is not only lodging, but where the Santa Cruz Beach, Boardwalk, and famous amusement park are located.

Watsonville was the epicenter of a an earthquake in 1989—and the turn-four grandstands had to be replaced when the tremor shook the structure apart. It was rebuilt with a better seating capacity and will now hold nearly 5,000 people. The biggest show of the year is a street stock special event at the end of the season, and a destruction derby during the fair. You can stay in Watsonville, but the best entertainment is in Santa Cruz.

GREAT WEST REGION

This region stretches east to Colorado and western South Dakota and to Oregon and Washington. Portland Speedway and Evergreen Speedway both feature two track lengths while Eagle Raceway in Lincoln, Neb., is the only dirt track in this region. Feature division classes include a combination of Late Model, Grand American, Super Stock, Limited Sportsman, and Grand American Modified. The tracks in the region are as follows: Colorado National Speedway, Eagle Raceway, Evergreen Speedway, Magic Valley Speedway, Portland Speedway, South Sound Speedway, Tri-City Raceway, Wenatchee Valley Raceway, and Yakima Speedway. Check previous listings as needed.

GREAT WEST REGION TRACKS

Eagle Raceway

Office: P.O. Box 30532
Lincoln, NE 68503
PH: (402) 420-7223
Location/Directions: eastern Nebraska, 11 miles from Lincoln, and 45 miles from Omaha.
From Lincoln, take U.S. 34 to State Route 63—the track is at the junction of SR 63 and U.S. 34.
Circuit: 1/3-mile clay oval; high banked.
Major races: NASCAR Great West Region Winston Racing Series; World of Outlaws Sprint Car Championship Shootout.

Eagle Raceway's Friday night regular racing is the main show, but it does host a round of the World of Outlaws, and several special racing events throughout the year. There are also a few Winged Prototype Modified races. Lincoln is the best bet for accommodations.

Kalispell Raceway

Highway 93
Kalispell, MT
Mailing: Larry Newland
19232 90th Ave NE.
Bothell, WA 98011
PH: (406) 257-7223
Location/Directions: Located on Hwy. 93, seven miles from Kalispell, MT, going toward Whitefish, MT.
Circuit: 3/8-mile high-banked paved oval.
Major races: NASCAR Winston Racing Series, Great West Region.

Kalispell Raceway Park has become NASCAR's 99th regional track out of the 100 in the system. It is the first NASCAR track in Montana, giving NASCAR a presence in 40 states. The track has been open since 1990, with regular Saturday night Late Model short track racing on a perfect new racing surface. In 1998, Kalispell hosted their first Northwest Tour race. All 4,000 seats sold out. You can stay in nearby Cavanaugh, or at the Outlaw Inn in Kalispell (406) 755-6100.

THE SUNBELT REGION

Stretching east from Tucson, Arizona, all the way to Florida's Volusia County Speedway (located near Daytona Beach), the Sunbelt region is by far the widest region in the country. Racers in this region rarely meet one another except at the year-end banquet in Nashville. The region is comprised of three tracks in Florida, two in Georgia, four in Texas, and one each in Arizona and Alabama. There are two dirt tracks, three clay tracks, and five asphalt ovals in the group. The tracks are as follows: Jax Raceways, Lanier National Speedway, Gainesville, Oglethorpe Speedway Park, San Antonio Speedway, St. Augustine Speedway, Summerville Speedway, and Volusia County Speedway. Check previous listings as needed.

SUNBELT REGION TRACKS

Jax Raceways

6840 Stuart Ave.
Jacksonville, FL 32205
PH: (904) 757-5425
Location/Directions: northeastern Florida, in Jacksonville.
Circuit: 1/2-mile clay oval/1/8-mile.
Major races: NASCAR Winston Racing Series, Sunbelt Region.

Jax Raceway has the same distressing southern humidity as Daytona—without the beach. But there are many places to cool off in the immediate area—like creeks, streams, and rivers—including St. Johns River.

Located just a few miles outside Jacksonville, the track seats 3,000 and an additional 3,000 can be accommodated for the dragstrip, which holds several annual Funny Car and jet car events. "Speedweek" in Jax, which starts Friday at the same time the 24 Hours begins at Daytona, runs a series of night Late Model racing. The Jax speedweek runs through the following Saturday, when the other local oval, Volusia Raceway, takes up the night racing.

Jacksonville is the most convenient place to stay, and the track can send you a list of the closest hotels. There is camping at the track's 65 acres, although there are no hookups for RVs.

Oglethorpe Speedway

267 Raymond Rd.
Tooler, GA 31322
PH: (912) 964-8200
(912) 964-7223
Office: (912) 964-7069
Location/Directions: eastern Georgia, 10 miles west outside Savannah. From Savannah, take I-95 (3 miles) to Exit 18, heading east on State Highway 80; proceed three miles to Dublin Rd., turning right and travelling one mile to the track.
Circuit: 1/2-mile clay oval.
Major races: NASCAR Winston Racing Series, Sunbelt Region.

Oglethorpe Speedway is located in a semi-residential area about three miles from the Savannah International Airport. The 3,500 seat facility runs a weekly NASCAR Saturday evening show, and rarely strays from that formula. The track is some four miles south of a large group of Motels—called "Gateway to Savannah."

San Antonio Speedway

Office: P.O. Box 1269
Helotes, TX 78023
Ph: (210) 628-1499
Office: (210) 695-8550
Location/Directions: located in South San Antonio, 3 1/2 miles south of Loop 410 on SR 16.
Circuit: 1/2-mile high-banked paved oval.
Major races: NASCAR Winston Racing Series, Sunbelt Region.

San Antonio's Saturday night show runs from March through September, with NASCAR Winston Racing Series Late Models, Super Street Stocks, Modifieds, Chargers and Thunder cars. The grandstands hold 4,200 and, for the bigger shows, sell out.

San Antonio has no shortage of rooms, unless you wish to stay around the river on any holiday weekend. Call the track for more information on lodging and accommodations.

MIDWEST REGION

This region is comprised of tracks from Iowa, Minnesota and South Dakota. In this region there are more dirt and clay tracks than any other. Only one of the nine tracks is paved. Most tracks feature the Late Model class. The racetracks are as follows: Adams County Speedway, Butler County Speedway, Crawford County Speedway, Dubuque Fairgrounds Speedway, Farley Speedway, Madison Speedway, Park Jefferson Speedway, Sunset Speedway, Viking Speedway, West Liberty Raceway. Check previous listings as needed.

MIDWEST REGION TRACKS

Grundy County Speedway

Office: 638 Nettle St.
Morris, IL 60450
PH: (815) 942-5043
Office/Fax: (815) 942-2510
Location/Directions: 1 mile north of I-80 on SR 47 (at the Grundy Agricultural District Fairgrounds).
Circuit: 1/3-mile paved oval; high-banked.
Major Races/Regular divisions: ARCA Lincoln Welders Midget Series; NASCAR Winston Racing Series, Midwest Region.

Racing at Grundy County Speedway takes place Friday nights beginning on the last week of April and continuing all the way through Labor Day. The track also hosts a few special events, and a half-dozen midget races on Saturday nights. In addition, there are special events during the fair, which is typically July 1–5.

The track seats 5,000 people, and is generally known as a comfortable and modern facility. The seats are packed occasionally for the weekly program, but are usually sold out for the bigger events.

In Morris, stay at the Holiday Inn, Super 8, or one of the four major motels within a mile of the track. Morris Municipal Airport. Denny's is a half-mile from the track, plus there are typical fast-food restaurants a few minutes from the fairgrounds.

Hawkeye Downs

**4400 6th Street SW
Cedar Rapids, IA 52404
Track: (319) 365-8656
www.hawkeyedowns.com
Location/Directions: eastern Iowa, just outside Cedar Rapids, off I-380 at Exit B-16, then a half-mile west to Sixth Street, and north to the track.
Circuit: 1/2-mile paved oval.
Major Races: USAC Midgets, ASA, NASCAR Winston Racing Series, Midwest Region.**

Hawkeye Downs, is located on the Iowa Fairgrounds in Cedar Rapids. It hosted its first Jalopy stock car race on Labor Day, 1925. The present grandstand was constructed in 1966, and can seat 8,000 people. Weekly and regional stock car racing are regular events, as are IMCA cars and an assortment of open-wheeled, full-bodied, and even motocross races. Cedar Rapids is a major city of with many hotel options.

Viking Speedway

**Alexandria, MN
Office: P.O. Box 462
Alexandria, MN 56308
PH: (320) 762-1559
Location/Directions: in Alexandria, at the Douglas County Fairgrounds, on SR 82, 8 miles west of SR 29.
Circuit: 1/2-mile semi-banked clay oval.
Major Races: NASCAR Winston Racing Series, Midwest Region.**

Viking Speedway features a regular Saturday night Late Model program during the racing season, with Modifieds, Super Stocks, Pro-4 Modifieds and Pure Stocks as intermediate divisions. The track holds some 2,700 people and sells out four or five times a year. The biggest show is the Fourth of July special.

You can stay in Alexandria or surrounding towns and there's a Days Inn, a Holiday Inn, a Comfort Inn, and an Arrowwood Resort. Call the track for more details.

MID-AMERICA REGION

This region extends from Minnesota through Wisconsin and into Illinois. The tracks are a combination of dirt, clay and asphalt, with lengths ranging from a quarter-mile to a more than half-mile oval. Although the varying track surfaces and track lengths make it difficult to achieve parity in points, each track in the region has Late Model as the featured class (except Tri-City Speedway, which runs Modified as the featured class). The tracks are as follows: Capital Speedway, Elko Speedway, I-94 Speedway, LaCrosse Fairgrounds Speedway, Peoria Speedway, Raceway Park, Rockford Speedway, and Tri-City Speedway. Check other listings as needed.

MID-AMERICA REGION TRACKS

Capital Speedway

P.O. Box 100
Holts Summit, MO 65043
PH: (573) 896-5500
www.capitalspeedway.com
Location/Directions: central Missouri, just north of Jefferson City, at the intersection of Hwys. 54 and OO in Holts Summit.
Circuit: 3/8-mile clay oval.
Major races: NASCAR Winston Racing Series, Mid-America Region; Late Model, Pro-Modifieds.

Capital Speedway hosts a weekly NASCAR Late Model program with a NASCAR Busch All-Star Tour race as its season feature event. Regular racing is held on Saturday night on the three-eighths-mile oval—considered one of the best in Missouri.

Located just south of Mark Twain National Forest, there are places to camp close by. Holts Summit has a few rooms, or try Jefferson City, or cross the Missouri River and stay in Frankenstein (no kidding!).

Elko Speedway

17816 Susan Ln
Minnetonka, MN 55345
Office: Racing Promotions Inc.
One Checkered Flag Blvd.
Shakopee, MN 55379
PH: (612) 445-2257
Location: southern Minnesota, 20 miles south of Minneapolis, off I-35.
Circuit: 3/8-mile paved oval.
Major races: NASCAR Winston Racing Series, Mid America Region.

Elko Speedway forms the first half of Shakopee Valley's dirt track weekend. The other paved NASCAR Winston Racing Series short track is Raceway Park, which operates Sunday night. Elko runs Saturday night. The track is located in the rolling farmland country of Minnesota, just a few minutes from Minneapolis.

The track operates from April through Labor Day and offers several shows besides NASCAR, including Figure-8s and Enduros.

Call the track for information on where to stay while in Shakopee Valley.

Peoria Speedway

3520 W. Farmington Rd.
Peoria, IL 61604
PH: (309) 673-3342
Circuit: 1/4-mile high-banked dirt oval.
Location/Directions: in Peoria, off I-74 at SR 8 and Farmington Rd.
Major races: NASCAR Winston Racing Series, Mid-America Division.

Peoria Speedway's regular Saturday night NASCAR show features Late Models, Sportsman, Street Stocks and Bombers and runs from April through October. The biggest show of the year is the Jon Hamilton Memorial, also called the Busch Illinois State Championships, usually run the first week of October.

The facility seats 3,000 fans and there is additional space in the pits, which is located on the other side of the track from the main grandstands and start/finish. The distinguishing feature, according to track owner Sherry Hamilton, is the food. "It's really good food," she says. "I taste everything before I let it in." She recommends the pork chop sandwiches.

You can stay in one of several motels in the Peoria area. Some recommended are the Days Inn and the Fairfield Inn, located 10 minutes off I-74 in East Peoria. Chili's is one of the racers' favorites, but some of the best food in Peoria is found at Boulevard Grill, next to the Paradise Boat in East Peoria, 15 minutes from the track.

Raceway Park

Office: 17816 Susan Ln.
Minnetonka, MN 55345
PH: (612) 445-2257
Location/Directions: in Shakopee, eastern Minnesota, 10 miles southwest of Minneapolis, off State Highway 101.
Circuit: 1/4-mile clay oval.
Major races: NASCAR Winston Racing Series, Mid-America Region.

Raceway Park is owned and promoted by the same folks who own Elko Speedway, the other NASCAR Winston Racing Series paved short track in the Shakopee Valley. While Elko runs Saturday night, Raceway Park runs Sunday night, completing the weekend in Shakopee. The facility seats 5,000, and is just ending its 36th year. It is just east of the Valley Fair Amusement Park and is touted as the area's "cornerstone of Shakopee's entertainment showcase." Call the track office for hotels in the area, or call the Minneapolis–St. Paul Chamber of Commerce Tourism Department at (612) 370-9132, or the Greater Minneapolis Convention and Visitors Association at (612) 348-4313.

Mid-America Region Tracks, continued

Tri-City Speedway

5100 Nameoki Rd.,
Granite City, IL
Office: P.O. Box 6024
St. Charles MO 63302
PH: (618) 931-7836
www.tri-cityspeedway.com
Location/Directions: located a half-mile south of I-270, on IL 203, just north of Granite City.
Circuit: 1/2-mile semi-banked dirt oval.
Major Races: NASCAR Busch All-Star Series; World of Outlaws Series; NASCAR Winston Racing Series, Mid-America Region.

Tri-City runs a Saturday show from April through September. The biggest show is World Of Outlaws, and there are usually two per season—one in May and one in June. There is also a NASCAR Busch All-Star race. The track first opened in 1960 and has remained the same basic layout since. Drivers typically applaud the continuity, saying the track is one of the finest half-miles in country.

The facility seats 4,500 and almost always sells out for the Outlaws. All seats are general admission. You can stay in Pontoon Beach, which is two miles from the track, the Super 8 or the Ramada Inn. There is nowhere to stay in Granite City.

THE HEARTLAND REGION

Getting into the heart of oval dirt tracking, this highly competitive region has produced the national champion five times. This region is comprised of tracks from southern Illinois, Indiana, and southern Missouri. There are a combination of track configurations out of the 10 in the region, but most tracks run Late Model as featured division. A partial listing of tracks includes: I-70 Speedway, Kil-Kare Speedway, Lebanon I-44 Speedway, Macon Speedway, Nashville Speedway, Winchester Speedway, Also, see previous listings for: Capital Speedway, Elko Speedway, I-94 Speedway, LaCrosse Fairgrounds Speedway, Peoria Speedway, Raceway Park and Rockford Speedway.

HEARTLAND REGION TRACKS

Kil-Kare Raceway

1166 Dayton-Xenia Rd;
Xenia, Ohio 45385
PH: (937) 426-2764
Location/Directions: located just off U.S. 35 between Dayton and Xenia on Dayton-Xenia Rd. Take U.S. 35 East from I-75 or 675 to Valley Rd., then north to Dayton-Xenia Rd. and the track.
Circuit: 3/8-mile paved oval.
Major races: ARCA Bondo series, NASCAR Winston Racing Series, Heartland Region.

Kil-Kare Raceway runs a Friday night non-NASCAR Late Model shows and an annual ARCA Bondo show. Although once a NASCAR track, the facility now features Late Model Sportsman, with Pro Stock Division, E-Modified Division, Pure Stock Division, Mini Stock Division and Figure Eight Division as secondary staples. The track also has a highly regarded dragstrip as well. You can stay in Xenia. Call the track for suggestions.

THE BLUE RIDGE REGION

The heart of NASCAR racing is right here. The region itself includes Kentucky and parts of Tennessee, Virginia, North Carolina and South Carolina, and its tracks vary from quarter-mile asphalt to half-mile paved. Asheville, Bowman Gray, Hickory; these are all tracks that big names in Winston Cup made their starts. If there is a place racing scouts would be looking for future starts, this is the region. Most run Late Model divisions as the featured class. A partial listing of tracks includes: Bowman Gray Stadium, Greenville-Pickens Speedway, Hickory Motor Speedway, Lonesome Pine International Raceway, Louisville Motor Speedway, New River Valley Speedway, Tri-County Motor Speedway. See previousl listings as needed.

BLUE RIDGE REGION TRACKS

Bowman Gray Stadium

4537 Country Club Rd.
Winston-Salem, NC 27104
(336) 716-2011
Location: northern North Carolina, in Winston-Salem, on Martin Luther King Blvd.
Circuit: 1/4-mile clay oval.
Major races: NASCAR Winston Racing Series, Blue Ridge Region.

Bowman Gray Stadium is nestled in a hilly area of North Carolina that, oddly, becomes dry and brown early in the normally humid North Carolina summers. But there is not much humidity here, making race watching a bit easier. The fifty two-year-old quarter-mile track is built around a football stadium, which is city owned, and used during the fall and winter by Winston-Salem State University, Reynold High School, and Parkland High School football teams. The stadium seats 17,000. The racing surface is wide, but completely flat. Racing doesn't interfere with football, although sometimes as rain outs occur the cars run past the goal posts at rescheduled events!

The regular show is run with Modified Street, and Buzz Bombers, and is occasionally sprinkled with a demolition derby or two. The biggest event is the Winston 200, followed by the Goodys 150—all run with Modifieds. There are plenty of rooms in the Winston-Salem area, which can be had by calling (800) VISIT NC.

Blue Ridge Region Tracks, continued

Lonesome Pine Int'l. Raceway

Coeburn, VA, 24230
PH: (540) 395-3338
FAX: (540) 395-5329
www.lonesomepineraceway.com
Location/Directions: on Old Route 58, in Coeburn, Virginia, Norton-Coeburn Rd. (two miles off Rt. 58 Alternate West) between Norton and Coeburn, VA.
Circuit: .375-mile asphalt.
Major races: NASCAR Winston Racing Series, Blue Ridge Region.

Lonesome Pine's three-eighths-mile paved oval boasts a beautiful setting with a modern and fast racetrack. The 15-degree banking in the turns and 50–70 feet of width makes it fast and safe. The track was opened in 1972 as a NASCAR Winston Cup facility track but now hosts mainly NASCAR Winston Racing events. But it has some history: Alan Kulwicki won his first ASA race here and still holds the track speed record (for full-bodied cars) with a speed of 84.375 mph.

Racing is scheduled April through September, with the regular program held on Saturday night. The facility is concrete grandstands on the frontstretch that hold a total capacity of 7,500.

There are several places to stay within a 15-mile radius, but the track recommends the Holiday Inn and Super 8 in Norton, or the Ramada Inn in Duffield.

New River Valley Speedway

Radford, VA
Office: 6749 Lee Hwy.
Radford, VA 24141
PH: (540) 639-1700
Location/Directions: located on U.S. 11, approximately two miles south of Radford, VA. Between Radford and Dublin.
Circuit: .416-mile high-banked paved oval.
Major races: NASCAR Winston Racing Series, Hooters Pro Cup Series, ASA.

New River Valley Speedway's regular Saturday show features NASCAR Late Model stocks plus four other divisions, and only varies from that formula a few times a season. When Winston Cup races on Saturday nights the track hosts a Sunday show. The facility seats 10,000 fans in the front grandstands—which is pretty tough to sell out no matter what the show.

Track officials call the venue "One of the finest short tracks in Virginia." Built in 1988 to its present configuration, the facility was originally a dirt track constructed back in the early 60s. It ran as a dirt oval with some of the greats like Curtis

Turner and the Wood Brothers and was a Busch Grand National track into the late 80s, but now runs mostly local racing.

You can stay in Radford, or there are several motels in Dublin, most notably the Super 8 (540) 731-9355, and Best Western (540) 639-3000. Race fans usually head to the Golden Corral in Radford for meals.

Tri-County Motor Speedway

Route 2, P.O. Box 517
Hudson, NC 28638
PH: (828) 728-7223
www.tricomotor.com/
Location/Directions: central western North Carolina, 15 miles north of Hickory, NC, on State Route 321.
Circuit: 3/8-mile paved oval.
Major races: NASCAR Winston Racing Series, Blue Ridge Region.

Tri-County Speedway is located on farmland, in a flat area of western North Carolina. The biggest race of the season is the Larry Smith Memorial with Late Model stocks, Limited Sportsman, Mini Stocks, Street Stocks, and Bud Cup racing. The regular program takes place on Friday nights. Accommodations can be found at Lenoir, which is a few miles from the track.

MID-ATLANTIC REGION

Another famous region in NASCAR history, with great tracks like South Boston and Myrtle Beach in the group. The region extends north from the southern tip of South Carolina through Virginia. Most tracks are paved, with lengths from .333 mile to .538 miles. Late Model stock car is the featured division of choice (except Summerville Speedway, which features Late Model Sportsman as the feature). Tracks are as follows: Florence Motor Speedway, Langley Speedway, Myrtle Beach Speedway, Old Dominion Speedway, South Boston Motor Speedway, Southern National Speedway, and Southside Speedway. See previous listings as needed.

MID-ATLANTIC REGION TRACKS

Florence I-95 Speedway

P.O. Box 1527
Hartsville, SC 29550
PH: (803) 346-7711
Location: central-eastern South Carolina, between Florence and Charlotte, NC, roughly 20 miles from Darlington, in Hartsville.
Circuit: 3/8-mile oval.
Major races: NASCAR Winston Racing Series, Mid-Atlantic Region.

Florence I-95 Speedway is primarily a Saturday night NASCAR racetrack that also hosts a series of twin-purse/twin-race events. There are also some lucrative $1,000 winner's purses for Florence demo-derbies, which attract a lot of crazy competitors.

Old Dominion Speedway

10611 Dumfries Rd.
Manassas, VA 22111
PH: (703) 361-7753
Location/Directions: 20 miles west of Washington, DC, in Manassas, VA, five miles south of I-66, off State Route 234.
Circuit: 3/8-mile paved oval.
Major races: NASCAR Winston Racing Series, Mid-Atlantic Region.

Old Dominion Speedway hosts a regular group of five racing divisions each Saturday night. The NASCAR sanctioned oval also has a dragstrip on the property and holds divisional and bracket drags frequently. An IHRA sanctioned event runs here as the biggest show of the drag racing season. The area has plenty of rooms—although they may be a bit expensive. Call the track for numbers of the cheaper inns.

Southside Speedway

P.O. Box 9606
Richmond, VA 23228
PH: (804) 763-3567
Location/Directions: central eastern Virginia, in south Richmond, off Highway 360 West.
Circuit: 1/3-mile paved oval.
Major races: NASCAR Winston Racing Series, Mid-Atlantic Region.

Just south of Richmond, in Chesterfield, Southside Speedway is known as the "toughest track in the South." The narrow oval is almost completely flat, which makes for some good bumping and jostling on any given race night. Its biggest event is the NASCAR Dash series, and for that one most of the 6,300 seats are filled. The regular Friday night shows are run with NASCAR Late Model stocks and Minis.

There are probably 50 motels within 20 miles of the track, but Chesterfield and Hanover are the closest. Some people camp—although there are no formal camping facilities—for the Dash.

THE NORTHEAST REGION

This region runs north from West Virginia to New York, with tracks in Pennsylvania and New Jersey. Although originally a region of mostly dirt tracks, it has become one with mostly paved ovals now. Only three are dirt anymore (Big Diamond Raceway, Grandview Speedway, and West Virginia Motor Speedway). Tracks are split between Modified and Late Model as the featured division. A partial listing of tracks includes: Big Diamond Raceway, Flemington Speedway, Grandview Speedway, Holland Int'l. Speedway, Jennerstown Speedway, Motordrome Speedway, and Riverhead Raceway. See previous listings as needed.

NORTHEAST REGION TRACKS

Big Diamond Raceway

P. O. Box 298
Minersville, Pa
PH: (570) 544-6434
FAX: (570) 544-6720
www.bigdiamondraceway.com
Location/Directions: located just outside Minersville. Heading south on I-81, take Exit 35 four miles to Minersville, then right on Primrose two miles through Forestville to the track.
Circuit: .333-mile clay.
Major Races: NASCAR Winston Racing Series, Northeast Region, Sportsman Modified, Sportsman.

Big Diamond celebrated its 28th year of auto racing in 1999 with a handful of Sunday shows and regular Friday night racing headlined by NASCAR Modified stock cars. NASCAR Sportsman and Roadrunners also join the Modifieds.

Big Diamond is also a part of Pennsylvania Spring Speedweek. You can stay in Minersville. Call the track for more information.

Grandview Speedway

218C Wilt Rd
RD1, Bechtelsville, PA 19505
PH: (610) 754-7688
http://www.grandviewspeedway.com/
Location/Directions: eastern Pennsylvania, on State Route 100, 20 miles north of Pottstown, on Passmore Rd. From Valley Forge, take Route 422 west to Route 100 north, then 10 miles to Passmore Road and a half-mile to the track.
Circuit: 1/3-mile clay oval.
Major races: NASCAR Winston Racing Series, Northeast Region, Modified, Late Model.

Grandview calls itself the "Greatest Show on Dirt." And as the home of the biggest and richest short track Modified stock car race in the Tri-state area, the claim may not be far from the truth. The purse for one race is over $35,000.

Saturday evening racing is the staple here, with sprints and micro-sprints often running with the NASCAR Winston Racing divisions. The track boasts of every seat being close to the action, and racing that can be clearly seen from any seat in the place; there is also a non-drinkers' seating section. The track is minutes from Allentown, Reading, Wilmington, Norristown, and Philly—all of which have rooms.

Motordrome Speedway

Hwy. I-270
Smithton, PA
Ph: (724) 872-7555
www.motordrome.com
Location/Directions: 25 miles south of downtown Pittsburg, 10 miles west of New Stanton, at exit 23 off I-270.
Circuit: 1/2-mile paved oval.
Major races: NASCAR Winston Racing Series, Northeast Region, Late Model, Pro Stock, Truck.

Opened in May of 1978 as "Motordrome 70 Speedway," the new track was a state-of-the-art half-mile banked dirt track. According to track lore, that first season was a disaster and, although the dirt track racing was entertaining, it was not lucrative.

In 1989, with an owner and promoter change, the track was paved and the pits moved to the infield. One of the remnants of that change is the drive-in theater style parking for fans to view the races from their automobiles from the old pit complex.

NEW ENGLAND REGION

Moving from New York north through Maine and comprising the northernmost region in the United States, the New England Region is known for its intense competition. The featured division of choice is Pro Stock, with the remainder mostly featuring Modified. Tracks include: Afton Raceway, Beech Ridge Speedway, Fulton Speedway, Lee USA Speedway, Thompson International Speedway, Monadnock Speedway, Riverside Park Speedway, Stafford Motor Speedway, and Star Speedway.

Although the Blue Ridge and Mid-Atlantic regions have probably produced more Winston Cup drivers than any other, up-an-coming drivers come from any of the regions. Check previous listings as needed.

NEW ENGLAND REGION TRACKS

Monadnock Speedway

Office: 137 Fair Oak Rd.
Springfield MA 01128
PH: (603) 239-4067
http://www.monadnockspeedway.com/
Location/Directions: In eastern New Hampshire, in Winchester. From Boston, take I-495 to Route 2 west to Route 140 north, turning north on Route 12 to Route 10 to the Speedway
Circuit: 1/4-mile paved oval.
Major races: NASCAR Winston Racing Series, New England Region.

Self-named the "fastest high banked quarter-mile in East," Monadnock Speedway holds a handful of special events in addition to the regular Friday night racing. The big show is the Budweiser Firecracker on Fourth of July, with NASCAR Winston Racing Series regulars running 200-lap races. Hotel information can be found by calling the track.

ARCA

**ARCA
(Automobile Racing Club of America)
P.O. Box 5217
Toledo, OH 43611
(734) 847-6726
(734) 847-3137**

All photos in this chapter courtesy ARCA.

In 1953, John Marcum, an ex-racecar driver and NASCAR official, decided to take on Bill France and NASCAR by organizing his own sanctioning body. It wasn't that Marcum wasn't happy working for France, he just wanted to go back home to Ohio. So he tried to reproduce the France series in the Midwest.

In 1953 he created MARC, the Midwest Association for Race Cars, which ran 20 races in that season. Richard Petty's uncle, Lee's brother, Julie, won races that year in MARC.

A few years later the series was up to an average of 30 races and beginning to compete

in NASCAR territory, with races in Georgia and other Southern states. The series title, therefore, had to go. In 1964 it was changed to ARCA, the Automobile Racing Club of America, which is what it has been known as since.

ARCA rules are very similar to NASCAR Winston Cup rules. In its current configuration, the series races on tracks from Daytona Beach to Pocono, Pennsylvania, and from Parkersburg, West Virginia, to Fountain, Colorado. Sometimes the races take place in one day—where unloading the cars, practice, qualifying and racing are done within twelve hours—but they also do three day events at superspeedways.

But probably the biggest feature of ARCA racing besides its heritage of being one of the premiere feeder series for serious would-be Winston Cup drivers is that the races are held on a combination of dirt ovals and paved ovals, and on everything from short tracks to superspeedways. The ARCA series is essentially the same today as NASCAR's Winston Cup (or what became Winston

Cup) was forty years ago.

Drivers are expected to be able to race on several types of tracks, from short paved to medium dirt to flat-out two-and-a-half-mile banked superspeedways. And when they get finished racing ARCA they should be ready for just about anything.

THE SERIES FORMAT

The ARCA season mirrors the Winston Cup, running for most of the year and on many of the same tracks. But there are a bunch of differences, including how points are scored.

ARCA also structures their events in many different event styles, that it sometimes seems like an Officer Candidate School drill just to make the race. For example, in August, the series races at Winchester Speedway in Indiana on a Saturday, then loads up the trucks and drives down to Charlotte, where, on Monday morning, they have to be ready to start practice and qualifying for the race at the Charlotte Motor Speedway, which takes place—oddly, on Wednesday.

One unique aspect of ARCA racing is that they also run on dirt ovals. The cars may be less expensive, but the racing is first class.

ARCA cars run on many of the same tracks as Winston Cup, including superspeedways like Talladega, above.

The complicated schedule has to do with where the series races and with whom. In Charlotte, the series raced with the Winston Cup and Busch series, and so the race happened the same day that the Busch teams ran for pole, which was Wednesday for a Friday night race. The ARCA series cars had to practice and qualify Monday and Tuesday and race Wednesday, the first day of Busch qualifying, Bud Pole Day.

But at some tracks, where the ARCA series is the featured series, the races are on Sunday. Daytona is on a Sunday as is Salem, Memphis, Toledo, Springfield, Du Quoin, and Salem. Daytona is on a Sunday because it runs a week before the Daytona 500, on the same day as the Busch Clash. The others are events where the ARCA Series is the featured series. But most of the dates are Saturday races, with a few Friday races and a few weekday races.

The races are broken into what ARCA officials call "short track" races, which are races run on tracks a mile and under; everything else is over a mile in length. The races are generally 200 miles or about the same number of laps at the smaller speedways. At

this point, races do vary, but ARCA is attempting to make all superspeedway races 200 miles (currently Talladega is 300 miles and Charlotte is 100 miles).

Just like most pro series, the events are broken into practice, qualifying and the actual race. Like most racing series, the fastest qualifier takes the pole and leads the race to the first corner. To get to qualify, the teams draw lots to determine the order, then they go out for one-lap runs for time. Fastest time gets pole, and second fastest is beside him and so on.

The races are run as any other series would, with red flags, yellow flags, white flags and so on, with the white flag signifying one lap to go, and the checkered at the end. Restarts are handled single file, and all laps run under yellow are counted as racing laps unless they are run at the very end of the event. The rule then is that competitors must see the green, white and checkered flags in that order to win—or finish—the race. So if an accident happens on the second to last lap, the cars would come around to the start/finish line for the yellow flag, but not get the white until the debris is cleared and

they could race to the finish. Once the track is cleared the white would fly with the green and the next lap the winner would take the checkered. Unless it is at a superspeeday. Then the race can end under yellow.

Points

Points toward the championship are scored slightly differently than most other series. The points are allotted like this: 200 for a win, then dropping in five-point increments back to the end of the pack. In addition, the pole winner gets 25 points for that performance, with the next four fastest drivers getting 20, 25, 10, and 5 points. Leading the race yields 10 points, and the driver who leads the most laps gets an additional 10 points.

That might differ from Winston Cup and Busch Racing but it tends to be fairly standard stuff. What follows is not all that common: Drivers are allotted 25 points just for showing up and competing. As long as the car takes to the track—regardless of whether it finishes—the driver receives 25 points.

Additionally, the series is broken into multi-race legs. These legs comprise sort of mini-seasons, which are then counted as points-paying performances. For example, five races may be packaged together as one "leg." If any driver competes in all five races, he receives 250 points. If he completes two "legs" without missing a race, he receives 500 points, and so on. Just by making all the races a driver can pick up a lot of points.

The champion will make something over $100,000 (in 1997 the championship was worth $110,000) and the champion made more than $300,000, including purses.

THE CARS

Like NASCAR's Busch Grand National and Winston Cup cars, ARCA cars can be identified with their street cousins. They can be slightly older than either of the NASCAR series cars, with vehicles that are six years old or newer, as opposed to three years old or newer for Winston Cup and Busch Grand National cars. The minimum weight is 3,400

ARCA cars are very similar to Winston Cup, and in fact, many are used Cup cars.

Many consider ARCA to be the ultimate breeding ground because the cars are so similar and because drivers run on so many different types of tracks.

lbs.—the same as Winston Cup. The wheelbase is the same as the Cup car, at 110 inches, and the track can be 60 to 60.5 inches (Winston Cup is 60.5; BGN is 60 inches).

Also like NASCAR, the series is set up so entrants are checked and rechecked to ensure a standard of "stock" competition. Of course, like NASCAR, the cars on the track are far from stock.

The ARCA cars use V8s between 339 cid and 358 cid. Compression is limited to 12:1. An additional rule regarding engines states that the body type must correspond to the engine manufacturer. In other words, you can't run a Taurus with a GM engine in it. All engine blocks must be cast iron from the original manufacturer's production line.

Of course, there is no turbocharging, no supercharging, no fuel injection or nitrous oxide and no fuel additives. The fuel is delivered via a single four-barrel carburetor, and fuel is limited to 22 gallons carried aboard the car. All fuel and oil are selected by the series and checked by ARCA officials. Because the cars run as fast as their Winston Cup brethren, the larger tracks (Daytona and Talladega) mandate use of roof flaps and restrictor plates.

Since the series runs on dirt tracks, you might assume they have designated dirt cars and speedway cars. Not true. As of 1999, all cars are superspeedway cars. That means the car that races at Talladega's 2.66 mile banked oval will be the exact same car that races on DuQuoin's dirt. It makes the entire field struggle the same with tuning—and makes for some great racing.

The series is as popular as it is because it is so close to Winston Cup. The cars used in ARCA are very similar to Winston Cup cars. Some cars are actually secondhand Cup cars, living a second life through the ARCA

series. And that makes sense for a few reasons.

First, ARCA allows someone with a limited budget to pick up a car that is no longer competitive in top-rank racing. It may be a Hendricks car or a Roush car, or whatever, but it is perhaps not competitive for whatever reason. Maybe it's just too old. But it finds a home in ARCA racing.

The typical ARCA race is 100 to 200 miles, depending on the track. The longest is the Daytona 200, which runs during Winston Cup Speedweeks, and comes the week before the Daytona 500. In addition to the Daytona race, ARCA runs with Winston Cup seven other times throughout the season.

That means an up-and-coming driver not only gets to network with Winston Cup regulars, they can also get into a real Winston Cup car, compete door-handle to door-handle in competitive circumstances without mortgaging the farm. More importantly, it gives the drivers the chance to get to know the machinery. Going from either a truck or a Busch Grand National car to a Winston

Cup car is not as easy as it may look. There are differences between them (as we've discussed in earlier chapters) and to be competitive in your first season in Winston Cup is a sure way to ensure your future as a race car driver. ARCA gives drivers a chance to be competitive the first time they step into a current Winston Cup car—they've basically already been there.

Another thing it does is give drivers a chance to compete on the speedways of NASCAR, like Daytona and Talladega. It gives them a taste of the biggest and the best and what it feels like to drive in a 20-car draft with restrictor plates on a superspeedway, experience that some may get to use in a Winston Cup car someday.

Competition is close and the racing is very tight, even though the series is lower budget. Many ARCA drivers make the move up to Busch and then Winston Cup.

ARCA BONDO SERIES TRACKS

As mentioned, ARCA races on many of the same tracks as Winston Cup and other series, so check previous listings for: Daytona International Speedway, Atlanta Motor Speedway, Lowes Motor Speedway, Memphis Motorsports Park, Michigan Speedway, Pocono International Raceway, Pike's Peak Int'l Raceway, Illinois State Fairgrounds, Texas Motor Speedway, Winchester Speedway and Talladega Superspeedway

Salem Speedway

P.O. Box 466
Salem, IN 47167
PH (track): (812) 883-6504
Location/Directions: central Indiana, 100 miles south of Indianapolis, on Highway 56, just outside Salem.
Circuit: 1/2-mile paved oval.
Major races: USAC Sprint Car Championships, ASA Championships, USAC Midgets, and ARCA.

Salem Speedway reopened in 1987 after a six-year lay-off with some substantial changes, making it one of the finest half-mile paved ovals in oval-rich Indiana.

The 52-acre facility was purchased by Don Gettelfinger, who immediately put buckets of money into new guardrails, new catch fencing, a new paint job, and upgraded grandstands. The track, which originally opened in 1947, was torn apart by a tornado in 1981, and had been only haphazardly repaired. As soon as Gettelfinger bought the facility, he completely repaired and immediately reopened it.

This track boasts of being the place that Mario Andretti won his first USAC race in 1964, and where Darrell Waltrip held a winning streak of six straight races. This is also the track where Rich Vogler lost his life. NASCAR once used this track, and Benny Parsons won several races here on the 33-degree half-mile banking. Salem has plenty of rooms.

Toledo Speedway

5639 Benore Rd.
Toledo, OH 43612
PH: (419) 727-1100
Location/Directions: northern Ohio, near the Michigan border, off I-75 at Exit 210.
Circuit: 1/2-mile paved oval.
Major races: ARCA, USAC Sprint Car Championships.

Racing at Toledo Speedway draws quite well from Ohio's metro area. Located just off I-75—just a few minutes away from Toledo—is easy to find and has several good races a season. The 900 Series, which is a nine-race series around a series championship that pays $150,000, is quite popular; or the ARCA Permatex 125 does well as a feature event for the racing season. There is also a quarter-mile oval in the center of the half-mile high-banks, plus a figure-eight track. All the racing happens Sunday night.

The facility sits on 52-acres of open field, so there is free camping, although there are only a couple of hookups for RVs. Toledo has plenty of rooms if camping is not your style.

ASA

10

THE ASA SERIES & TRACKS

ASA
American Speed Association
550 North Pendleton Ave.
Pendleton, IN 46064
(765) 778-8088

All photos in this chapter are courtesy of ASA.

All the American Speed Association founder Rex Robbins wanted to do was own a racetrack. After making an offer on a racetrack, the previous owners suggested he begin his career as an owner by learning how to promote races. Heck, they told him, maybe he even ought to start a series, just to get the hang of the sport and how it works. In 1972, the ASA was born.

Like the ARCA series, the ASA is known for bringing up young, potential Winston Cup Champions. Former ASA standouts include Mark Martin, Darrell Waltrip, Neil Bonnett and Rusty Wallace, among others. Some, like Wallace and Martin, were ASA champs.

In 1998, Adam Petty set a record in the ASA ranks by becoming the youngest driver to win an ASA event at I-70 Speedway in June of 1998. He was 17. Of course Petty

Jimmie Vaughn in the Pennzoil Chevy leads a train in pursuit of the leader, typical of tight ASA racing action.

added some more notoriety to the series by becoming the first (known) fourth-generation driver to win in stock car racing (Lee, Richard, Kyle, and then his son, Adam).

The series is now known as the best short track series in the nation, with intense battles on 1-mile or shorter facilities. All races are held on paved ovals; unlike ARCA, which has some races on dirt ovals.

THE CARS

The cars are similar to Winston Cup cars in that they are Pontiac Grand Prixs, Chevy Monte Carlos, Ford Tauruses (and Thunderbirds) and so on. But unlike Winston Cup, which uses sheet metal bodies, the ASA cars are all fiberglass. They are physically smaller than their NASCAR counterparts in either Winston Cup or Busch Grand National, with shorter wheelbases and lighter minimum weights.

ASA cars are built upon a chassis, which is essentially a common center section, set of frame rails and roll cage. The chassis are "spec" chassis and all built by a company in Twin Lakes, Wisconsin, called Five Star Stock Cars, which builds all ASA chassis. They are all built to the same specs and everyone must run the same car. The car is inspected by ASA officials and receives an ASA serial number. The team then builds its type of car on the chassis, be it Ford Chevrolet, or Pontiac.

Specs

The engines are V6s. The reason for this is far more progressive than either NASCAR or ARCA. ASA officials realized that Detroit was looking for a series that could race-test a V6 engine. So in 1982, V6s became standard equipment on ASA race cars. V6s are more fuel efficient, lighter, and (at least at the time) seemed to be the engine of the future. Most American manufacturers back then were using V6s to power their cars.

The ASA engines have a 9:1 compression ratio, with less horsepower than the comparable Winston Cup or BGN car. These cars develop approximately 500 horsepower, and they use unleaded racing fuel. NASCAR still uses leaded gas.

From the outside, ASA cars look like their street-based cousin: Taurus, Monte Carlo, or Pontiac Grand Prix. But underneath they are identical. All ASA cars are built to the same specs by a single manufacturer. Teams can then put the fiberglass body of their choice on top. This controls costs and competition.

Races are long enough to require pit stops, which gives crews and drivers real world training for moving up to larger series. Short tracks make for tight racing (below).

The other major difference in engines is that ASA cars use mufflers. Due to noise restraints at some tracks, competition was shortened or otherwise cancelled. With muf-fled cars, racing coexists with trackside residents a lot better.

RACES

There are approximately 20 to 22 races a year, depending on the schedule, and most are two-day events, with an occasional one-day event thrown into the schedule.

As mentioned earlier, for the most part the races are short track races. There are currently two races on one-mile tracks (Pikes Peak and Milwaukee), but the remainder are held on shorter tracks like Salem Speedway and Berlin Raceway.

The races are similar to any other form of oval track racing in that you have two laps of single-car qualifying, where the best of the two laps is recorded for a grid position. The qualifying order for the first 20 cars is set by grid position; the next four will be set by current race points. So if a driver leads the series but finds himself in a position where he can't make the qualifying session, or

worse, spins in the session, he will end up no worse than 21st.

Positions 25–34 are set via a last chance qualifying race, which is a 12 to 15 lap race on the same day as qualifying. The race will take the top 10 finishing positions and grid them at the back of the field. If there are still more entrants, two final spots will be award-ed to 98 championship contenders based on points.

The fields are usually limited to 36 starters, although the series likes to stay at 32 if possible. By the time all the serious races qualify the field is usually set at 32, since if there are no points leaders not qual-ified, positions 21 to 24 will be open to the top ten finishers of the last chance race. The field is usually 32 cars.

The events themselves are usually held in two days, with qualifying and the last chance race on Saturday, and racing on Sunday. At the one day events, the cars will show up in the morning, practice at 9 A.M., qualify at 11 A.M., and get the green at 1 P.M.

One of the most unique parts of an ASA race is the Autograph Session at the beginning of a few select races. Instituted in 1994, the auto-graph sessions were created to give fans a bet-ter look at their favorite ASA drivers.

ASA fans are given the opportunity to walk onto the starting grid an hour before the race begins and talk with their favorite drivers, who are standing next to their cars, just waiting and willing to talk with whomever walks up. They are available for autographs, photos or just plain chitchat. Most fans never get a chance to meet the drivers; nor do they ever have a chance to go down to the starting line prior to the race, where the energy and tension of the event is indescribable. With the ASA you can do both at the same time. You may not be talk-ing with someone as famous as Bill Elliott

An ASA on-track autograph session. This is one of the few places fans can walk down on the starting line just prior to a race.

Points are similar to Winston Cup, so finishing the race is important. ASA drivers also receive points for the position on the grid, not just for pole, so qualifying is pretty intense as a result.

or Dale Earnhardt, but given the series' popularity and the fact that so many Winston Cup drivers have come from here, you may just catch them before they become famous.

Points System

Points are very similar to the NASCAR Winston Cup points system. A driver earns 175 points for a win, 170 for second, and so on, losing five points at a time until 11th place, where the incremental drop is four points at a time to 20th, then three points through 30th spot, and two points through 40th position. Also like NASCAR racing, ASA gives five points to a driver who leads at least one lap, and five points to the driver leading the most laps.

Additionally, ASA drivers are awarded points for appearing at the track, regardless of whether they qualify or race. They are allotted 10 points for one-mile or shorter racetracks, and 15 points for tracks longer than a mile. They also receive 10 points for showing up with a car that meets all the requirements of competition (i.e., having the right decals on the car) and meeting the required standards of competition (in other words, having the right patches on the driver's suit and being on the grid on time).

ASA drivers also receive points for qualifying. Unlike NASCAR, an ASA driver will receive points for his position on the grid. If he qualifies first, he receives five points, second, four, and so on back to fifth qualifying position, which pays one point.

ASA currently races at Daytona, Lowe's Motor Speedway, Michigan Speedway, Pocono Speedway, Toledo Speedway, Kentucky Speedway, Berlin Speedway and Winchester Speedway, among others. Check previous track listings as needed.

THE WORLD OF OUTLAWS

11

The World of Outlaws (WoO), the national championship sprint car series, will be the focus of this chapter. Although WoO is just one of many sprint car series across the U.S., we will only feature this one, primarily due to space contraints, and because it is the most popular. What follows is really a primer on the sport of sprint car racing, with the World of Outlaws as the premium example.

The series is named as it is for the reputation the drivers have (perhaps stretched a little for promotional purposes) as unfair participants. The series has nearly 72 events a year across the U.S, so these guys are rarely home. Many of the tracks are routine, small Saturday-night race tracks, except when the Outlaws come to town. The purse offered is usually the highest the track will see all year, and, even though anyone with a WoO-legal sprint car can compete, as many locals do, it is usually the series' regulars that "grab the money and run, " robbing the locals of a chance at the biggest purse of the year. Thus, the term "outlaws." A typical event will draw 40 to 50 cars to compete for the 24 starting spots in the A-Main, the feature race of the evening.

Outlaw racing is sprint car racing in its highest form. A WoO car is purebred for its style of competition. It has a short wheelbase, open-wheeled, open-cockpit, front-

WoO racing is all about getting sideways, and frequently, upside-down.

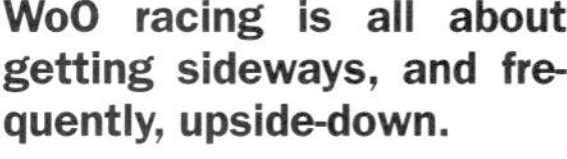

A typical Saturday night at an Outlaws track. The transporters are lit up, the paddock is busy and buzzing with the sounds of portable generators and the best seats are up on top.

Not the most glamorous of paddocks, Outlaw teams do their work in the dirt while waiting for the next heat. Note the difference in wheel sizes on this car. This extreme example of stagger is specific to sprint cars.

The master, Steve Kinser, passes down low. Kinser will go down as the greatest sprint car driver of modern times. Photo courtesy World of Outlaws/Ken Simon.

engine, rear-drive and is V8-powered. The car looks like a completely modern race car and an old wind-up toy at the same time. It appears to be a makeshift dune buggy, but then has aerodynamic wings and spoilers that seem as large as the car itself. Funny looking as they are, these cars are exceptionally powerful and fast, and a handful to drive.

World of Outlaws cars always drive on dirt, unlike other sprint car series. Mario Andretti, A.J. Foyt and Bobby and Al Unser drove sprint cars on their way to IndyCars. The driving is tough, the competition is tough, the cars are primitive, and if you could dominate in sprint cars you could race anything. And these men did, winning in everything from NASCAR and Indianapolis to Le Mans and Monza.

But back when Andretti, Unser and Foyt were racing sprint cars, the only sanctioning body was USAC, but USAC races paid mostly in prestige—the purses were quite small. A championship wasn't worth much if nobody wanted to pay for it. The World of Outlaws changed that in 1978 when it became the first national sprint car championship with an eye on the cash. The biggest purse is the Knoxville Nationals—which existed prior to the WoO's formation—

Good view of opposite lock. World of Outlaws cars are rarely pointed in the direction they are headed, but the drivers know what they are doing. The sprint car driving technique is to powerslide through corners. This is an excellent example. Photo courtesy World of Outlaws/Jeff Jones.

which pays an incredible $605,000 for the four-day show. But the smallest purse allowed by the series is $40,000 for a one-day event; $75,000 for a two-day race; and $115,000 for a three-day event (Knoxville is the only four-day race on the tour). Of that, the minimum for a win is $7,000 (for a one-day race).

RACES

Sprint car races are fast-paced and last a short time and almost always are held at night. They also compete, generally, on short tracks when the premium is to put the power down to the dirt as efficiently as possible over a short distance.

A sprint car race is set up in stages or heats, then there are features. You'll typically have several races leading up to the featured event, which is called the "A Main" or the "A Main Feature." It is typically the last event in the evening and pits the best drivers from all the heat races against one another for the big bucks. The day of the week can vary, but the fairly consistent fact is that it is night racing. There are usually one or two day races per year, but that's about it.

A typical race evening works like this: Practice and qualifying are held in the early evening—on the same day as the race. Qualification laps are done in two-lap intervals, with each car being timed, and the fastest of the two laps being recorded. The drivers are then pitted against each other in heat races.

Race organizers try to separate the top drivers into different heats so they all have a good chance of making it to the final feature. There are usually four heats. The winners of the heat races—four to five per heat (four if there are five heats; five if there are four heats, for a total of 20 cars)—move on to the A-Main. 24 cars are allowed into the A-Main. But wait a second, four times five equals 20, not 24. So there is another way into the A-Main. More about that in a second.

Prior to the A-main, The Channellock Dash is held. The Dash is set up for the eight fastest qualifiers. The third and fourth quickest in each heat will likely not make it to the Dash, but the two fastest in each heat—or

the eight fastest altogether—will take a run at each other in a five to seven lap shootout. The final finishing is where the first eight in the grid will start in the A-Main.

But before the grid is set for the A-Main, The Channellock Dash inverts the start for the first six drivers. So the driver who qualified first is sixth, the driver who was sixth is first, but seventh and eighth are the same as they qualified. The heat races are generally 8 to 10 laps.

If a driver wasn't able to qualify in the other heats, they have a chance in the B Main race. This is usually a four-lap race with the first four finishers going on to the A-Main and race against the big boys.

The actual A-Main feature is usually 40 laps, but that depends on the track. A third-mile oval will be 40 laps; a track less than a third but not more than a half is usually 30 laps and a track a half-mile or more is usually 25 laps.

That's how the races work if they are one-day shows. But the series races more than just one-day shows. For a two-day show, there would be more heats, which would in the case of a multi-day race, be called "Prelims." Frequently, the field will simply be split so there are essentially two different races taking place at the same racetrack.

The races are traditional dirt track, running counterclockwise. There are pits in the middle of most tracks, but frequently they are not used to the same extent as in other types of racing. Pits are not usually marked by sophisticated banners or stenciling, and in most cases pits are in the center of the track. Because the fans still need to see across the tracks, the pits are often cleared of vehicles and most people. Since the races are short, there isn't going to be a lot of stopping during the race anyway. Spares are used only if there is an opportunity to fix something during a race should it be stopped for some reason.

That brings up another point: based on the video clips on TV lately, you'd figure sprint cars flip over every few laps, or at least once a race. That isn't true. Yes, they flip over more frequently than a Busch car, but they certainly don't expect to do it every race. If that happens during a race it becomes an automatic red-flag situation and all racing stops. If there are crashes or spins, the yellow comes out just as it would at any other oval track race and the cars slow and proceed with caution until the debris or car is removed. Then racing commences again.

Sammy Swindell takes the outside line. Swindell has been involved since the series' inception. Photo courtesy World of Outlaws/Owen and Lynne Richards.

A typical sprint car puts out 750 horsepower but only weighs 1,200 pounds, so you can imagine what a handful these cars are to drive.

Points

An Outlaw driver accumulates points throughout the season to rank in the standings at the end of a full season. But generally only about 20 drivers will enter every race in order to win the championship. The average title-winning driver can amass as many as 10,000 to 11,000 points. They are based on the following finishes: 40 points for a win in a heat or prelim, dropping one point down to final finisher. The A-Main wins are worth 150 points, with second spot getting 146, third receives 143, then the intervals drop in two-point increments. The driver leading the most laps in the A-Main gets four points, so the most possible in the A-Main is 154 points. The World of Outlaws Championship has a points fund of $750,000, and $150,000 of that goes to the champion.

THE CARS

World of Outlaws cars, as mentioned earlier are very specialized race cars. They are set up to race not just on ovals but on dirt ovals. They therefore have special components that allow them to do both things well (race on dirt and around in circles).

First, the specifications of a World of Outlaws car is as follows:

Engine: 410 cubic inches
Horsepower: 750 horsepower
Speed: up to 160 m.p.h.
Transmission: in/out direct drive with quick-change rear end
Lubrication: dry sump oil system
Fuel: methanol
Fuel system: fuel injection
Wheelbase: 89 inches
Weight: 1,200 pounds
Chassis: light chrome-moly frame
Suspension: full torsion bar
Tires: most World of Outlaws sprinters race on Goodyear tires
Wheels: chrome
Steering system: power steering
Brakes: disc brakes

Probably the first thing you'll notice about these sprint cars is the huge wing. The wing is designed to produce downforce at the direction the car travels into the corner—namely sideways. Mounted on each side of the main center wing, left and right side as twin vertical parts of the wing, are called sideboards. They only work as the car turns, provided the car is turning correctly, with the wheels cocked in full-lock and the car sliding through the corner.

Most of the pictures you'll see of a World of Outlaws car are with the car going one direction and the front wheels going the opposite direction. That's the way they drive, in full opposite lock in almost every turn. To go around a left turn, you aim the steering wheel to the right. Sounds logical, doesn't it?

They essentially give lateral stability and push the car toward the inside of the track, while the centrifugal forces are pushing the car to the outside. The huge surface that is perpendicular to the track keeps the car pushed down toward the track itself, acting just like any wing on any other race car.

Wings have another purpose as well: they add as a safety device of sorts. Sprint cars, with all their power, are prone to flipping over. A car without a wing on top will tend to roll over far more violently than one with a wing. The wing tends to slow the rotation and thereby makes the rollover much less hazardous. The second thing it does is it adds another layer of metal to crush in an impact. Modern race car designers use things like carbon fiber and other composites that will remain stiff until an impact, when they fail totally, adding a type of crush zone. Outlaws cars do not have such zones.

They are safe, with stiff roll cages surrounding the driver, but in an extreme impact there is little to cushion the driver in the impact. The crushable wing structures allow some give in an extreme impact.

Finally, the wings sure do allow a great surface to paint sponsor's names on.

Donuts

Since the cars have no actual transmission, they also have no clutch. Since they have no clutch they have an obvious problem with starting and idling. The cars won't do either task without some help. To start a sprint car, one needs a push. So at the beginning of each race, you'll see 24 push trucks pushing their drivers off to get them fired up. The car's in gear, the truck pushes it along, and compression fires it up. Off it goes, ready to race.

When sprint cars get in trouble on the track, for instance when they get into a corner too deep and start to spin, they have to do some extreme driving to keep going. In most series, the rule is "in a spin, both feet in," meaning put your feet on the brake and the clutch, allowing the car to stop without stalling.

Not so in sprint cars. Again, there is no clutch nor onboard starter. But they still have to keep the car running. How do they

The brakes on a sprint car are inboard, a single disc in the rear. Sprint cars don't do a lot of braking anyway. They just pretty much feather the throttle and power-slide through the turns. If someone gets in the way, oh well.

do that? The best way is to keep their foot on the throttle and keep the steering wheel cranked over. So the end result of this is that you'll see cars doing donuts all over the place in the attempt to stay in the race.

The driver slides out, knows he's going to back into the wall, so he cranks the steering wheel into the spin and plants his foot. The revs come up, the wheels spin and the car loses more traction, eventually spinning even worse than before—sometimes spinning the wrong direction so the driver must figure out a way to get it going toward the direction of traffic. As one could imagine, this frequently causes more problems with oncoming traffic. But that's how sprint car racing works, and that's part of the fun.

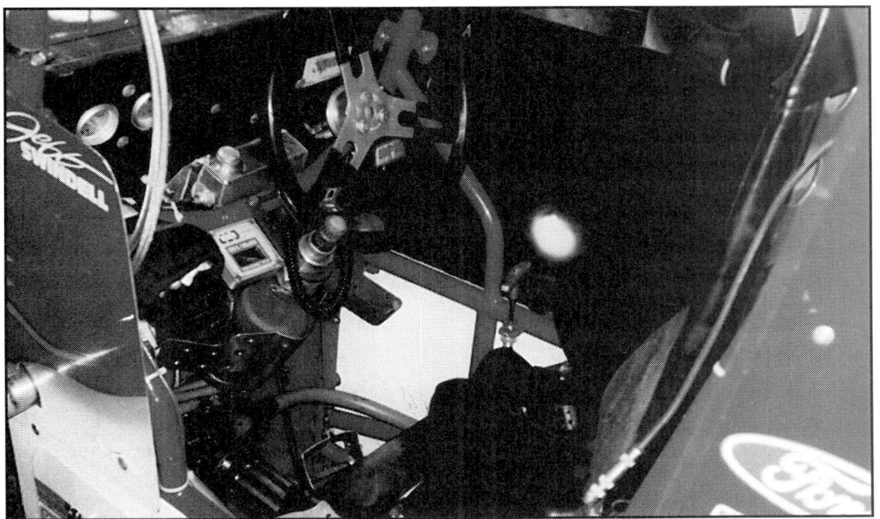

The cockpit of a sprint car is tight and spartan, and there are no fancy LED readouts and such.

12

Also, see previous listings for: Tri-City Speedway, Eagle Raceway, Las Vegas Motor Speedway, I-80 Speedway, and Lebanon Valley.

Battleground Speedway

Houston/Highlands, TX
Office: P.O. Box 330034,
Houston, TX 77233-0034
PH: (800) R-A-C-E-I-N-G
Office: (713) 946-7223
FAX: (713) 747-6745
Location/Directions: east, Texas, East of Houston, in Highlands. From I-10 East, take the Highland exit #787, then head north approximately four miles.
Circuit: 3/8-mile, high-banked clay oval/1/8-mile dirt oval.
Major races: World of Outlaws Series.

Battleground's regular show is held on Saturday nights with Street Stocks, Stock Cars, Thunder Bomber, Sprints, and occasional UMP Modifieds. SUPR Late Models. The short track runs Dwarfs, Turfs, Mini-Dwarfs and Midgets. The biggest show of the year is when the Outlaws come through town, but there are also IMCA Sprints and IMCA Modifieds.

Racing runs March through October in the humidity of East Texas—which is hot and opressive. The stands hold 5,000, and 3,317 are reserved seats, with grandstands in pits that have another 1,700 non-reserved seats. The track has plans on adding 2,000 more seats. You can stay at the Fairfield Inn, located at Mercury and I-10 on the north side of the Freeway, and the track suggests dining at Ye Olde Highlands Inn in Highlands.

Beaver Dam Raceway

7086 N. Raceway Rd.
Beaver Dam, WI 53916
PH: (920) 887-1600
Location/Directions: in Beaver Dam, WI, on SR 33. From Milwaukee, take I-94 west to Hwy. 26 to Hwy. 33, then west into Beaver Dam, and past the Dodge County Fairgrounds approximately two miles to Raceway Rd.
Circuit: 1/3-mile, high-banked clay oval.
Major races: World of Outlaws Series.

Home of the Saturday Night Thunder and the United Sprintcar Association, Beaver Dam Raceway's regular show is a Saturday night (what else?) Late Model series but hosts several outings of the Hav-A-Tampa Late Models, as well as a USAC National Midgets tour stop. But the biggest attraction is the annual WoO race. Your best bet is to stay in Beaver Dam, so call the track for more information.

Bloomington Speedway

351 Church Ln.
Bloomington, IN 47401
Office: 5185 Fairfax Road
P.O. Box 239
Clear Creek, In 47426
PH: (Track) (812) 824-7400
(Office) (812) 824-7862
http://www.turn2.com/bloomingtonspeedway/
Location/Directions: central Indiana, approximately 35 miles south of Indianapolis, and south of Bloomington. From Indianapolis, take State Route 37 to Bloomington and Dillman Rd., then proceed a quarter mile east, then north a mile-and-a-half, then a quarter-of-a-mile east on Church to the track.
Circuit: 1/4-mile clay oval; semi-banked.
Major races: World of Outlaws.

Bloomington Speedway doesn't host a weekly dirt show. And there are only a half dozen or so races at the circuit per year. But the few races run are set in place with fat purses, and are quality events—like the WoO show. Bloomington Speedway has been in existence since 1923.

Bloomington has plenty of rooms, and finding one is not a problem—even when arriving late. Camping is permitted at the track, but there are no hookups. There is no reserved or advanced seating, but you can set up lawn chairs on the grass.

Calistoga Speedway

P.O. Box 344
Calistoga, CA 94515
PH: (707) 942-5111
Location/Directions: in Northern California's Napa Valley, 70 miles north of San Francisco. From San Francisco, take U.S. Highway 101 to Highway 37 west. From 37, head north on 29 toward Napa, to Fair Way and the Napa County Fairgrounds, where the track is located.
Circuit: 1/2-mile clay oval; semi-banked.
Major races: World of Outlaws Sprint Car Championship Shootout.

Calistoga Fairgrounds Speedway is located in scenic Napa Valley, and hosts only a handful of events each year —but all are excellent shows. Northern Auto Racing Club racing dominates the action when the World of Outlaws is not in town. Local racers are talented, but it's the beautiful, warm Napa Valley Summer nights that make the visit worthwhile.

Do some wine tasting up the road in St. Helena or Sonoma, or stop in following a day at Sears Point (about 20 minutes away) for a quality dirt track show. Rooms are available in either Napa or Vallejo.

Cedar Lake Speedway

Somerset, WI
PH: (715) 248-7119
Office: (715) 246-5631
www.racingonline.com/cedarlake
Location/Directions: western Wisconsin, 60 miles east of Minneapolis, MN. From Minneapolis, take Interstate I-94 to State Route 65 to SR 64. From SR 64, go four miles east to County Route C to Country Route CC in Somerset, then two miles west to the track.
Circuit: 1/2-mile clay oval; high-banked.
Major races: World of Outlaws Sprint Car Championship Shootout.

Cedar Lake Speedway's annual World of Outlaws race regularly packs in upward of 8,500 people, and the quiet farms surrounding the speedway come alive with a different kind of horsepower. In addition, Cedar lake regularly hosts WISSOTA Late Models, WISSOTA Sprints, WISSOTA Modifieds and WISSOTA Super Stocks, and claims to be the only facility in the USA to host all four top WISSOTA classes on a weekly basis. There are not only bleachers in the facility, but spectators can sit in their cars in tiered parking areas and watch racing from there as well.

The best place to find rooms is in nearby Richmond, or you can camp by the side of the track, or in the parking lot under the shade trees. There is running water and bathrooms, but no hookups for RVs are available.

Devil's Bowl Speedway

1711 Lawson Rd.
Mesquite, TX 75181
PH: (972) 222-2421
Office: (972) 222-2818
Location/Directions: Fifteen minutes east of Dallas off 635. Take 635 East to Terrell Exit (Hwy. 80) to Lawson Rd., then three miles to the track.
Circuit: .25-mile dirt oval.
Major races: World of Outlaws.

Devil's Bowl Speedway hosts a regular Saturday night program with Late Models and Street Stocks, as well as regular Sprint and USA Modified schedule. It has several special shows throughout the year, with the Outlaws being the major show.

Devil's Bowl sits right across the street from a catfish farm, so you can go buy or fish during the day and watch racing during the evening . . . smelling a little bit of fish perhaps. Or a few yards down is a gun range. Folks stay in Dallas for the bigger shows, or there's a La Quinta and a Holiday Inn in Garland, closer to the track.

Eldora Speedway

Office: 13929 State Route 118
New Weston, OH 45348
PH: (937) 338-3850
www.hotlaps.com
Location/Directions: southeastern Ohio, 60 miles northwest of Dayton, and 140 miles north of Cincinnati, in Rossburg. From Cincinnati, take I-75 through Dayton to U.S. 36 West to Greenville. From Greenville take State Route 118 North ten miles to Rossburg. The track is two-and-a-half miles north of Rossburg on SR 118.
Circuit: 1/2-mile clay oval, high-banked.
Major races: World of Outlaws Sprint Car Championship Shootout, USAC Sprint Cars, Midgets, and Silver Crown Championships.

Eldora Speedway is one of the most impressive dirt tracks in the county, and is certainly the best in Ohio. The farm area around it belies its stature, as the little track has purses of $50,000 for a King's Royal win. It hosts all sides of the USAC Championships series, as well as a couple of WoO shows. Another big event here is the World's 100 for Sprint cars, which attracts the WoO drivers. But the Ohio Speedweek—which is a seven-race series held at seven different tracks, and sanctioned by the All-Star Circuit of Champions—is the most popular of the Eldora season. The seven include: Millstream Speedway; Buckeye; Speedway 7; Attica; Sharon Speedway; Fremont Speedway; and concluding at Eldora Speedway.

Fourteen miles north of Eldora is Greenville, and most stay there for a race. Other places to stay include Versailles, Salina, Dayton, Sydney, and Sepique. The track recommends the Holiday Inn in Wapakoneta, OH, at (439) 738-8181.

Hagerstown Speedway

15112 National Pike, Rte 40
Hagerstown, MD
Office: P.O. Box 712
McConnellsburg, PA 17233
PH: (301) 582-0640
FAX: (301) 582-3618
www.hagerstownspeedway.com
Location/Directions: northwestern Maryland, approximately 70 miles from Washington, DC, six miles west of Hagerstown. From Washington, DC, take I-70 west to Huyett's exit, then Route 40 west, and four miles to the track.
Circuit: 1/2-mile clay oval, semi-banked.
Major races: World of Outlaws Sprint Car Championship Shootout.

Amid rolling greenery and the scenic forests of western Maryland, Hagerstown Speedway looms like a hilltop citadel. The track is enclosed on all but one side by woods (the side not bounded by trees is dominated by grandstands) making it a unique place to watch a dirt race. It is one of the best dirt tracks in the country, hosting both motorcycles and cars (WoO, sprinters, ARCA, and Late Model stockers).

Track owner Frank Plessinger was the first in the country to offer a $50,000 prize for a dirt track win. Later he created a speedweek worth $200,000. Hagerstown is constantly being updated, and its modernization—as well as its large prize money—make it a regular favorite on television.

The track also holds a handful of interesting races you won't see elsewhere—like big-rig truck racing on the dirt. The track has been a longtime host of World Of Outlaws, and occasionally running AMA Grand National events. Hagerstown has a handful of rooms, and you should have no problem there, or try Fredrerick, which is 28 miles away. The Host Hotel Ramada can be found at (301) 733-5100, the Days Inn at (800) 422-2754, Econo-Lodge (301) 791-3560, Super 8 (301) 739-5800, Quality Inn (301) 733-2700, Howard Johnson (800) 732-0906, Venice Inn (800) 283-6423, Four Points Hotel (800) 325-3553. Make sure to ask for the Speedway Discount.

Huset's Speedway

Sioux Falls, SD
Office: P.O. Box 130
Brandon, SD 57005
PH: (605) 582-3536
(605) 582-3819
http://www.husets-speedway.com/
Location/Directions: eastern South Dakota, east of Sioux Falls. Take I-90 East to Exit 406, then head south three miles on State Route 11 to the track.
Circuit: 3/8-mile clay oval; high-banked.
Major races: World of Outlaws Sprint Car Championship Shootout.

Huset's Speedway is located in the arid, high desert of South Dakota, and is one of the biggest attractions of the immediate area. The WoO show is the biggest of the year, generally filling the 4,500-seat facility as the open-wheeled cars come through. There are plenty of rooms in Sioux Falls, and more information regarding accommodations can be found by calling the Sioux Falls Convention and Visitors Bureau at (605) 336-1620.

I-55 Speedway

P.O Box 614
Pevely, MO 63070
PH: (636) 479-3219
Location/Directions: eastern Missouri, thirty miles from St. Louis. From St. Louis, take I-55 south past Pevely to Exit 178.
Circuit: 1/3-mile clay oval, high-banked.
Major races: World of Outlaws Sprint Car Championship Shootout.

I-55 Speedway sits between two hills in the midst of lots of greenery, and would be secluded, except it's right off the interstate. The track runs mostly Late Model stocks on Saturday nights, but it holds one round of the WoO Sprint car championships.

The 6,500-seat facility has camping for those who wish to follow the Outlaws, or you can stay in Festus, which is two miles south of the track.

Illinois State Fairgrounds Speedway

2000 E. Cornell
Springfield, IL 62703
PH: (217) 753-8866
Tickets: (217) 782-1979
Location/Directions: central Illinois, north of downtown Springfield, off Business Route 66.
Circuit: 1-mile clay oval.
Major races: AMA Grand National Championship Camel Pro Series, World of Outlaws Sprint Car Championship, USAC Silver Crown and Midget Championships.

Illinois State Fairgrounds Speedway is one of the few dirt tracks to host the big three dirt shows, with WoO, AMA, and USAC shows all running at least once during the season. The dirt oval seats 14,000, and the one-mile facility is one of the best in the country.

As with most fairgrounds circuits, parking in the wrong place will give you a three-mile hike—and Springfield's fair is no different. Gate seven, off Taintor Rd. is the best way to get to the circuit, and will get you in and out fast. The tunnel to the infield can be reached by using gate six—also off Taintor Rd.

For a concise list of hotels in the area—including prices—call the Springfield Convention and Visitor's Bureau at (800) 356-7900 (from Ill.) or (800) 545-7300 (elsewhere).

King's Speedway

801 South 10th Ave.
Hanford, CA 93230
Office: P.O. Box 14
Hanford, CA 93232
PH: (559) 582-3478
Location/Directions: central California, mid–Central Valley, roughly between Fresno and Bakersfield, approximately 140 miles north of Los Angeles. From Bakersfield, take State Route 99 to 198 west to Hanford and 10th Av. exit, following 10th Ave. one mile to the King's County Fairgrounds and the speedway.
Circuit: 1/3-mile clay oval; slightly banked.
Major races: World of Outlaws Sprint Car Championship Shootout.

Track officials just call it "central valley flat," meaning grapes and cotton may be more at home in the valley heat than race cars. Average summer days range from 100 to 105 degrees at Hanford's Kings Speedway—but of course, it's considered a dry heat.

Some of the best California sprint car drivers compete here often, including Chuck Miller and Jimmy Sills, who both race cars owned by gentlemen who live in Hanford. The facility seats 4,300, and when WoO comes to town it occasionally fills to 5,000. Stay in downtown Hanford, or at the Holiday Inn in Visalia 30 miles from Hanford—which is the headquarters for WoO when they're in town. For more hotel information call the track.

Knoxville Raceway

Marion County Fair
P.O. Box 347
1000 N. Lincoln
Knoxville, IA 50318
PH: (515) 842-5431
(515) 842-3220
FAX: (515) 842-2899
http://www.knoxvilleraceway.com/
Location/Directions: central Iowa, approximately 30 miles from Des Moines, on State Route 14 in the Marion County Fairgrounds.
Circuit: 1/2-mile clay oval; semi-banked.
Major races: World of Outlaws Sprint Car Championship Shootout.

Knoxville has a full calendar of events, with racing usually occurring four days a week, and with everything from motorcycling to sprint cars racing here. The season starts in April and features racing every Saturday through August. The 24,000-seat facility often has televised races, and most top racers have been on Knoxville's banks at one time in their career. This is a premier sprint car oval—and is touted by some experts as absolutely the best in the country.

Now that California's Ascot Park has closed, Knoxville certainly becomes the best dirt facility west of the Mississippi—and even in their heyday, Ascot officials conceded that position to Knoxville.

While you're in Knoxville, check out the National Sprint Car Hall of Fame and Museum, located right next to the raceway. For more information on the museum, call (800) 874-4488, or just stop by. The area gets crowded when the bigger shows come through, and will likely be packed for the Knoxville Sprint Car Nationals, usually in August. The other big event is the Iowa Ethanol Classic over the July 4 weekend.

There should be plenty of rooms even if you have to travel as far as Des Moines. Knoxville has several hotels, but if booked try: Newton, which has seven hotels; Pella, which has three inns; Chariston, with three; Oskaloosa's five lodgings are conveniently located; and there is at least one hotel each in Indianola, Prairie City, and Albia.

Lernerville Speedway

Office: 278 N. Pike Rd.
Sarver, PA 16055
PH: (724) 353-1511
(724) 353-1714
http://www.lernerville.com/
Location/Directions: western Pennsylvania, 20 miles north of Pittsburgh. From Pittsburgh, take I-79 to State Route 68 north, then take SR 356 south 11 miles to the track.
Circuit: 1/2-mile clay oval; semi-banked.
Major races: World of Outlaws Sprint Car Championship Shootout.

Lernerville Speedway officials boast of being a more successful than both the Pittsburgh Pirates and the Pittsburgh Penguins on a per-night basis. With five divisions of racing weekly, the oval has plenty of variation—and a lot of activity.

World of Outlaws headline the season, but the 9,000 seat grandstands usually fill close to capacity every week—making the purses lucrative, and the driver rosters full of top hotshots.

Of the 9,000 seats, the track boasts of some 4,500 reserved, a non-alcoholic section, corporate and hospitality boxes, handicapped facilities, and camping at track. There are no hookups. The outskirts of Pittsburg also has plenty of rooms, with several within a few minutes of the track.

Lincoln Speedway

New Oxford, PA
Office: 765 Carlisle
Hanover, PA 17331
PH: (717) 624-2755
(717) 697-1321
www.lincolnspeedway.com
Location/Directions: southern Pennsylvania, 20 miles south of Baltimore, in New Oxford, PA. From Baltimore, take MD State Route 30 to SR 94 south to Race Track Rd., then left just over a mile.
Circuit: 3/8-mile oval; semi-banked.
Major races: World of Outlaws Sprint Car Championship Shootout.

Lincoln Speedway is located in eastern Pennsylvania farmland in an open field. The track is a D-shaped oval, which makes for an interesting show, while playing havoc on race setup—especially when WoO racing comes to town. The regular show is a Saturday racing schedule with Super Sprints and Thunder Cars.

The track is actually in New Oxford, where there are rooms. Also try Hanover.

Oklahoma Fair Speedway

Office: P.O. Box 74943
Oklahoma City, OK 73147
PH: (405) 948-6796
(405) 948-6700
Fax: (405) 948-6828
www.oklafair.org/speed.html
Location/Directions: central Oklahoma, off I-40 on May Ave., a half-mile north of city center. From I-35 north or south, exit I-40 west, proceeding to May Ave. exit. Then go north a half-mile to the speedway.
Circuit: 1/2-mile clay oval; semi-banked; 1/4r-mile clay.
Major races: World of Outlaws Sprint Car Championship Shootout, Super Sprints, Pro Stocks, Modifieds and Factory Stocks.

Oklahoma State Fair Speedway's 9,000-seat grandstands are filled for the two WoO races per year. The track also holds an AMA Supercross and a NCRA Sprint Car show—although Friday night's four-division racing is the staple, with three of the four racing every week.

The track, built in 1954 and hosting regular Friday night racing in the early '60's has become one of the best tracks in the southwest. Grandstand are covered and the track surface, a slightly banked clay oval has seen speeds up to 120 mph. Lodging is available at I-40 and Meridian area, where there are several choices of motels.

Orange County Fair Speedway

239 Wisner Ave.
Middletown, NY 10940
PH: (914) 342-2573
Office: (315) 834-6606
http://www.orangecountyspeedway.com
Location/Directions: southern New York State, approximately 50 miles northwest of New York City. From New York City, take Palidades Parkway north to State Route 6, and west through Harriman State Park, then north on SR 17 to Middletown. Take Exit 120, and head west on SR 211, turning southwest on local 96 to the track, which is a half-mile from the junction of SR 211 and 96.
Circuit: 5/8-mile clay oval; semi-banked.
Major races: World of Outlaws Sprint Car Championship Shootout.

Orange County Fair Speedway, at the Orange County Fairgrounds, is located just outside Middletown, 55 miles from NYC. The track is set in a commercial area, surrounded by shopping centers, housing developments, and light industry.

Racing occurs Saturday nights from April to October, and is sanctioned and promoted by the successful eastern DIRT organization. The biggest race of the season, outside the World of Outlaws race, is the Eastern States 200 in October. The track office will give you more information on where to stay in the area, or call the New York Division of Tourism office at (800) 225-5697.

Perris Auto Speedway

Lake Perris, CA
Office: 18700 Lake Perris Dr.
Perris, CA 92571
PH: (909) 943-7181
http://www.perrisautospeedway.com/
Location/Directions: in southern California, at the Lake Perris Fairgrounds in Perris, California, on the Ramona Expressway, two miles east of the 215 freeway.
Circuit: 1/2-mile clay oval; semi-banked (also a 1/4-mile clay oval).
Major races: World of Outlaws Series.

PAS calls itself the "cleanest, well kept (sic) dirt track in the U.S.," which, according to track lore, is a condition of the racing surface. The track is made of imported clay, which is said to be almost dust-less and has a great deal of adhesion.

The major race here is the World of Outlaws, which fills the place to capacity. Race-watching can be done from the stands, which are built to hold some 4,500 fans, and the back straight is raised so anyone in the stands can see the entire racing surface. Call the track for information on accommodations and dining.

Red River Valley Speedway

Office: Route 2
East Grand Forks, MN 56721
PH: (office) (218) 773-2120
Track: (701) 282-2200
Ticket info: (218) 773-9221
Location/Directions: eastern North Dakota, just west of Fargo. From Fargo take I-94 to Exit 85, then a quarter-mile east on SR 10 to the track.
Circuit: 1/2-mile clay oval; high-banked.
Major races: World of Outlaws Sprint Car Championship Shootout.

Red River Valley Speedway, in the Red River Valley Fairgrounds, sits in the western city limits of Fargo. Set in a nice, rural, open, grassy area, with sparse buildings, the track hosts some terrific racing. The three-decades-old facility seats 6,000 people, and fills up for the Outlaws, which is the speedway's biggest event of the season. There is camping at the track, or Fargo has plenty of rooms

Rolling Wheels Speedway

Elbridge, NY 13060
Mailing: 278 North Pike Rd.
Sarver, PA 16055-9735
PH: (315) 689-7809
Office: (716) 334-5959
www.dirtmotorsports.com
Location/Directions: central New York State, eight miles from Syracuse, 11 miles southeast of Butler on SR 356. From Syracuse, take I-90 west to State Route 31C to Elbridge.
Circuit: 1/2-mile clay oval; semi-banked.
Major races: World of Outlaws Sprint Car Championship Shootout.

Rolling Wheels Speedway sits in a forested area eight miles from Syracuse, in Elbridge, off Highways 5 and 20. WoO is the biggest show of the season. There are only 13 races a year here, but most races are at least 50-lappers. The regular show is held on Friday nights. The most frequently run classes are Street Stock, Sportsman, and Modifieds.

Rooms are available in Syracuse.

Route 66 Speedway

Joliet, IL
PH: (815) 722-5500
http://www.rt66raceway.com/
Location/Directions: from Chicago, take I-55 South to I-80, exiting at Exit 132A, heading south on Route 53 South three miles to the track.
Circuit: 1/2-mile clay oval; 3/8-mile paved oval.
Major races: World of Outlaws Championship, NASCAR Winston Racing Series

Route 66 Raceway is yet another illustration of America's growing interest in motorsport. The track was reconstructed from an older, less significant circuit between 1997 and 1998 at a cost of $24 million, and is now one of the newest Outlaws tracks in the series, as well as home to an annual NHRA drag race.

Sitting atop 240 acres of land at the intersection of Chicago St. and Route 53, the track is not just for motorsport, but also for concerts and other entertainment, boasting the ability to hold up to 60,000 spectators.

For Outlaws fans, the facility has 8,000 seats at the oval track, all with backrests. Rooms are easy enough to find in Chicago, or call the track for a list of closer accommodations.

Santa Maria Speedway

Office: P.O. Box 1270
Morro Bay, CA 93442
PH: (805) 922-2233
Office: (805) 466-4462
Location/Directions: southern California, between San Luis Obispo and Santa Barbara, approximately 110 miles from Los Angeles. Located in Santa Maria, at the Maricopa exit, then one-quarter mile to the track, which is located on Hutton Rd.
Circuit: 1/3-mile clay oval; high-banked.
Major races: World of Outlaws Sprint Car Championship Shootout, USAC Midgets.

Santa Maria Speedway is located 12 miles from the Pacific coast, one mile from Santa Maria—just past the Santa Maria river (dry). An half-hour north of San Luis Obispo, the track is a nice spot for a California getaway.

Built in 1964, the speedway is located under a coastal mesa, and is right at, or possibly below, sea level. Although water is a problem in the winter, it never floods in the summer months. During the summer the temperatures get up to about 100 degrees, and the clay has to be watered three times a week.

There are 1,500 permanent seats, but the hillsides can accommodate another 1,500 or so—so bring a blanket or lawn chair. Ramada Inn acts as headquarters when the Outlaws come to town; call the track for information on other hotels in the area.

Silver Dollar Speedway

(Office) 704 Vine Ave.
Roseville, CA 95825
Silver Dollar Fairgrounds
Fair St.
Chico, CA
PH: (916) 969-7484
Location/Directions: northern California, in the Northern Central Valley, approximately 100 miles north of Sacramento, and 170 miles northeast of San Francisco. From Sacramento, take State Route 99 North (which joins SR 70 and SR 149) through Marysville to Chico to Park Ave., heading west on Park Ave. one half-mile to the Chico Fairgrounds, and the racetrack.
Circuit: 1/4–mile clay oval; high-banked.
Major races: World of Outlaws Sprint Car Championship Shootout.

Silver Dollar Speedway is one of Northern California's few stops for the World of Outlaws tour. Those who miss the one day show at Calistoga generally make the drive north for a two or three day WoO show at Silver Dollar Raceway.

Although Chico isn't exactly the tourism capital of California, and even though the college's (Chico State University) 14,000 students has inspired hotel construction, you'll likely need to arrive early before an event to find a room (or book by phone).

Things are usually filled in Chico for WoO shows so you might consider staying in Oroville, Marysville, Paradise, or Orland. Camping is also an alternative here. The track can accommodate 144 motorhomes with complete hookups—and on occasion can be changed to accommodate as many as 500. Call the track office for details.

Southern Oregon Speedway

6900 Kershaw Rd
White City, OR
PH: (541) 772-6264
Location/Directions: located on the outskirts of White City, 15 minutes from downtown Medford, OR, at the Jackson County Sports Park. Take Hwy. 62 into White City, then right onto Hwy. 140 toward Klamath Falls, and right again on Kershaw Road to the speedway, a quarter mile up.
Circuit: 1/3-mile, high-banked clay oval.
Major races: World Of Outlaws.

Stock car racing is the staple of Southern Oregon Speedway, but the track's major race of the season is the World of Outlaws race in August, which is by far the biggest draw. Grandstand Capacity at the facility is 2,600, with an additional 2,400 spaces on a grassy knoll off turn one. There's a non-smoking and non-drinking section as well.

The track suggests the Reston Hotel (Home of "Rock and Rodeo"), at 2300 Crater Lake Highway Medford, OR 97504, (800) 779-7829; and ask about Race Fan Special Rate. If you have an RV, try Medford Oaks RV Park, at 7049 Hwy. 140, Eagle Point, OR 97524, (541) 826-5103. For dining, try one of four Pappy's Pizza Inns (one in Medford, one in Crater Lake and two in White City), or try Canton Dynasty for Chinese in Medford.

Tri- State Speedway

Rural Route 2
Haubstadt, IN 47639
PH: (812) 768-5995
Office: (812) 768-6025
Location/Directions: southwestern Indiana, approximately 145 miles from Indianapolis. From Indianapolis, take I-65 South to I-64 west to State Route 41, heading north—the track is on SR 41, three miles from the junction of I-64 and Highway 41.
Circuit: 1/4-mile clay oval; semi-banked.
Major races: World of Outlaws Sprint Car Championship Shootout, USAC Sprint cars.

Set in the flat, rural surroundings of western Indiana Tri-State Speedway's 5,000-seat facility hosts an Outlaw show—the biggest of the year—and usually fills the place to capacity. There is camping here, but there are no RV hookups. You can stay in Princeton, which is some 10 miles from the track, or Evansville, which is 15 miles away.

Tulsa Speedway

Office: P.O. Box 76
Hwy 75 North & 66th
Owasso, OK 74055
PH: (office) (918) 272-6120
Track: (918) 425-7551
Location/Directions: northeastern Oklahoma, on the outskirts of Tulsa. From I-75 north, take the 66th St. exit and head east to the track.
Circuit: 3/8-mile clay oval; high-banked.
Major races: World of Outlaws Sprint Car Championship Shootout.

Tulsa Speedway, located six-and-a-half miles north of downtown Tulsa, is hot and dry. Friday is factory stock night, with full-bodied racecars, while the open wheeled sprints run Saturday nights. The Outlaws race twice a year in this 4,500-seat facility.

Although the track is closer to downtown then to the Tulsa International Airport, which is just east of the track, the only motels downtown are the high-dollar business type. Try around the airport first.

West Plains Motor Speedway

US Hwy 63
West Plains, MO
PH: (417) 257-2112
http://www.westplains-speedway.com/
Location/Directions: located on U.S. Highway 63, six miles south of West Plains, MO.
Circuit: 3/8-mile clay oval; semi-banked.
Major races: World of Outlaws.

West Plains Motor Speedway is located on a 100-acre tract of land a couple of hours from the Ozarks, making it a very attractive place to watch racing, with high rise bleachers giving a great view of racing.

The regular Saturday night program is with IMCA Modifieds, Super Stocks, Hobby Stock cars and trucks, Cruisers and the top class at the speedway, the Super Late Models. But the biggest show is the World of Outlaws Sprint cars. There is also the "Show-Me 100," a Late Model event that offered a big paycheck to the winner and draws Late Model drivers from across the country.

A campground is located on the premises, complete with enclosed bathrooms and hot showers. Or a few rooms are available in West Plains.

Williams Grove Speedway

1 Speedway Dr.
Mechanicsburg, PA 17055-9514
PH: (717) 697-5000
Or: (717) 766-4778
FAX: (717) 795-7216
http://www.wmgrove.com/
Location/Directions: central Pennsylvania, four miles south of PA Turnpike. Take Route 15 South to first light (Lisburn road) turn right at the second stop sign. Track is a tenth-mile up.
Circuit: 1/2-mile clay oval; semi-banked.
Major races: World of Outlaws Sprint Car Championship Shootout, 410 Sprints, Second division 358 Sprints, USAC Midget Championships.

Williams Grove Speedway's 8,500 seat facility hosts a regular Friday show, which is headlined by 410 Super Sprints. The track also has a World of Outlaws race seven times a year and a USAC Midget race annually. In addition, the September Fram-Autolite National Open is one of the biggest races in the state—featuring invitational sprint car racing, and attracting some of the country's best drivers.

The green Pennsylvania farmlands racetrack is directly across the street from the Williamsport Amusement Park, and there are plenty of places to stay in the area. The best are in Mechanicsburg, or up the road in Carlisle. The track recommends the following: Days Inn (717) 766-3700, Amber Inn (717) 766-9006: Econo Lodge (717) 766-4728 or (717) 249-7775; Best Western (717) 766-0238: Embers Inn (717) 243-1717 and the Holiday Inn (717) 245-2400.

The track also recommends the following restaurants: Country Kitchen (located on Route 11 at the Camp Hill Mall), Bert Brothers (located on Route 15), Baker's (located on Route 15), and the Golden Corral (located on Route 11).

HANDBOOKS

Auto Electrical Handbook: 0-89586-238-7

Auto Upholstery & Interiors: 1-55788-265-7

Car Builder's Handbook: 1-55788-278-9

Chevy S-10/GMC S-15 Handbook: 1-55788-353-X

Powerglide Transmission Handbook:1-55788-355-6

Street Rodder's Handbook: 0-89586-369-3

Street Rodder's Chassis & Suspension Handbook: 1-55788-346-7

Turbo Hydramatic 350 Handbook: 0-89586-051-1

Welder's Handbook: 1-55788-264-9

BODYWORK & PAINTING

Automotive Detailing: 1-55788-288-6

Automotive Paint Handbook: 1-55788-291-6

Fiberglass & Composite Materials: 1-55788-239-8

Metal Fabricator's Handbook: 0-89586-870-9

Paint & Body Handbook: 1-55788-082-4

Sheet Metal Handbook: 0-89586-757-5

INDUCTION

Bosch Fuel Injection Systems: 1-55788-365-3

Holley 4150: 0-89586-047-3

Holley Carburetors, Manifolds & Fuel Injection: 1-55788-052-2

Rochester Carburetors: 0-89586-301-4

Turbochargers: 0-89586-135-6

Weber Carburetors: 0-89586-377-4

PERFORMANCE

Aerodynamics for Racing & Performance Cars: 1-55788-267-3

Baja Bugs & Buggies: 0-89586-186-0

Big-Block Chevy Performance: 1-55788-216-9

Big-Block Mopar Performance: 1-55788-302-5

Bracket Racing: 1-55788-266-5

Brake Systems: 1-55788-281-9

Camaro Performance: 1-55788-057-3

Chassis Engineering: 1-55788-055-7

Chevrolet Power: 1-55788-087-5

Chevy Trucks: 1-55788-340-8

Ford Windsor Small-Block Performance: 1-55788-323-8

Honda/Acura Performance: 1-55788-324-6

High Performance Hardware: 1-55788-304-1

How to Build Tri-Five Chevy Trucks ('55~–'57): 1-55788-285-1

How to Hot Rod Big-Block Chevys: 0-912656-04-2

How to Hot Rod Small-Block Chevys: 0-912656-06-9

How to Hot Rod Small-Block Mopar Engines: 0-89586-479-7

How to Hot Rod VW Engines: 0-912656-03-4

How to Make Your Car Handle: 0-912656-46-8

John Lingenfelter: Modifying Small-Block Chevy: 1-55788-238-X

Mustang 5.0 Projects: 1-55788-275-4

Mustang Performance (Engines, '79–'93): 1-55788-193-6

Mustang Performance 2 (Chassis, '79–'93): 1-55788-202-9

1001 High Performance Tech Tips: 1-55788-199-5

Performance Ignition Systems: 1-55788-306-8

Performance Wheels & Tires: 1-55788-286-X

PHR's Small-Block Chevy Performance Trends: 1-55788-334-3

Race Car Engineering & Mechanics: 1-55788-064-6

Small-Block Chevy Performance: 1-55788-253-3

Super Chevy's Nova Handbook: 1-55788-339-4

ENGINE REBUILDING

Engine Builder's Handbook: 1-55788-245-2

Rebuild Air-Cooled VW Engines: 0-89586-225-5

Rebuild Big-Block Chevy Engines: 0-89586-175-5

Rebuild Big-Block Ford Engines: 0-89586-070-8

Rebuild Big-Block Mopar Engines: 1-55788-190-1

Rebuild Ford V-8 Engines: 0-89586-036-8

Rebuild GenV/Gen VI Big-Block Chevy Engines: 1-55788-357-2

Rebuild Small-Block Chevy Engines: 1-55788-029-8

Rebuild Small-Block Ford Engines: 0-912656-89-1

Rebuild Small-Block Mopar Engines: 0-89586-128-3

RESTORATION, MAINTENANCE, REPAIR

Camaro Owner's Handbook ('67–'81): 1-55788-301-7

Camaro Restoration Handbook ('67–'81): 0-89586-375-8

Classic Car Restorer's Handbook: 1-55788-194-4

Mustang Restoration Handbook ('64 1/2–'70): 0-89586-402-9

Tri-Five Chevy Owner's Handbook ('55–'57): 1-55788-285-1

VW Beetle Restoration Handbook (1949–1967): 1-55788-342-4

GENERAL REFERENCE

A Fan's Guide to Circle Track Racing: 1-55788-351-3

Auto Math Handbook: 1-55788-020-4

Ford Total Performance, 1962-1970: 1-55788-327-0

Guide to GM Muscle Cars: 1-55788-003-4

Stock Cars!: 1-55788-308-4

MARINE

Big-Block Chevy Marine Performance: 1-55788-297-5

Small-Block Chevy Marine Performance: 1-55788-317-3

TO ORDER CALL: 1-800-788-6262, ext. 1
HPBooks
A division of Penguin Putnam Inc.
375 Hudson Street
New York, New York 10014